Aspects of Education in the Middle East and North Africa

Aspects of Education in the Middle East and North Africa

Edited by

Colin Brock & Lila Zia Levers

Oxford Studies in Comparative Education
Series Editor: David Phillips

SYMPOSIUM
BOOKS

Symposium Books
PO Box 204 Didcot Oxford OX11 9ZQ United Kingdom
the book publishing division of wwwords Ltd
www.symposium-books.co.uk

Published in the United Kingdom, 2007

ISBN 978-1-873927-21-2

This publication is also available on a subscription basis
as Volume 18 Number 2 of *Oxford Studies in Comparative Education*
(ISSN 0961-2149)

Typeset by wwwords Ltd
Printed and bound in the United Kingdom by Cambridge University Press

Contents

Acknowledgements

We would like to express our sincere thanks to all those who contributed to the seminar series and presented their papers for publication, as well as those who responded to our subsequent invitation to add chapters for this volume.

We would also like to thank most sincerely our editorial assistant, Jenny Hsieh, for all the hard work she contributed in order to enable us to produce a final manuscript. Thanks are also due to Dr Roy Levers for checking the statistics and to Shirley Brock for proof reading the final script.

Colin Brock & Lila Zia Levers

Introduction

COLIN BROCK & LILA ZIA LEVERS

This volume, being within the series *Oxford Studies in Comparative Education*, arose from a series of seminars held at St Antony's College, Oxford. These seminars gave rise to seven papers, and the remainder have been commissioned. They do not represent the whole of the Middle East and North Africa, as such a collection would have been too large for one volume. Rather, the selection here is intended to present different perspectives on a range of educational issues, relevant to a particular focus or country, or common to a number of countries in the area. There is no overarching theme beyond that which is common to most of the countries in this area, such as modernity versus tradition; the spread of education effecting sociological changes – most pronounced in the rural and tribal areas; the changing fortunes and roles of women; the aspiration and expectation of youth; and the state having become the major player in providing education. These are all shared by most of the countries represented here.

We are happy that amongst the education systems and issues covered in this study we have been able to include contributions concerning Israel in general, the Negev Bedouin within Israel, and Palestine. All too often, Israel, and issues related to it, has been excluded from Middle Eastern collections, while Palestine suffers from not yet technically being a state and with many of its people internally or externally dislocated in more than just a spatial sense. Other countries and issues represented are: Iran, Turkey, United Arab Emirates, Saudi Arabia, Morocco and Algeria. In this volume, connections between the role of education and women, and their position and increasing visibility in non-traditional roles inform four of the chapters. Two such chapters (Finlaw and Mazawi) focus on higher education and the empowerment of women as they become key players in the socio-economic changes that are transforming their countries in the Gulf region. Another investigates the role of education in bringing about cultural change and fostering leadership amongst a select group of powerful 'first-generation professional' Arab, Muslim women (Kirdar). These three chapters illustrate extremely varied fortunes as between the different groups and individuals who are the subjects of each piece of research, ranging from the cultural and institutional constraints on women within the Saudi Arabian tertiary sector to the beneficial effects of having experienced and retained complementary aspects of Islam and Western education.

We commence the collection, however, with the contribution of Barbara Stowasser, which examines the general perception of Islam as a religion that accords an inferior position to women. The Qur'an is often quoted to support this position, especially the Sura 4:34 in which the treatment of women appears. Stowasser examines the reaction of modern educated, Muslim female university students to this Sura and its interpretation by Islamic scholars. She describes her experience of teaching traditional and modern Qur'anic exegesis (Tafsir) literature at Georgetown University and the role it plays in the educational experience of modern educated religiously-minded Muslim women. She states that most of the students in her seminars were female, and active in 'rethinking Islam'. Some were foreign students, and many others first or second generation immigrants to the USA. Her course centred on the study of Arab Tafsir literature in chronological order, as well as focusing on specific Qur'anic themes for textual comparison, such as issues of gender, for example, the men's 'guardianship' over women, which appears in the Sura 4:34. She goes on to examine the classical interpretation of Sura 4:34, through the writings of al-Tabari and al-Baydawi and other pre-modern Arab Sunni scholars, and describes the reaction of her students to the classical interpretations of Sura 4:34, in which male superiority and supremacy is emphasised, as being 'uniformly negative'.

She also examines the modern scholars (from Abduh [1905], to Rida [1935] and al-Rahman [1988]), and the work of women scholars in the second half of the twentieth century. She indicates that unlike the earlier pioneers among female religious scholars, most of the contemporary women writers are 'engaged in an effort to "unread" patriarchal interpretations of the Qur'an'. They consider that in the area of Tafsir, women's contribution is essential to opening up the Islamic discourse on gender as a whole and that 'feminism' 'within the context of Islam can provide the only path to empowerment and liberation that avoids challenging the whole culture'. She touches on the works of Muslim women scholars who at present live in the West and write in English, such as Amina Wadud, Asma Barlas, Reffat Hassan, and Nimat Hafez Barazangi. These and other 'activist scholars', she points out, often question or even reject being identified as 'feminists' as they consider this term to apply to women in the West who are secularist while fighting male domination. Nevertheless, Stowasser says:

> there is a liberationist tenor to their work that perhaps does merit
> use of the epithet in the new sense of an 'Islamic feminism'. This
> new spirit makes the connection between women's rights and
> democracy, human rights and economic justice, and it is thus
> conceived as the absolute antithesis to the patriarchal, paternalistic
> and hierarchical framings of the pre-modern Tafsir.

She ends the chapter by giving the Internet sites where the Qur'an and gender are discussed, and concludes that 'the whole of Sura 4:34 is at present a regular staple in this new world of electronic communications, and that the verse's electronic interpretations tend to reflect the new hermeneutics of gender-equal readings of the Qur'an'.

The contribution of Serra Kirdar, 'The Impact of Educational Empowerment on Women in the Arab World', based on a larger piece of research, illustrates just how far some Arab women have travelled along the emancipation route. Although the record is extremely varied, she has been able to find remarkable cases of outstanding success in a variety of country contexts: Saudi Arabia, Bahrain, Morocco, Egypt and Jordan. The author is not concerned, however, only with a single cultural context; rather, she is examining the effects of a dual religious-cultural experience – what she terms 'the merging of cultural traditionalism and modernity within individuals. The women represent Arab professional female role models, having 'used their educational experiences to redefine their own identities and engender changes'. She places this initially in a global as well as regional perspective and emphasises the significance of female educational development for development overall. However, in the Arab social context, opportunities for women are still class related. Nonetheless, those who have a voice are using it more to challenge the status quo. Indeed, 'many women who have aligned themselves with the Islamic revival movement in different Arab countries have gone to considerable lengths to proclaim their independent initiative', for it is traditional social norms rather than religious regulation that constrain educated women from fully utilising their knowledge and skills. This, Kirdar comments, is basically no different from the Western societies where 'the glass ceiling' certainly still exists. The high-achieving respondents to Kirdar's interviews indicated that while they had been given opportunities to succeed, they had to do so in a spectacular way, and then once in a key professional position they tended to feel isolated because of their gender. But they did not, as Western women have tended to do, 'abandon the feminine in order to ascertain the masculine'. All interviewees believed that further change and opportunity is inevitable but will take time.

Kirdar moves on to consider the issue of 'a female empowerment'. Possibly partly due to the breakthrough of the generational band she had interviewed, these are elite women, but what about the growing and emerging middle classes? They are looking for a new way, but not necessarily the Western way. They are setting new benchmarks and assisting the new middle-class Arab men to progress as well.

Sally Findlow's chapter on 'Women, Higher Education and Social Transformation in the Arab Gulf' looks at how a particular group of Arab women are engaging with rapidly expanding higher education opportunities at home and abroad, and conceptualising this engagement as part of a wider regional project of social change. Set in a historical context and against broader discussions about the social functions and gendered inequalities of higher education, it challenges over-simplistic stereotypes of the opportunities available to Arab, particularly Arab Gulf, women. It draws on policy analysis and the first-hand accounts of local women to describe how the United Arab Emirates higher education system interacts with issues of tradition, modernity, religion and family to produce complex patterns of aspiration, empowerment and tension among young women. The marginalisation of women in higher education is addressed, so while in absolute number there has clearly been an increase, the fields of study in which the majority of women are engaged are fairly limited and circumscribed. Nonetheless, Findlow shows this is not uncommon in a global perspective.

The Gulf States are the focus of this study and were, even by regional standards, slow starters in development terms, though for at least two decades public rhetoric has extolled the social roles of women. In some instances certain devices have been used to deal with traditional considerations, such as locating a new campus for women miles inland from the main centre or offering distance learning modes. One impressive feature is the apparent success in attracting large numbers of women to technical education. Sally Findlow summarises this situation as a 'feminist/ internationalist orientation, constrained only by residue social conservatism'. She interviewed female university students and found that enrolling in higher education was often seen as an alternative to merely staying home. It is at least an option available to women, even if, as yet, only a few avail themselves of it. However, barriers to utilising qualifications and experience in higher education are widespread, the marriage imperative being the foremost. As Findlow puts it, 'Economics, lifestyle and status are all involved in this mismatch. The more educated a woman is, the higher her bride-price'. She also found that mothers are encouraging their daughters to enrol in higher education and once there to be careful to conform to a traditional lifestyle. So it would appear that social adjustment to increased opportunities is under way and the voices of educated women in the Gulf are beginning to be heard.

Andre Mazawi is also concerned with women's higher education opportunities in the Gulf Arab States. As he points out, women constitute more than 75 per cent of all higher education students, but less than 30 per cent of Faculty members. Furthermore, their presence in both regards is highly concentrated in certain disciplinary fields. He refers to them, despite their number, as a subordinate and politically weakened social group. Their situation is not assisted by their issues being marginalised in the literature – hence the significance of the chapters in this volume by Mazawi and Findlow. Mazawi's chapter concentrates on three main issues: (a) a spatial political economy of academic opportunities; (b) globalisation and the privatisation of emancipation; and (c) academic opportunities as topographies of struggle. The first of the three concentrates on Saudi Arabia, concluding that women are not normally admitted to disciplines which are associated with industry and technology or with the production of religious knowledge. Rather the promotion of women in Gulf higher education is an emblematic representation of a cultural product. It is a construction of an ideal-typical 'modern-yet-authentic Gulf woman' who represents a cultural product of modernity endorsed by a benevolent state.

The third focus is on women's increased activism in post-Gulf War social debate. Overall the picture is one of struggle to gain the maximum possible benefit from such liberalisation as has occurred. Mazawi's overall conclusion is that it is not yet clear how the increased participation of Gulf women in academia will be able to relate to the resolution of issues of social justice, fairness and equity in the wider societies.

Another focus within this collection is Iran, a complex country, multiethnic and multilingual. One particular feature is the multifaith nature of the population – while the vast majority are Shi'i Muslims, the remainder are Christians, Jews and Zoroastrians. These aspects of Iranian plural society are examined in the chapters by Mehran and Mohammadi-Heuboeck. Iran was declared an Islamic Republic in 1979 and Iranian schools have ever since aimed at creating pious and politicised schoolchildren, because the aim of the Islamic leaders since the Revolution has been to create politically aware and devout Muslim citizens. The education system has been regarded as the principal instrument through which this is to be achieved. In the aftermath of the Revolution, a major revision of school textbooks took place. Islamic themes, references to Islamic personalities, and episodes in the history of Islam were introduced into the majority of school texts, especially those of the humanities. Religious studies itself came to form a major part of the curriculum. Given the overtly Islamic nature of the education system, it may be asked how the minority faiths fare within it. The answer to this question we find in the chapter by Golnar Mehran, on 'Religious Education of Muslim and Non-Muslim Schoolchildren in the Islamic Republic of Iran'.

The system of education in Iran, since the establishment of a modern system of education in the first half of the twentieth century, has been highly centralised and this is still the case under the Islamic Republic. There is a standard curriculum throughout the country and teachers are trained in state-sponsored teacher training centres. The textbooks are also uniform throughout the country, with the exception of religious textbooks. The Ministry of Education prints separate religious textbooks for the Muslim and non-Muslim schoolchildren between the ages of seven and sixteen, the period of formal compulsory schooling.

The purpose of Mehran's study is twofold: to identify the goals of state religious education and to determine whether these are intended to bring unity or disunity among the different faiths. Hence, she undertakes an in-depth study of religious education in schools by examining the pictorial and textual content of religious education textbooks during the 2004-05 academic year for both Muslim and non-Muslim students. She addresses the following themes: how religious diversity is treated in the textbooks; messages conveyed to students of different faiths; and the similarities and dissimilarities of religious education for the majority and minority faiths. Her findings reveal that state religious education aims at bringing about unity rather than division, by emphasising 'commonalities' and ignoring dissimilarities, among monotheist religions. Another of her findings is that religious education in Iranian schools is also characterised by a policy of silence that deliberately excludes potentially divisive issues, and avoids acknowledging and addressing the religious diversity that exists in contemporary Iranian society.

Another prime characteristic of Iran is its multiethnic and multilingual composition, and Iran Mohammadi-Heuboeck examines the question of ethnicity, language and identity through impacts on the Iranian Kurds in contemporary Iran. In 'Aspects of Bilingualism in Iranian Kurdish Schoolchildren' she begins by listing the Iranian ethnic groups, all with their different languages, and points out that the Persians, Azeris and the Kurds comprise the largest groups. The question then arises, given the highly centralised nature of the state and its education system, and the emphasis on Persian as the language of instruction in schools and communication in local and national administrative structures, how is this multilingual factor accommodated? She examines this question by focusing on a case study of the Iranian Kurds with particular reference to the new generation of Kurdish youth. With the establishment of a modern centralised state under Reza Shah (1925-41) and the aim of creating a unified country, the Persian language became the official language and school textbooks came to be published only in Persian. Mohammadi-Heuboeck argues that this development put Persian 'in close contact with a variety of regional languages, giving rise to politically motivated situations of bilinguilism throughout the country'. After the Revolution of 1979 the ethnic peoples of Iran hoped for a certain amount of autonomy, especially with regard to their language and culture. But under the Islamic Republic this was not to be. Despite many debates and discussion, as well as the official recognition (article XV of the Constitution) of the right of the minorities to teaching in their own languages, Persian remains the language of instruction in Iranian schools. Mohammadi-Heuboeck traces the long periods of struggle by the Kurds for the right to receive education in their own language, and examines the impact of a centralised school system on the new generation of Kurdish youth. She writes that the dynamic of identification of the new generation is not the same as it used to be for the previous generation, socialised mainly within the family circle. School life forms a considerable part of the Kurdish youth experience and the family circle is no longer the only place of identity and cultural reference.

Mohammadi-Hueboeck goes on to examine the changing attitude of even the older generation to the dual linguistic identity and the increasing acceptance of Persian as the 'language of our children', even though in many cases their own knowledge of Persian is rather poor. This has become even more widespread under the Islamic Republic as a result of the increase in the population and the Islamic Republic's drive to increase literacy. Therefore the transmission of the Kurdish language is gradually on the decline, and the younger generation's linguistic identity is oriented more and more towards Persian, the official language. As a consequence, not only has a conflict been created within the Kurdish communities, but also between its rural and urban areas – the urban increasingly becoming Persian speaking and therefore regarded as educated, and the rural still dominated by Kurdish and regarded as backward. She states that this stigmatised stereotype of the Kurdish language can be seen in schoolchildren, who regard Kurdish as the language of farmers, and therefore there is no reason for them, living in urban areas, to speak it. This attitude by most of the younger generation to the language also applies to the Kurdish culture itself, which is regarded as dispensable and no longer relevant to a modern Persian-speaking society. The fact that they speak Persian as their first language is seen as a sign of modernity and social prestige.

She further analyses the sociolinguistic interaction of the young or middle-aged parents, from different socio-economic backgrounds, with their children. The parents' ambitions for their children to climb the social ladder influences their attitude to Persian, to the extent of adopting it as the language of communication in the home, even to young children, so as to prepare them for school and interaction with their peers. Her contact with families in the Kurdish communities gives her an insight into the complexity of their lives in the face of the interplay between the old linguistic aspirations and the requirements of the socio-economic dynamics in today's Iran. She examines the conflict that the young experience in this cultural duality. The majority of the youth, who have assimilated the national identity by speaking Persian, either in a local or Tehrani accent, like to conceal their Kurdish origin, but nevertheless live under the constant threat that their Kurdish origin might be revealed in public. The feeling of discomfort and shame towards their parents or their family, who may not speak the Persian language well, is common among them, and they put much effort into concealing their parents' Kurdish identity.

Mohammadi-Heuboeck points out that this crisis of identity is not only limited to Kurdish children speaking Persian, but also extends to the children speaking Kurdish itself. The experience of being Kurdish in schools where Persian language and culture is dominant has resulted in the emergence of ethnic nationalism amongst some of the new generation. They regard the institution of school as a symbol of political domination by the state in the Kurdish area. Fear of loss of their Kurdish identity creates either passive or active antagonism towards the central government. They wish to be recognised as Kurds and strongly believe that Kurdish language and literature should also form part of the curriculum along with other subjects. Mohammadi-Heuboeck concludes that this can only be achieved if the article XV of the Constitution, granting the right to the minorities to be taught in their own language, is realised in practice.

Yossi Dahan & Yossi Yonah, in their chapter on 'Israel's Education System: equality of opportunity – from nation building to neo-liberalism', begin by stating that the value of equal opportunity has always been the guiding principle of the founders as well the prominent political leaders of the state of Israel in the formulation and implementation of public policies in the sphere of education. This value was also regarded as essential for realisation of a cohesive society and creation of solidarity among the members of the emerging new Jewish state, the geographical origins of which are extremely diverse. They go on to pose the questions: 'how has this value fared in Israel's education system over the years', and 'to what extent does it receive meaningful expression in Israel's education policies?' They begin by examining the State Education Act of 1953, which formally nationalised Israel's education system. This was to provide equal opportunity and equal treatment for children regardless of their ethnic origins and social background. However, in practice, this was not the actual outcome: Dahan & Yonah maintain that from the outset 'geographical segregation and systematic discrimination against various social groups' took place. This was seen in areas such as allocation of resources, teaching personnel, and school curriculum. The severest form of discrimination was against the Arab children. The Israeli Arab citizens lived under the military rule that followed the establishment of the state of Israel, and their children were allocated to segregated schools and severely discriminated against in the allocation of resources. In the case of the other Israeli citizens, Mizrahi and Ashkenazi Jews, the pattern of geographical segregation in their lives was upheld by the education system. Most of the Mizrahi children attended poorly equipped schools where academic achievement was low, while Ashkenazi children, whose parents were mainly of European origin, attended privileged schools, with high-quality teaching and facilities, preparing the pupils for higher education and consequently a privileged position in society. Therefore, Dahan & Yonah, state, 'the education system has generally resulted in reproducing existing patterns of geographical segregation and structural inequalities between Mizrahi and Ashkenazi children, thus practically creating two educational sub-systems characterised by a display of material conditions and different school curricula'. Hence, this led to the emergence of wide scholastic gaps among children belonging to different social groups, which became a worrying factor for education policy makers, who perceive it as undermining attempts to cultivate a cohesive Jewish community.

Dahan & Yonah proceed to focus on the reforms that were initiated to remedy the initial shortcomings of the education system, the two most important being the Integration Reform, implemented in 1968, and the 'Dovrat Reform', endorsed by the government in 2005. Both reforms, they state, despite their different ideological and political nature, 'decree that educational policies are desirable only to the extent that they significantly contribute to the realisation of the value of equal opportunities'. According to this value, every child, irrespective of social background, including nationality, ethnicity, race, gender, family milieu and economic status, should be granted educational opportunities. They show that both these reforms fail to implement the principle of educational equality of opportunity, considered 'one of the main constitutive building blocks of Israel's state ideology', though they meet the aim of creating a strong national Jewish identity by adopting a strong nationalistic curriculum which rules out any reference to multiculturalism and does not allow expressions of other national identities that exist in the state of Israel.

Richard Ratcliffe's contribution is a fascinating insight into certain educational experiences of a very special and distinctive group, the Bedouin of the Negev in Israel, who he clearly shows have exhibited a keen political interest in education. As with the chapters on gender discussed above, the issues of concern in education for this group reflect wider social trends and problems. As he puts it, Bedouin educational politics was significant in relation to wider politics within the community at large. Ratcliffe indicates that the Negev Bedouins, until recently, have been peripheral within the Arab world, indeed even 'romanticised'. In relation to education in particular they have become politically active. They have, according to Ratcliffe, 'come to symbolise the internal Arab threat, in terms of demography, land, security, and perhaps even the existential impossibility for social interpretation'. He discusses in particular what he terms 'the moment' for Bedouin education: the educational contestation of 1994-2005, including a sustained campaign for the improvement of Bedouin education in Israel, which also brought much 'new knowledge' to light about their plight, by showing clearly that 'the low status of Bedouin education was not caused by "cultural" reasons, but rather by unequal material conditions and discrimination'. This sustained campaign had the additional effect of symbolising the discrimination against Palestinian Arab citizens of Israel in general. Ratcliffe analyses what he terms the technopolitics approach of the campaign, concentrating on practical issues of neglect and discrimination rather than ideological and rhetorical stances. He describes it as having an 'integrationist logic', revolving around issues of development, land, gender, demography and segmentary politics. It was tactically partial, pliable and patient. Nonetheless, it was still a struggle and the struggle goes on. For Ratcliffe this campaign, this moment, 'marked the internationalisation of Bedouin politics' in Israel/Palestine; with the focus on competing national projects, this transformation is often overlooked.

Bilal Barakat's chapter analyses 'The Struggle for Palestinian National Education Past and Present'. It is viewed here in the context of anti-colonialism and modernisation in what he rightly describes as 'a highly exceptional position'. This, of course, is due to the historical developments behind the present conflictual situation in education commencing in 1846 with the Ottoman education laws modelled on the French system. He examines the progress of both public and private provisions and access, noting the social class implications, including the limited expansion of public schooling and the British mandate from the early 1920s to 1948. He shows

17

this partiality to be a deliberate policy, with the prime objective being to educate potential teachers and bureaucrats. This approach failed completely to meet the technical needs of the Palestinian community. However, schools were active in other respects, for example, in the Arab revolt of 1936-39, when the British responded by constraining physical access – a forerunner of what has happened with the construction of the war in contemporary Israel/Palestine. The 1967 seizure by Israel of the West Bank and Gaza Strip greatly increases control of regulated space, subsequent to which 'authority was severely abused'. Provision was reduced to a minimum and systematic development curtailed. Such severe limitation raged from primary to university levels. Nonetheless, the Palestinian universities have *de facto*, if not *de jure*, served as features of a nascent 'rational authority' for Palestine in supplying high-level, professional expertise.

Barakat describes how the Oslo Accords of the early 1990s formally transferred control of the educational system in the Occupied Territories to the newly formed Palestinian National Authority. This enabled the increase of provision at primary level to reach near universal enrolments and progressed through the secondary stage as well. The outcome he regards as favourable as compared with Arab schools within the state of Israel itself, when 'internal colonialism' brings additional constraints. However, in the Occupied Territories there has been considerable physical damage and human casualty due to military action.

Turning to the issue of education in relation to liberation, Barakat poses the question: 'Whose liberation, and from what?' Is the kind of education that assists a revolutionary struggle appropriate for assisting social and economic well-being in a broader sense? Such tension can also be portrayed as being between education for individuals and education for the community as a whole. But there are many Palestinian communities as well as social classes. Only in the universities of the West Bank, apparently, has 'the individual' and 'the national' been reconciled.

Issues of identity and historical records have been severely and adversely affected by Israeli destruction of research documents, archives and central records. Through such assaults, Palestinian identity 'as political, historical, intellectual or cultural beings is sought to be minimised if not eliminated'. Nonetheless, educational provision in contemporary Palestine has helped so far to prevent the total realisation of Israel's strategy of attacking Palestinian identity. So Barakat concludes that education remains a potential contributor to the realisation of the Palestinian state and its national development.

Abdelkader Ezzaki, in 'Formal Schooling in Morocco: the hopes and challenges of the current educational reform', commences by quoting the United Nations Development Program's 2003 Human Development Report's figures on education. These show that, in Morocco, despite the fact that the educational expenditure forms more than 25% of the government's total budget (about 5.5% of gross domestic product), it ranks as one of the low-performing countries in North Africa on the human development indicators, behind Egypt, Algeria and Tunisia. Clearly, it became necessary to remedy the shortcomings of the educational sector by introducing a reform programme. Ezzaki proceeds to review and discuss the educational reform in Morocco following the setting up of a Special Commission of Education and Training in the mid-1990s which addressed the problems bearing on all sections of the education sector. This led to the drawing up of a Charter, which was officially adopted in 1999. This Charter came to form the basis for all the reform initiatives taken by different educational authorities in the country. It deals with a full range of educational matters such as universal education, the curricula, methods of teaching and evaluation, language teaching, and information and communication technology (ICT). He describes each section of the report against the relevant sector of the education system and examines the extent to which the proposed reforms have been implemented.

Ezzaki finds that, despite improvements in each of these areas, they still fall short of the standards and targets set out under the Charter. The illiteracy rate, for example, is over 40%, one of the highest in the Arab world: about 2.5 million children of school age, mainly female in rural areas, are still out of school; grade repetition rates have increased; the already weak pre-schooling system has further declined leading to inadequate language and skill development required for the next stage of schooling. In the area of curriculum change the reform stipulated the integration of new areas of study into the curriculum, such as human rights, environmental issues, citizenship, technology and computing. However, Ezzaki regards this reform as problematic in that it leads to overloading of the curriculum, increasing the cost of schooling for parents, while the outcome may be superficial learning, resulting from this multiplicity of contents. Another aim was to include practical skills into the curriculum. This, however, is being achieved through such initiatives as the project '*la main à la pâte*' (hands-on learning) supported by the French cooperative programme in Morocco. It aims at enabling students to learn academic content through practical activities. The challenge is to incorporate such initiatives formally into the curricula and, as Ezzaki says, 'to create a new pedagogical culture centred on learning "relevance"'.

Having examined each section of the reform against its implementation, Ezzaki concludes that the Charter is a sound document and highly relevant to the needs of the education system in the country. It has brought about much needed improvement in many sectors of the education. However, certain implementation difficulties are reducing the success level of the reforms. He puts forward a number of policy initiatives to remedy the shortcomings.

Ayse Kok has explored a very different theme from the other chapters in 'Computerising Turkey's Schools'. Information technology is, of course, making its mark throughout the Middle East and North Africa, but in Turkey it is coinciding with a major project to bring basic opportunity for all.

In all countries ICT impacts on education in two major ways: first, it requires a certain threshold of technical competence to install and utilise it, and then once installed, it becomes a valuable medium for the development of learning at all levels.

After discussing certain theoretical and technical issues that apply globally, Kok turns to the context of Turkey itself and especially the social transformation of recent decades. There have in fact being a number of national bodies involved in ICT projects, but the key objective now is to integrate ICT into a centralised education system. This is proving a massive and challenging task, given disparate levels of infrastructure and understanding across the country. It is not just a technical challenge but a curricular one as well. In general the installation of technical capacity is well ahead of understanding how it can support curricular development. So two programmes, Basic Education Phase One (1998-2003) and Phase Two (2000 onwards) have been under way, looking to Turkey's future, including possible membership of the European Union. Indeed, this is a driving force behind the ICT development. But as Ayse Kok concludes: 'What this would mean in respect of Turkey as a Middle Eastern country is another issue'.

The Qur'an and Women's Education: patriarchal interpretations of Sura 4:34 and their unreading by educated Muslim women

BARBARA FREYER STOWASSER

This chapter explores some of the roles that traditional and modern Qur'anic exegesis (Tafsir) literature plays in the educational experiences of modern, educated, religious-minded Muslim women. It also seeks to document some recent female-authored efforts, projects, and publications in the field of Qur'anic interpretation. The present topic is the result of several seminars that I have taught at Georgetown University, where we study the Arabic Tafsir literature in chronological sequence while also focusing on specific Qur'anic items for textual comparison; prominent among the latter are issues of gender, such as the Qur'anic notion of men's 'guardianship' (*qiwama*) over women, legislated in Sura 4:34. Most of my students in these classes are Muslim, female, and active in 'rethinking Islam'; some are foreign students, many others first- or second-generation immigrants to the United States. It is most frequently the Muslim students (male or female) who present their modernist-liberal interpretations of Qur'anic passages – especially on issues of politics and gender – as reflective of the one and only 'true meaning' of the text, and who generally find their encounters with the classical Tafsir literature upsetting. Indeed, reading the pre-modern Sunni exegetic literature on Sura 4:34 proved time and again the most controversial part of the course; it also led to our most fruitful class discussions regarding the relationship between scripture and culture, and the essence and role of cultural paradigms.

The Qur'anic verse of 4:34 reads: 'Men are in charge of/are guardians of/are superior to/have authority over/ women, because God has endowed the one with more/has preferred some of them over others/, and because they spend of their means. Therefore the righteous women are obedient, guarding in secret/guarding the secret/ by what God has guarded. As to those from whom you fear rebellion, admonish them and banish them to separate beds, and beat them. Then if they obey you, seek not a way against them. For God is Exalted, Great'.

Pre-modern Sunni interpretations of Sura 4:34

According to the early Qur'anic exegesis of al-Tabari (d.923), whose work is mainly based on Hadith ('narrative traditions'), this verse primarily concerns the domestic relations between husband and wife. It legislates men's authority over their women, which entails the male's right to discipline his women in order to ensure female obedience both toward God and also himself. al-Tabari deemed this system equitable in that it also sets out the man's obligation to pay his women's dower, and then provide for them while they are his wives. al-Tabari's reading of the phrase 'because God has endowed the one with more/has preferred some of them over others' rests mainly on the men's economic ability to support their wives, and their concomitant obligation to do so. In addition, however, there are several traditions quoted by al-Tabari (at the end of his Tafsir on this issue) that also indicate that men 'in general' (as males) have 'precedence' of 'excellence' over women; but he does not develop this theme.

Further, according to al-Tabari, female obedience consists of: marital fidelity, friendly behavior toward the husband and his family, and good household management. 'Rebellion', or 'disobedience' (*nushuz*), is interpreted to mean female appropriation of superiority over the husband, undue freedom of movement, objection to sexual contact when desired by the husband, and other acts of defiance. If men fear such behavior on the part of their wives, they should, first, verbally admonish them; al-Tabari suggests that 'the husband threaten his recalcitrant wife with God's punishment'. Second, they should 'leave the marital bed'; the traditions and lexical definitions assembled by al-Tabari to interpret this item range from the obvious meaning of literally separating beds to 'refusing to talk to the wife while having sex' (a meaning that al-Tabari himself finds astonishing), to 'using strong and rude language while in bed', to 'tying the woman up like one shackles a camel, in the sense of confining her to the home'. Third, then, is the beating: al-Tabari interprets this last resort as 'to strike her without hurting or disfiguring her' (al-Tabari, 1972, pp. 290-317).

Two hundred years later, in the twelfth century, Sunni Muslim exegetes had begun to ponder the 'reasons behind' the legislation of 4:34 in new ways. They provided explanations for why 'men were in charge of/superior to' women. Most of their explanations in this context were cast in mental, physical, spiritual, and political terms. The diagram that 'elevated' men 'above' women was expanded from the private to the public sphere, as the issue of men's *qiwama* ('guardianship') over women turned from a functionalist interpretation of 4:34 – how to apply the verse to the functions of the genders in the family – to an essentialist interpretation of the 'inherent power and value' of men over women, in absolute terms. The scholastic theologians al-Zamakhshari (d.1144), al-Razi (d.1209/1210), and al-Baydawi (d. around 1286), whose tafsir is a concise recapitulation of theirs, all followed this essentialist paradigm in which men and women are essentially different from one another and essentially unequal.

In al-Baydawi's commentary on 4:34, men's 'guardianship of' or 'superiority over' women is likened to the superiority of rulers or sovereign political leaders over their male subjects. Part of this superiority derives from innate abilities, and the other part derives from acquired abilities. The phrase 'God has endowed the one with more' in 4:34, therefore, means that God has favored men over women by endowing them with a perfect mind, good management skills, and superb strength with which to perform practical work and pious deeds. Men alone are naturally gifted with superior attributes that range from intellect and determination to literacy and the ability to ride. Hence, to men (alone) were allotted prophethood, government (the larger imamate), the leading of prayers (the lesser imamate) and the performance of (other) religious ceremonies, witnessing in all (legal) matters, the duty to fight for the sake of God (*jihad*), attend Friday prayers, the right to wear the turban, receive the greater inheritance share, and hold the monopoly in matters of marriage and divorce. The implication is that women are excluded from playing any of these roles because they are mentally deficient and religiously and legally incapacitated (religiously, because they may neither pray nor fast when menstruating, and legally, because they may not give witness in cases of *hudud* ['canonical legal offenses'], and so forth) (al-Baydawi, 1968, pp. 207-208).

The later medieval Hadith-based Tafsir sounds very similar themes. Like the rationalist interpreters just mentioned, the Hanbali authority Ibn Kathir (d.1373) defines the male as the woman's superior, superintendent, and sovereign who disciplines her when she goes astray. Because the man is better than the woman, prophethood is exclusively assigned to men, as is kingship, the latter in accordance with the Prophet's words, 'a nation ruled by a woman will not thrive', that were transmitted by Abd al-Rahman ibn Abi Bakra from his father Abu Bakra and recorded as a sound Hadith by al-Bukhari. In addition, God Himself proclaims the innate excellence of men over women by saying, 'and men have a degree above them' (Sura 2:228) (Ibn al-Kathir, n.d., pp. 490-491). In presenting their sets of criteria for gender differences, these classical Sunni authorities thus conflate biological and socially constructed qualities and potentials to where men and notions of masculinity are constructed as rationality, intellect, and spirituality, while women and femininity connote the irrational, the emotional, the carnal, and the sexual. The biological differences between men and women thereby come to signify much more than just political categories of gender. As the contemporary Islamic feminist Sa'diyyah Shaikh has written, 'this dichotomy translates into a hierarchical understanding of humanity which prioritises mind over body, reason over passion, spirituality over carnality, and male over female' (1997 [the electronic text of this article does not indicate page numbers]).

By likening the authority of the male over the female to the authority of the sultan over his (male) subjects, the pre-modern Tafsir also established parallels between public and private authority. This went hand in hand with a redefinition of the concept of 'obedience' along gender lines, which said, 'Men's obedience is to God, His Prophet, and the holders of authority' (Sura 4:59), while women's obedience is to the husband; and it is by way of her obedience to the husband that her obedience to God is verified and measured. When read in chronological order, the early Tafsir literature defines woman's *ta'a* ('obedience') first as her obligation toward God, and thereafter as her duty toward her husband; but soon the husband takes pre-eminence, and it is through obedience to him that a woman's obedience to God manifests itself. In the autocratic world of medieval Islamic politics, the Tafsir thus sees the ruler's authority over his subjects mimicked by that of the male over the female, and in either case, the relationship is marked by dominance of the one and subjugation of the other.

As the woman's obedience to her husband becomes instrumental in her relationship with God, male supremacy and gender hierarchy are sacralized in a manner that parallels a higher command structure; here, God's supremacy rests directly on God's first-tier agents, the male believers, who carry out His laws toward the women (and slaves) under their authority (Shaikh, 1997). A woman's ultimate sin, then, is *nushuz* ('rebellion' – against the husband) while a man's ultimate sin is *shirk* ('rebellion against God's Oneness'). The sacralization of gender relations on the concept of *ta'a* in these Tafsir works of the classical age has a narrative, negative mirror image in the apocalyptic Hadith materials that largely pre-date them and where in some instances *kufr* ('unbelief, blasphemy, hybris, infidelity; also: ingratitude') becomes the operative term in denoting the sin because of which so many women are condemned to hell. In identifying the 'minor signs of the hour', the apocalyptic Hadith lists objectionable gender practices and relations that signal the end-time disruptions of moral social order. They provide a reversed, 'upside-down', warning vision of what godly society is, or should be, such as that women will outnumber men fifty-to-one; men will have to work for women; men will have to obey women; women will be the superiors of men; a man will obey his wife and disobey his mother; women will appear nude in public even though they are clothed (because their garments do not cover their ritually-defined 'areas of nakedness'); illicit sexual relations will be prevalent; and the like (Stowasser, 2004, pp. 49-52; Smith & Haddad, 1981, pp. 160-161). Most of the inhabitants of hell are women. Prevalent among their many sins is their failing of *kufr*, 'ingratitude' – not toward God but toward their husband. Clearly, the Hadith here serves to legitimate social control of males over females by suggesting that a woman's relationship to God is somehow determined by her relationship to her husband (Smith & Haddad, 1981, p. 163).

In this increasingly sacralized paradigm of male–female relations, the male's right to 'beat' the recalcitrant female into obedience (based on his sultan-like authority over her) must somehow be squared with the fact that he, himself, is ultimately responsible to God for his actions; the same, of course, is true for the sultan. This notion modifies how the man may choose to carry out his right to physical punishment. For al-Tabari, quoted above, 'beating' the wife was to be 'striking her without hurting her or disfiguring her' (al-Tabari, 1972, vol. 8, pp. 313-316) and al-Razi adopts the same position, while adding that desisting from the beating is better, and that the Prophet said that 'men who beat their wives are not among the better men' (al-Razi, 1934-1962, vol. 10, p. 90). Al-Zamakhshari quotes a Hadith (that he proclaims weak because of its faulty chain of narrators) according to which the Prophet said to a husband: 'hang your whip in such a place that your family can see it', but he adds that even though men have power over their women, God's power over themselves is much greater, and he follows up with a Hadith according to which the Prophet saw how a man was about to hit a slave and said to him: 'Abu Mas'ud, God has more power over you than you have over that slave', and Abu Mas'ud threw away the whip and freed the slave (al-Zamakshari, 1953, vol. 1, p. 292).

The Pre-modern Sunni Tafsir of Sura 4:34: theology, legislation, or history?

My students' reactions to reading these classical interpretations of Sura 4:34 were uniformly negative. Why would women be depicted as, or judged as being, mentally, physically, and spiritually inferior to men, when no such legislation existed in the Qur'anic text – when, indeed, the Qur'an contained so many verses on the essential equality of men and women in their shared humanity and dignity, obligations and rewards, as believers? Why, also, did the classical exegetes 'generalize the specific' rather than 'historicize the specific', which would have led them to focus on the revelations' moral purpose? The classical texts also prompted the students to debate the nature of this discourse and how to classify it. Is this 'old Tafsir' theology? Is it law or legislation? Does it bear traces of the social realities within or against which it was written? Why, for example, would the exegetes of the twelfth century and later be more patriarchal in their interpretations of Sura 4:34 than were their predecessors, such as al-Tabari in the ninth century? Did they perhaps translate the autocratic practices of the political systems of their own time into a more normative, discriminatory gender ideology? Or, more likely, did the rise of the largely state-sponsored *madrasa* educational system in the eleventh century provide the *'ulama* ('lawyer-theologians, scripturalist experts') with a newly defined corporate status that reconstituted their class as jurists, emphasized scholarly methods of jurisprudential nature, and reinforced the influence of the previously standardized and canonized Hadith, much of which had come to reflect a patriarchal and paternalistic world-view? The latter would explain the Tafsir's definitions of women's obedience in terms where female insubordination toward the husband came to equal female sin toward God. These are difficult questions. To answer them will require the collaboration of specialists in the fields of history and literature, Tafsir, Hadith, and law.

Strictly speaking, the pre-modern Tafsir on gender is neither theology nor legislation, nor is it a source for the study of social history, even though it contains aspects of all three. It represents a consensus-based intellectual discourse by theological and legal experts who offer opinions and verdicts on an abstract, ahistorical relationship between gender questions on the one hand and moral society on the other. In their role as self-appointed guardians of communal morality, the scholars employ scripture to anchor their vision of moral society as a hierarchical order in which males occupy the upper tiers and women are excluded from all aspects of public life. Sometimes the scholars find no scriptural basis for their value judgments and socio-political agenda, at other times they drastically alter the context and meaning of the Qur'anic laws, but their intellectual discourse embodies one of the major traits of '*ulama* scholarship, reliance on *ijma*' ('scholarly consensus') across time and place; here it is noteworthy, for example, that while some of the exegetes quoted above lived hundreds of years and thousands of miles apart, they phrased their Tafsir texts on Sura 4:34 in largely identical language. This suggests that they were writing not about how society was/is, but how in their opinion it should be. It also suggests that the Tafsir on gender is not a source of concrete social historical data but of an intellectual history that consists of specific, long-lived, clerical pronouncements on an issue that was, however, not considered worthy of much interest or intellectual effort. There were no women's voices privileged to contribute to this discussion.

So far, it has been between difficult and impossible to reconstruct an alternative discourse voiced by women, or even one that is representative of Muslim women's lives in the medieval period, since history writing was also a male domain. As Denise Spellberg has shown, Tafsir, Hadith, *Tabaqat* ('biographical dictionaries') and *Tawarikh* ('chronicles') were all male-authored literary genres that propagated androcentric definitions of gender power relationships (Spellberg, 2005, p. 4). Nevertheless, Ruth Roded has unearthed sizeable records in pre-modern biographical dictionaries which indicate that medieval Muslim women were active in scholarship and teaching, Sufism and politics, commerce and the financing of pious endowments (Roded, 1994, pp. 63-114). Even in the largely atomistic (one-item-at-a-time) collections and handbooks of classical Islamic jurisprudence usually framed in the language of precedence (quotations from Qur'an and Hadith), there is a great deal of variation in definitions of women's social and economic rights, some of which appears to overshadow, indeed to negate, the heavily patriarchal paradigm of the medieval Qur'anic Tafsir. Pre-modern *fatawa* (sing. *fatwa*, 'formal legal opinions') also provide some information on how gender issues did, indeed, play out in more egalitarian forms at any given moment (Haddad & Stowasser, 2004, pp. 5-6).

How much history, then, do we learn from the classical Tafsirs of 4:34? From the limitations of the classical Tafsir literature, we learn much about pre-modern, consensus-based Islamic cultural values enshrined in gender categories. We can perhaps even surmise that the normative, misogynistic. nature of the medieval interpretations was linked to the fact that all existing state systems during their authors' lifetimes were autocratic and hierarchical, which mimetically colored their world-view. We can also learn the fact that women were not privileged to contribute to this discourse. It is only in the modern period that 'the female silence of the medieval male master narrative has been challenged ... by Muslim women who have begun to overwrite centuries of gendered silence' (Spellberg, 2005, p. 13).

Modernist Interpretations of Sura 4:34

The modernist-reformist Tafsir that emerged in the Arab world in the late nineteenth and early twentieth centuries influenced how women have now studied the Qur'an, both by way of methodology (hermeneutics) and doctrine (the Qur'anic paradigm of gender equivalence). The Egyptian theologian and jurist Muhammad Abduh (d.1905), Islamic modernism's most important early representative in the Arab world, saw Islam as eminently compatible with modernity. His main goal was to 'renew' Muslim morality and reform the traditional social structures of his day by way of a return to the dynamic faith and pristine morality of Islam's first generations. Although familiar with the classical Tafsir literature, to which he frequently referred, Abduh's approach to the Qur'an in his own exegesis showed a new attention to the literal meaning of the Qur'anic verses and also their contextualization, both within the particular Sura as well as the entire Qur'an. At the same time, he cut back on usage of the Hadith as a whole and most especially its isra'iliyyat ('Bible-derived and extra-biblical traditions'). Abduh's Tafsir was a collaborative effort with his editor, commentator, and later spokesman Rashid Rida (d.1935). Their interpretation of Sura 4:34 introduced the students in my classes to the modern and still prevailing notion that the sexes are not inherently unequal, but that they are complementary – equal but different. Since it is part of God's creational plan that each fulfills specific biological and social functions, none can be elevated or denigrated above or below the other. Abduh's and Rida's notion of gender equivalence, rather than gender equality, continues to inform traditionalist and also Islamist discourses, where it has profound implications for their formulations of women's social and political rights. Islamic equal rights proponents therefore frequently regard it as problematic, because it emphasizes women's domesticity and maintains that, in order to function, both family and society at large require a hierarchical structure of male control.

Abduh and Rida placed Sura 4:34 back into the domestic context, saying that in the God-willed order of the family, the man is charged with *qiwama* ('leadership') to protect domestic life and well-being. He is to the wife as the head is to the body. Men merit this 'superiority' because of qualities they alone possess, some innate and some acquired. Men, for instance, are given a stronger, more perfect, more complete, and more beautiful constitution, as is the case with the males in all species. This physical constitution is also linked to a stronger mind and sounder perceptions, the ability to earn money and administer affairs in a creative way. Women, in turn, should be gratified that their dependency, even though a matter of their own natural constitution, is actually rewarded with 'remuneration' or 'wages' (dower and maintenance). The husband's *qiwama* over his wife consists not of acts of tyranny but of guidance toward righteous behavior, education, domestic efficiency, houseboundness, and fiscal responsibility within his budgetary guidelines. This enables the woman to keep her house in order and safety, and bear and raise her children. God has not 'preferred' men over women. In individual cases, wives can even surpass their husbands in knowledge, work, bodily strength, and earning power. But it is by their biological and social functions in the family that the sexes as a whole are addressed and organized in Sura 4:34. From this system follows the man's leadership in concluding the marriage contract and deciding upon divorce. Man's exclusive obligation to fight holy war also derives from his role as protector of the woman, and his larger inheritance share relates to the fact that his expenses are greater. According to Abduh, all other prerogatives mentioned by the classical interpreters (prophethood, government, prayer-leading, religious ritual, call to prayer, sermonizing on Fridays), while following from the man's more perfect disposition and lack of preoccupation (with other things), have nothing to do with his 'guardianship' of women (of Sura 4:34), because even if the law had endowed women with all these prerogatives, by innate nature men would still be 'in charge' of them in the family (Rida, 1973, vol. 5, pp. 66-80). I reminded my students that in the nineteenth century when Western cultural norms and ideas were being propagated in Egypt and thought to represent 'modernity', they came in the form of Victorian models and paradigms that were themselves quite averse to notions of gender equality, and that this Victorian-derived 'modernity' certainly influenced how Abduh and Rida perceived of 'modernity' at that time.

More important in the long run than Abduh's and Rida's specific interpretation of the meaning of men's *qiwama* over women in the family (of Sura 4:34) was the fact that they developed a theoretical and methodological system, or model, of Qur'anic exegesis in which the doctrines of the faith (*'aqa'id*) and the laws of ritual and worship (*'ibadat*) were deemed beyond human reinterpretation, while the Qur'an's socio-political laws (*mu'amalat*) required constant reconsideration in order to ensure that the Qur'anic laws enhance rather than harm the public well-being (*al-maslaha al-'amma*) of the

Muslim community. By focusing on the concept of public weal, Abduh and Rida made the connection between revelation and history. Their dimension of 'history' included both the history of seventh-century Arabia, where the revelation was first received, and the Arab world of the nineteenth century, where its laws needed to be applied for the benefit of all, in the rigorous manner that Abduh's and Rida's reformism envisaged. In defining the 'meaning' of the Qur'an's social laws in this manner, their paradigm rested on the notion that the first Islamic community of the righteous forefathers (*al-salaf al-salih*) had been a republic of virtue in which both men and women lived profoundly moral lives. Their own nineteenth-century Egyptian society was a far cry from that seventh-century Arabian model; therefore, some of the Qur'anic rules on *mu'amalat* had to be reinterpreted to fit the needs and possibilities of this later situation (Stowasser, 1993, pp. 8-9). Their formula on the relationship between revelation (as God's eternal word) and the era where it was first verbalized presented the first of many modern Arab-Islamic stances on the thorny issue of the 'historicity' of scripture. This theme has been central to the methodological approaches of Qur'an interpreters during the twentieth century and beyond.

But Abduh's legacy was complex, and Islamic modernism has come in many forms, as have its exponents, who range from progressive-liberal intellectuals to fundamentalist activists. Unlike Abduh, who was a member of the *'ulama* establishment, most later exponents of Islamic modernism have had educational backgrounds in areas other than theology and law. Experts on Islamic history and culture, philosophers, cultural anthropologists, sociologists, linguists and specialists in literary criticism and, even, engineering have all brought new methodologies to bear on how to read the Qur'an. A major voice in the modernist hermeneutic literature of the 1950s to the 1980s was the Pakistani scholar Fazlur Rahman (d.1988), Professor of Islamic Studies at the University of Chicago, who defined the intellectual process of 'rethinking' (*ijtihad*) the Qur'an's applicability to modern socio-political concerns as the act of rational differentiation between the Qur'an's 'literal laws' (which are time-bound), on the one hand, and the 'reasons behind the laws' (*rationes legis*, which lead us to comprehend the enduring values that underlie those laws), on the other hand (Rahman, 1980, 1982). The very considerable Muslim modernist literature on the Qur'an and gender that has appeared during the past few decades both in the Middle East and the West has sounded similar themes.

Women's Voices Rising

During the second half of the twentieth century, Muslim women scholars began to work in the classically male-dominated areas of Qur'anic exegesis and the study of Hadith. Female-authored Qur'an-based studies, especially on gender questions, have proliferated over the past decades. They have followed a trend that, in its modern incarnation, goes back to the preference for thematic Tafsir over the traditional interlinear (verse-by-verse) Tafsir and which was manifested in mid-century *'ulama* works by the likes of Mahmud Shaltut (d.1963), the Egyptian modernist Rector of al-Azhar from 1958 to 1963 who approached the Qur'anic text as an organic whole, emphasized interpretation by themes, considered the Hadith at best a secondary source of interpretation and legislation (with large parts of it unreliable), and stressed the need to rethink the Qur'an's laws on socio-political issues with the purpose of moral reform of the community (Stowasser, 1998, pp. 36-37).

Women have produced Tafsirs (Zaynab al-Ghazali), partial Tafsirs (Bint al-Shati'), documents of textual Hadith criticism (Fatima Mernissi), and many thematic Qur'an-based gender studies in which Sura 4:34 was and is a pivotal item. Unlike the earlier pioneers among female religious scholars, most contemporary women writers and activists today are engaged in the effort to 'unread' patriarchal interpretations of the Qur'an. They believe that women's work in the area of Tafsir is absolutely essential to opening up the Islamic discourse on gender as a whole and that 'feminism' within the context of Islam can provide the only path to empowerment and liberation that avoids challenging the whole culture.

A'isha Abd al-Rahman, who chose to write under the pseudonym Bint al-Shati' (1913-1998), was the daughter of an Azhar-educated shaykh and teacher in a local mosque in Dimyat, Egypt; she later became the student and then wife of the Fu'ad/Cairo University scholar of Arabic literature and linguistics Amin al-Khuli (d.1965), who is credited with developing a literary approach to Qur'anic exegesis based on both text and context. Between 1962 and 1969, Bint al-Shati' published a two-volume literary (as opposed to traditional) interpretation of fourteen selected Suras of the Qur'an under the title of *Al-Tafsir al-Bayani lil-Qur'an al-Karim* of which the first volume deals with Suras 93, 94, 99, 79, 100, 90, and 102 (in that order), and the second with Suras 96, 68, 103, 92, 89, 104, and 107 (Screslet, 2003, pp. 6-7). By selecting these early Meccan Suras as the focus of her interpretations, Bint al-Shati' avoided having to deal with gender and other legal matters. Between 1961 and 1965, however, she also authored some substantial biographical tomes on the Prophet's wives, his mother, daughters, and several exemplary women among the second Islamic generation (Hoffman-Ladd, 1995, pp. 4-5). Unlike her Qur'anic work, which is methodologically modernist, Bint al-Shati''s Hadith-based accounts on the women of the Prophet's household and family are religiously conservative. Even though Muhammad's wives, for example, are presented with a modern focus, their exemplary qualities are found in their supportive strengths in the domestic arena (Stowasser, 1994, pp. 119-132).

The Islamist activist and scholar Zaynab al-Ghazali (1918-2004) is the author of a two-volume Tafsir, but she is better known for her activism than her scholarship. 'She called herself the "mother" of the Muslim Brotherhood, a reference to her seniority in age and her leading role as teacher and propagator of the Brotherhood's cause in Egypt' (Hoffman, 1985, p. 233). At the end of the 1940s, she joined her own feminist political activism to the activities of the Muslim Brothers in Egypt, a fact that later put her into Nasser's prison where she suffered acts of torture (al-Ghazali, 2005, pp. 62-63). Zaynab al-Ghazali's life story, related in her autobiography, *Ayyam min Hayati* (1984), is a personalized tale of gender-egalitarian religious activism that continues to inspire contemporary Islamic equal-rights advocates. In a 1981 interview, she stated that 'Islam has provided everything for both men and women. It gave women everything – freedom, economic rights, political rights, social rights, public and private rights. Islam gave women rights in the family granted by no other society ... the Muslim woman must study Islam so she will know that Islam has given her all her rights' (Hoffman, 1985, pp. 234-235). She herself had founded the Muslim Women's Association when she was eighteen years old, in order to acquaint women with this fact and convince them that the (secular, nationalist) women's liberation movement was but a deviant innovation that occurred due to the Muslims' backwardness. Zaynab al-Ghazali used the Muslim Women's Association as an instrument toward the Islamization of Egyptian society in a dual manner: by offering Qur'anic instruction for women, and also providing charitable support for the needy. This pattern continues among many Islamist associations today.

But motherhood remained central to al-Ghazali's notion of womanhood. She stressed that a woman's 'first, holy, and most important mission is to be a mother and wife' (Hoffman, 1985, p. 237). To fulfill their role as the educators of their sons, women need to be educated and well knowledgeable themselves (Hoffman, 1985, p. 236). Many scholars have remarked that al-Ghazali herself did not seem to follow what she preached. She divorced her first husband because he interfered with her work, and had a written agreement with her second husband that he would not do likewise (Hoffman, 1985, p. 237). Indeed, al-Ghazali's enduring legacy in Egypt and beyond derives from her political activism and her emphasis on the importance of women's participation in public life, including politics.

A yet very different record of Islamic female scholarship on scripture and canonized tradition emerges from the textual-critical oeuvre of the Moroccan sociologist Fatima Mernissi. In her *Le harem politique* (English translation by Mary Jo Lakeland *The Veil and the Male Elite: a feminist interpretation of women's rights in Islam,* 1991 and also published under the title *Women and Islam: an historical and theological enquiry*) Mernissi attacked age-old authoritarian readings of the Qur'an as mere male manipulations of the sacred text. She also engaged in classical Hadith criticism to prove the *in*authenticity of the (presumably Prophetic) tradition 'a people who entrust their command to a woman will not thrive', because of historical problems concerning the date of its first transmission, and moral deficiencies recorded of its first transmitter, the Prophet's freedman Abu Bakra (Mernissi, *Veil,* 1991, pp. 49-61).

New Strategies

Not all women's educational activities that focus on the Qur'an are liberationist in intent or political in motivation. During the 1970s and 1980s, female participation in mosque-held Qur'anic study groups rose sharply. Mosques, religious centers, and private settings in the Middle East and the West are presently providing opportunities for women to memorize the Qur'an, and some of these venues also facilitate more formal lectures by Muslim women for Muslim women on matters of doctrine, ritual, and morality issues inherent in the Qur'an and the Traditions. In Egypt, for example, the female instructors in the *maqra'at* ('Qur'an memorizing centers') in government-controlled mosques are generally graduates of religious schools and academies variously affiliated with the traditionalist al-Azhar University, and their academic degrees are at best on the level of a Bachelor of Arts. On the other hand, in most local mosques and organizations that are not controlled by the government, the teaching is carried out by professional women who have no formal religious education themselves but often hold advanced degrees in a science or applied science. In either case, the lessons tend to be supportive of a traditionalist gender paradigm. The institutional backdrop behind this relatively new phenomenon of large-numbered women's collective study programs of the Qur'an is the emergence of a new female profession, the female preacher (*al-mar'a al-da'iya*). Women preachers are expected to teach women their obligations and responsibilities, and most do so in a conservative mode, by prevailing upon the women in the audience to wear Islamic dress, condemning the notion of women's work outside the home, emphasizing women's duty of obedience toward their husband, engaging them as volunteers in charitable endeavors, and the like. It is said that the Qur'anic study centers have been behind the greater popularity of Islamic dress in Egypt during the recent past.

Very different from these conservative venues of Qur'anic education are the new female intellectuals who combine scripturalist scholarship with gender activism. Though indebted to the older female scholars like Bint al-Shati' and Fatima Mernissi, mentioned above, the present generation of gender-liberationist Muslim women (and some men) have greatly intensified their quest for a more fully realized Islamic community that grants full rights of active citizenship to its women. Their work is informed by knowledge of the patriarchal legacy of Tafsir and their desire to gain a new and fresh approach to the Qur'anic text in order to unread this tradition. In addition, their scholarship bears the mark of the transformative force of global Islam that derives from international connections and an awareness of social, political, and intellectual events transcending the local. The women who work and publish in this field are now connected to one another over several continents and languages, share the ability to read (and often write) in English, and are Internet-savvy.

Some Female Scholars on Gender and the Interpretation of Islamic Sources in Egypt

Among present-day activist scholars in Egypt, successors to Zaynab al-Ghazali, are Heba Raouf Ezzat and Omaima Abu Bakr. Heba Raouf Ezzat teaches political science at Cairo University and is generally hailed as a proponent for indigenous gender equality (Stowasser, 2001, pp. 99-119) who sees Islam as the primary and general solution not only for women's rights but also for democracy, human rights, and economic justice. She maintains that this will require a new interpretation (*ijtihad*) of Qur'an and Sunna ('the Prophet's exemplary precedent' related by way of the Hadith); but since the Hadith – in Raouf Ezzat's opinion – is 'the books of man', the Qur'an is the far more important source for the new gender-equal paradigm (Ezzat, http://islam21.net/main/index.php?option=com_content&task=view&id=294&Itemid=39). While the family is an important social institution that needs to be protected, this should not occur at the expense of women's freedom; indeed, a truly Islamic family needs to function by mutual consultation (*shura*) between the husband and the wife, which 'democratizes' gender relations within the family and allows women to balance their domestic and public lives (Hafez, 2003, pp. 34-35).

Omaima Abu Bakr teaches English Literature at Cairo University and is also co-founder of a non-governmental organization, the Women and Memory Forum, dedicated to rewriting the histories of prominent Muslim women whose stories have survived only in androcentric chronicles and other such historical sources. Abu Bakr stresses the egalitarian nature of the Qur'an's message and warns against the cultural trappings that have been 'incorporated and canonized' into religion. In so far as the true principles of Islam differ from the way that Islam is actually practiced, attention needs to be paid to the divergences between theoretical statements about women's Islamic rights and the actual implementation of these rights; developing an indigenous framework will then, however, liberate Muslim women from having to 'subscribe to any foreign Western agenda or discourse on feminism and gender' (Abu Bakr, 1999).

Muslim Women's Qur'anic Scholarship in the West

There are several important Muslim women scholars who presently work on gender issues in scripture, live in the West and write in English; for the most part, they are also profoundly influenced by Fazlur Rahman's methodology. By way of their impact on the global discourse on Qur'an and gender, special mention should here be made of Amina Wadud, the African American author of *Qur'an and Woman: rereading the sacred text from a woman's perspective* (1992); Asma Barlas, author of *'Believing Women' in Islam: unreading patriarchal interpretations of the Qur'an* (2002) and Reffat Hassan, both of Pakistani background; and Nimat Hafez Barazangi, author of *Woman's Identity and the Qur'an: a new reading* (2004). Even though these

33

and other activist scholars often question or even reject being identified as 'feminists' – since, as they point out, (Western) feminists are secularists who are fighting male domination – there is a liberationist tenor to their work that perhaps does merit use of the epithet in the new sense of an 'Islamic feminism'. This new spirit makes the connection between women's rights and democracy, human rights and economic justice, and it is thus conceived as the absolute antithesis to the patriarchal, paternalistic and hierarchical framings of the pre-modern Tafsir.

From among this new, female-authored literature, I am choosing Amina Wadud's book on *Qur'an and Woman* as an example of present-day gender-equal hermeneutics that also provides a novel reading of Sura 4:34. Wadud's theoretical stance regarding Tafsir consists of the differentiation between two textual levels in the Qur'an, the historically and culturally contextualized 'prior text' and the wider 'metatext' of essential or culturally universal relevance. In the latter, gender distinctions (based on early Arabian precedent) are superseded by the Qur'an's emphasis on gender equality (Cornell, 1994, p. 392).Wadud distinguishes three categories of Qur'anic interpretation: the traditional, reactive, and holistic. 'Traditional' exegesis is faulted for its atomistic methodology and lack of recognition of the Qur'an's structure of thematic unity; its main fault, however, lies in the fact that all traditional Qur'an interpretations were written by men. 'Reactive' interpretation is largely how feminist and other ideologically motivated individuals have used the Qur'an in order to 'vindicate the position of women on grounds entirely incongruous with the Qur'an's position on women'. Finally, the 'holistic' category, chosen by Wadud herself, involves consideration of the context of a Qur'anic revelation, the grammatical and semantic composition of its given text, and also the overall Qur'anic world-view (Wadud, 1992, pp. 1-4). Every Qur'anic 'reading' in part reflects the intentions of the text as well as the 'prior text' of the one who makes the 'reading', that is, the reader's own perspectives, circumstances, and background. While a large variety of readings can thus coexist, mere relativism is prevented by the permanence and continuity of the Qur'anic text itself, on which all readings converge; 'it is not the text or its principles that change, but the capacity and particularity of the understanding and reflection of the principle of the text within a community of people' (Wadud, 1992, p. 5). No interpretation involving the separation of principles and their applicability, however, can ever be final, because to impose a single cultural perspective – even that of the original community of the Prophet – contradicts the essential nature and universal purpose of the Qur'an (Wadud 1992, pp. 10 and 6).

Within this framework, Wadud's reading of Sura 4:34 begins with an inner-Qur'anic, context-focused study of essential lexical items in this verse, which are also found as operative items in other Qur'anic verses on gender-specific economic legislation such as inheritance shares and specific spousal support legislation. While Wadud follows the Islamist Sayyid Qutb (d.1966) and others in understanding this verse as legislative on the functional relationship between man and husband (protector and provider) and woman and wife (mother of his children), she then also extends those principles of 'gender equality *qua* mutual dependency in the family' to society at large. Here, in the societies of the modern world, Wadud finds the verse's meaning revealed as the expression of an ideal obligation of men to create a better society by bettering their relationships with women, which constitutes part of their God-given obligation to establish human trusteeship (*khilafa*) on earth (Wadud, 1992, pp. 69-78).

Sura 4:34 on the Internet

Some of the female scholars mentioned above have published articles on or about Tafsir in electronic form that we have here accessed for this book chapter. Many other electronically available Qur'an-related texts, be it in the form of scripturalist exegesis or specific *fatwas* ('formal legal opinions'), however, are not signed so that their authorship remains obscure. Among the web pages and Internet sites that yield ample information to the educated Muslim female regarding the Qur'an and gender are the following:

- Islamonline.net;
- jannah.org/genderequity;
- mwlusa.org, site of the Muslim Women's League that has several entries regarding verse 4:34 labeled 'The Verse of Abuse, or the Abused Verse';
- wluml.org, Women Living under Muslim Laws, who had a six-day workshop on Qur'anic Interpretations by Women in 1990 of which proceedings were first published in 1997 and then reprinted in 2004, and in which Sura 4:34 took up three of the formal presentations on gender issues.

And then there are many others, such as:

- islamicity.com;
- muslimwomenstudies.com;
- maryams.net;
- islam21.net;
- crescentlife.com

And there are many more.

Many Islamic feminist readings of Sura 4:34 available in this medium converge in problematizing the *daraba*-phrase of this verse that grants men the right to 'beat' recalcitrant females (or 'beat' those females of whom they fear recalcitrance). Some of the feminist interpreters endeavor to redefine the connotations of the specific vocabulary item of *daraba*, insisting that *daraba* has many other meanings than just 'beating' or 'hitting'. But beyond that is the scripturalist issue of why and how the historical meaning of hitting or

35

striking one's women in the seventh century (an act of domestic authority) is now regarded as domestic violence in the twenty-first century. The latter formula, an item of modern gender sensitivity, is how the issue is dealt with in the web page of *Domestic violence in the Qur'an.* But it is also noteworthy that the whole of Sura 4:34 is at present a regular staple in this new world of electronic communications, and that the verse's electronic interpretations tend to reflect the new hermeneutics of gender-equal readings of the Qur'an.

References

Abu Bakr, O. (1999) Gender Perspectives in Islamic Tradition.
http://www.crescentlife.com.thisthat/feminist%20muslims/gender_perspectives_in
_islamic_tradition.htm

al-Baydawi, A. (1968) Anwar al-Tanzil wa-Asrar al-Ta'wil, in H.O. Fleischer (Ed.)
Reproductio Phototypica Editionis 1846-1848, vol. 1. Osnabruck: Biblio-Verlag.

al-Ghazali, Z. (1984) *Ayyam min Hayati*, sixth printing Beirut: Dar al-Shuruq.

al-Ghazali, Z. (2005) The Mother of Men, *Islamic Horizons*, November/December,
62-63.

al-Razi, M. (1934-1962) *Al-Tafsir al-Kabir*, vol. 10. Cairo: Al-Matba'a al-Bahiyya al-
Misriyya.

al-Tabari, A.(1972) *Jami' al-Bayan 'an Ta'wil 'Ay al-Qur'an*, vol. 8, 290-317, ed.
Mahmud M. Shakir & Ahmad M. Shakir. Cairo: Dar al-Ma'arif.

al-Zamakhshari, M. (1953) *Al-Kashshaf 'an Haqa'iq Ghawamid al- Tanzil*, vol. 1, ed.
Mustafa Husayn Ahmad. Cairo: Matba'at al-Istiqama.

Barazangi, N.H. (2004) *Woman's Identity and the Qur'an: a new reading.* Gainesville:
University Press of Florida.

Barlas, A. (2002) *'Believing Women' in Islam: unreading patriarchal interpretations of the
Qur'an.* Austin: University of Texas Press.

Cornell, V.J. (1994) Qur'an, in John Esposito (Ed.) *The Oxford Encyclopedia of the
Modern Islamic World*, vol. 3, 392. New York: Oxford University Press.

Domestic violence in the Qur'an. http://209.157.64.200/focus/f-news/1359865/posts

Ezzat, H.R. Women and the Interpretation of Islamic Sources.
http://www.islam21.net/pages/keyissues/key2-6.htm

Haddad, Y.Y. & Stowasser B.F. (Eds) (2004) *Islamic Law and the Challenges of
Modernity*, 5-6. Walnut Creek: Altamira.

Hafez, S. (2003) The Terms of Empowerment: Islamic activists in Egypt, in *Cairo
Papers in Social Science*, 24(4), 34-35. Cairo: The American University in Cairo
Press.

Hoffman, V.J. (1985) An Islamic Activist: Zaynab al-Ghazali, in Elizabeth W. Fernea
(Ed.) *Women and the Family in the Middle East*, 233. Austin: University of Texas
Press.

Hoffman-Ladd, V.J. (1995) *The Oxford Encyclopedia of the Modern World*, vol. 1, 4-5,
ed. John L. Esposito. New York: Oxford University Press.

Ibn Kathir, I. (n.d.) *Tafsir al-Qur'an al-'Azim*, vol. 1, 490-491. Cairo: Dar Ihya' al-Kutub al-'Arabiyya.

Mernissi, F. (1991) The Veil and the Male Elite: a feminist interpretation of women's rights in Islam, trans. Mary Jo Lakeland. Reading: Addison-Wesley.

Rahman, F. (1980) *Major Themes of the Qur'an*. Minneapolis: Bibliotheca Islamica.

Rahman, F. (1982) *Islam and Modernity*. Chicago: University of Chicago Press.

Rida, M.R. (1973) *Tafsir al-Qur'an al-Hakim al-Shahir bi-Tafsir al-Manar*, vol. 5. Beirut: Dar al-Ma'arif.

Roded, R. (1994) *Women in Islamic Biographical Collections: from* Ibn Sa'd *to* Who's Who. Boulder: Lynne Rienner.

Screslet, R.J. (2003) Meaning and Method: Bint al-Shati''s Tafsir al-Bayani. Unpublished Graduate Seminar paper, Georgetown University.

Shaikh, S. (1997) Exegetical Violence: nushuz in Quranic gender ideology, *Journal for Islamic Studies*, 17, 49-73. http://theothervoices.org.za/Religionsa/jotafs.htm

Smith, J.I. & Haddad, Y.Y. (1981) *The Islamic Understanding of Death and Resurrection*. Albany: State University of New York Press.

Spellberg, D. (2005) History Then, History Now, in Amira El-Azhary Sonbol (Ed.) *Beyond the Exotic: women's histories in Islamic societies*. Syracuse: Syracuse University Press.

Stowasser, B.F. (1994) *Women in the Qur'an: traditions, and interpretation*, 119-132. New York: Oxford University Press.

Stowasser, B.F. (1993) Women's Issues in Modern Islamic Thought, in Judith E. Tucker (Ed.) *Arab Women*, 8-9. Bloomington: Indiana University Press.

Stowasser, B.F. (1998) Gender Issues and Contemporary Quran Interpretation, in Yvonne Y. Haddad & John L. Esposito (Eds) *Islam, Gender, and Social Change*, 36-37. New York: Oxford University Press.

Stowasser, B.F. (2001) Old Shaykhs, Young Women, and the Internet: the rewriting of women's political rights in Islam, *The Muslim World*, 91(1 & 2), 99-119.

Stowasser, B.F. (2004) The End is Near: minor and major signs of the hour in Islamic, in Abbas Amanat & John J. Collins (Eds) *Apocalypse and Violence*, 49-52. New Haven: The Yale Center for International and Area Studies.

Wadud, A. (1992) *Qur'an and Woman: rereading the sacred text from a woman's perspective*, 1st edn. Kuala Lampur: Penerbit Fajar Bakti Sdn., Bhd.

Women Living under Muslim Laws (1997, reprinted 2004) *For Ourselves: women reading the Qur'an*. London: Women Living under Muslim Laws.

The Impact of Educational Empowerment on Women in the Arab World

SERRA KIRDAR

In no area has the force of tradition been felt more strongly and the effect of globalisation been more apparent than that of the status and roles of women. The position of women in the Arab world, in particular, is neither uniform nor static. Whereas some societies in that region have encouraged women to work in professional fields, other more traditional societies have limited women's work and areas of study to the arts and humanities, hoping thereby to preserve their roles as wives and mothers. My previous research indicates that professional careers available to women in many communities have tended to be mere extensions of their traditional roles (Kirdar, 2006). The purpose of the research from which this chapter was drawn (Kirdar, 2004) was to investigate the role of education in the engendering of cultural change and leadership amongst a select group of powerful, 'first generation professional', Arab, Muslim women, and specifically, the role and impact of their dual educational/cultural experiences, both Arab and 'Western'. The empirical dimension specifically deals with a small echelon of educated Muslim women from different Arab countries who are not representative of all Muslim Arab women; it is not the intent of this chapter to make generalisations about 'Muslim Arab women'. The women selected as samples come from: Saudi Arabia, Bahrain, Morocco, Egypt and Jordan. However, the issues and themes which this chapter attempts to address are not simply relevant and limited to this small echelon of society. Indeed, issues pertaining to the quality of a nation's educational system, the changing roles of women and the challenges they face as they seek empowerment, both within their respective societies and in their professions, can be applied to many cultures, communities and nations. The impetus of this chapter is to analyse the merging of cultural traditionalism and modernity and how their dual education has enhanced the ability of these women to become leaders in their professional careers, and within their respective communities, whilst still maintaining strong ties to their culture, religion and traditions, albeit to varying degrees.

Gender issues and the quality of education are of vital importance to a nation's development. Indeed, 'improving the quality of education is the most rewarding investment a country can make' (Roudi-Fahimi & Moghadam, 2003). It is of even more significance to the Arab nations where only 20 per cent of women in the Middle East region take part in the labour force, the lowest level of any world region (Roudi-Fahimi & Moghadam, 2003, 4). By comparison, Indonesia, having the largest Muslim population of any country, has a profile where women constitute 38 per cent of labour force participation (United Nations, 2000). To maintain living standards in a region where more than half the population is under the age of eighteen, it is imperative that governments improve labour productivity and increase female participation in the workforce. The future advancement of women in the Arab world is inextricably linked to the socio-economic progress of the entire region (Kirdar, 1997). However, in the Gulf States women have the lowest representation rate in the labour force as a consequence of the more traditionally and conservatively held views of women. In Saudi Arabia, for example, women comprise a mere 7 per cent of the labour force. Education and employment have been the main channels that provided women of all classes with mobility and self-awareness, but access to either or both has been largely constrained by the economic and political systems of their respective countries:

> It is clear that the women of the wealthy upper class ... have
> utterly different concerns than those of the economically less
> fortunate classes. (Seikaly, 1998, p. 178)

There are a large number of women from Arab countries who have had the privilege of education in their own countries as well as in the West. However, gender constraints and pre-defined gender roles still very much dictate the society in which these women operate. The patriarchal system is omnipresent. The challenges facing educated Arab Muslim woman, in reconciling certain traditional mores and intellectual and educational exposure, has only served as a greater impetus for the need to focus on the changing role of women and education in the Arab world. Middle-class urban Arab Muslim women have particularly enjoyed improved levels of education and social mobility, yet this has not translated into significant power in civil society, where women have been excluded or marginalised from decision-making processes. As a result, it is only women of the educated elite who have been able to step outside these circumscribed boundaries (Roudi-Fahimi & Moghadam, 2003).

The working women in the Arab world tend to be elite and middle class, many of whom have been educated in the West. It is from the examination of the perceived experiences of this category of women, through qualitative procedures and a selected sample of cases, that I connected with broader problematic issues of education and development in the Arab world.

Often, it has been political conflicts that have fundamentally impacted the way active and educated women view the world and their own role in the process of change. Nationalism has helped project women into the public arena and has acted as a means for emancipation. Although males were the initial advocates for women's emancipation at the turn of the twentieth century in Egypt, it was not long before women themselves, through newly established women's organisations, called for religious, educational, political and social reforms. The influence of 'modernisation' during the twentieth century is evident in the legal reforms, voting rights, and educational and employment opportunities that altered and broadened women's roles and positions in their respective societies. Active, conscious and politicised educated women are demanding the restoration of control over their own lives and over their ability and power to make their own decisions and choices (Chu & Radwan, 2004).

No longer are women simply wives and mothers; today they have entered different areas of public space, ranging from politics to the professions. However, one must caution against generalisation. Such progress is not true for all women; in fact, it is only a relatively small percentage of Arab Muslim women to whom this applies, and even within the group it varies greatly from one region to another. Today, there are women who have forged this working balance between the traditional and the modern. Amongst these are the ten women chosen as samples. They have created their own paradigm that has allowed them to work within their respective systems and cultures whilst embracing the modern world. These women are among a rising number of high-achieving women from different countries in the Arab region that are fast emerging as living role models of empowered and influential women who have made the system work for them and who have gained much stature internationally. Women from the educated elite are now challenging the status quo and demanding equality in family and society, calling for women's economic, political and social empowerment. The feminist discourse has reached new levels. No longer must a woman fighting for her rights as an equal citizen fit the 'Western' secular paradigm. On the contrary, many women who have aligned themselves with the Islamic revival movement in different Arab countries have gone to considerable lengths to proclaim their independent initiative. These Islamic women, in continuing their fight for equality, see no conflict between the conventional roles of mothers, wives and professionals. Indeed, the subjugation of women does not have its source in Islam; rather, 'it is a manifestation of the region's vulnerability to many of the dictatorial and authoritative regimes under which human rights, those of women included, are repressed' (Kirdar, 1997, p. 4). Today, there exists dual pressure in calling for political reform and economic pressure, and changes that recognise the need to bring forth the women from the safety of their homes into the public arena.

I have personally witnessed two incidents that indisputably illustrate this revolutionary change in women's empowerment. The first happened to be *muhajabbat* women protesting in the streets of London calling for the wearing of the hijab as a matter of choice. (*Muhajabbat* is the Arabic name given to the women who wear the Islamic headscarf to cover the hair. This is often incorrectly referred to as the 'veil'. 'Hijab' is the Islamic headscarf worn by women.) The second incident was an article in the *Wall Street Journal* by a prominent Saudi businesswoman, 'ranked among Fortune's top 50 powerful women outside of the USA' (Jeddah Economic Forum, 2004). She spoke out about the future of Saudi Arabia's economy and growth at the main regional event of 2004, in the presence of her male counterparts. The fact that Saudi Arabia calls for sex segregation and does not routinely host mixed conferences in which women themselves are keynote speakers only further reinforces this notion of change and empowerment that women themselves are demanding, even in the most conservative of societies.

The Arab world, that is to say, those countries that have an affinity with the Arabic language, Islam and Arabic culture, has struggled to redefine women's roles in society and identify ways of reconciling tradition and modernity. Increasingly, leaders of these Arab countries have recognised the need for modernisation and change, often drawing inspiration from the West and overcoming the force of tradition, regarded by many as an obstacle to change. Nonetheless, they have remained cognisant of the pre-eminent role that Islam holds amongst their people, and have had to contend with subscribing to and abiding by religion as a source of a cohesive transnational Arab identity, recognising it to be a source of legitimacy and popular mobilisation: 'no place has the tension and conflict between tradition and modernity been more prevalent and evident than in the ambivalent and contradictory paths pursued with regard to women's role and emancipation' (Esposito & Haddad, 1998, p. 16). Thus, while education and family reforms were pursued by some Arab governments, there was also a continued pursuit of traditional values in tandem. In other cases, as in the Gulf States, there was a stricter adherence to tradition, as illustrated in the strict laws of sex segregation in Saudi Arabia.

However, it is arguable that such differences are as much related to the political economy as they are to religion and culture. In the non-oil-producing countries, with weak economies, women often found employment opportunities, spurred on by financial necessity that served to alter their role, both within the societal and the familial domains. Nonetheless, in many such circumstances, when the demand for extra labour subsided, the newly emancipated professional woman was expected to resume her place within the walls of her home. The result of the emergence of oil wealth and cheap foreign labour in many of the Gulf States resulted in a reinforcement of traditional cultural norms and values regarding a woman's place in her society, her family and socially acceptable professions.

It is the interaction between the region's economic structure and its conservative culture, in which traditional gender roles are strongly enforced, that is largely responsible for the lower levels of female education and labour force participation. It must be noted that these 'traditional cultural norms' are arguably more related to tribal customs than to Islam itself. Though Islamic law did stipulate parameters for behaviour, the Qur'an did not replace Arabian, patriarchal tribal society and customs. In fact, many of the customs practised today were a result of local contexts and social class, which varied from urban to rural and from one country to another. The challenge facing countries and individuals in the twenty-first century is to find a working balance between the preservation of identity and community while at the same time taking part successfully in a globalised system. What is needed is a reconciliation of culture within a globalised environment; a creation of a synergy and co-existence of globalisation with the preservation of cultural identities.

The women selected for this research as examples of this developmental change have gained recognition within their respective professions, within their communities and in the international arena. Their professions cover academia, business, sports, biotechnology, human resource development and education. They have created their own formula that has resulted in a sense of empowerment and leadership. Their sense of empowerment has come through their educational achievements and experiences and the challenges and conflicts that they have encountered along the way. The purpose of this chapter is to cast new light on this group of high-achieving Arab women and to understand how certain first-generation professional Arab women have managed to forge that balance and redefine their identities within a 'glocultural' dynamic. Today there exist many women who are redefining and renegotiating their immediate circumstances to suit their needs and their ambitions.

Whereas in the past it was essentially a male movement that called for women's rights, or women's education or women's issues in the Arab world, predominantly in Egypt in the 1950s, this is no longer the case. The change may be subtle to the outside observer. But whether the women are covering their hair or calling for equal pay and opportunities, it is they who are now pushing their agenda forward. For example, many women in the Arab Muslim world have opted to wear the hijab. The reasons vary, but amongst the many given there are those who cite freedom to move around, work and be taken seriously. They do not want to be objectified as sex objects, nor do they wish to be harassed when they go to work, as more women in the Arab world are taking part in the workforce. For them, it is a way to reap the benefits of modernisation and modernity without sacrificing their cultural traditions. To them, it is a source of empowerment. For other empowered women, they do not feel compelled to take such protective measures. They push their agendas forward by being keynote speakers at local and international conferences, speaking their minds and pursuing their objectives. Neither paradigm is less or more of a female movement. Both are pushing forward their own objectives and agendas. These women have become their own architects and executives of their empowerment. No longer are the men drafting women's movements. Perhaps men started it for their own nationalistic interests and to serve political rhetoric. Yet change is imminent. These women are the driving force, covered and not covered; the destination is clear and the will, education and determination are there. Not only do greater numbers of women seek access to higher education and the professions, they now want to ascend the ranks and break the 'glass ceiling'. But it will take time.

It is imperative to reinforce the understanding of contextual issues and localised feminism, as well as the need to draw certain parallels between the existing glass ceiling notion that plagues 'Western' female professionals and the professional opportunities and roadblocks encountered by their Eastern female counterparts. In fact, many professionally ambitious women in the Arab world and in the West face similar barriers to senior management positions. Though the 'Western' world may appear to have a more 'egalitarian' view of men and women, in the final analysis, there are still very few women who get beyond the glass ceiling without forfeiting their femininity and their familial duties as wives and mothers.

Indeed, there is no denying that women in the Western hemispheres have and do enjoy a much more liberated society where, as women, they enjoy equal rights and opportunities, and are free to make their own decisions. Has patriarchy been completely abolished here in the liberated 'West'? Throughout the course of the interviews, respondents stated that these conflicts are indeed prevalent, even in the most 'liberal' of societies, yet the difference is simply a matter of varying degree.

Among the various observations made by the respondents in this study regarding their views on the challenges facing them as women within their work environment were two points that echoed the findings from 'Western' psychologists. The first observation made by the respondents was that they felt pressured to perform better than their male counterparts in order to constantly prove themselves to be capable and command respect. This was in accord with research findings based on 'Western' societies which stated that women who are a minority in their workplace are likely to face greater performance pressures as well as to be constantly under 'observation'. As a result, women may experience stress from feeling that they have to perform better than their male colleagues.

The second experience some of the respondents mentioned related to feeling isolated from their co-workers as a result of being a woman. Some of the women noted that the gender divide was so apparent that it strained and in some cases, impeded their interactions with the men. In one case, a respondent claimed that her exclusion and total lack of support from her Arab male colleagues brought her very close to abandoning her project and quitting. Again there was a correlation between the experiences shared between these select professional Arab women and professional 'Western' women; the findings stated that women who are in the minority in male-dominated industries end up isolated from the main male group, which leads to their resignations in some cases.

However, it must be noted that although women appear to face similar challenges and obstacles regardless of culture, there appears to be one fundamental difference. 'Western' psychology purports that 'sex stereotypes place women into a double bind situation' whereby if they adopt a stereotypically masculine style of leadership 'they are considered abrasive or maladjusted' and if women assume stereotypically feminine styles of leadership then 'they are considered less capable and competent' (Gardiner & Tiggerman, 1999, p. 2).

Yet, drawing from the personal experiences and observations of the women interviewees in this research, only initially did there exist challenges to prove their capabilities, authority and gain the respect of their male colleagues. This required them to assume a concept of self that was not solely dictated and shaped by gender. Nevertheless, in none of the cases did the women feel compelled to choose between 'masculine' or 'feminine' styles of leadership. They very much embraced their femininity whilst also making concerted efforts to be recognised for their qualifications, expertise and professionalism. In fact, they felt that over time they were recognised and respected for their professionalism without ever having to abandon their self-identities as women, whether in terms of appearance or behaviour. This is in stark contrast to 'Western' thought that calls for women to abandon the feminine in order to ascertain the masculine. The Arab Muslim women interviewed for this study did not feel the two to be mutually exclusive. The interviewees for this study all believe in embracing their roles as women but did feel that they had to cast aside their self-identities as women and assume the role of 'the professional' when at work; the professional but not the masculine. Perhaps this first generation of senior management professional women has managed to find a balance that so far has escaped 'Western' women in senior management positions.

The notion of the 'glass ceiling' appears to be a distinctly gender-specific phenomenon. Despite allegations that a glass ceiling no longer exists in impeding women's success in the corporate world in the United States, a report was issued on corporate women that highlighted the persistence of a glass ceiling'(Cotter et al, 2001). However, it is necessary to define what a glass ceiling and its criteria mean. The first criterion is the presence of barriers reflecting discrimination that 'keeps minorities and women from rising to the upper rungs of the corporate ladder, regardless of their qualifications or achievements'; it is an unexplained inequality that is not due to the qualifications of women and minorities (Cotter et al, 2001, p. 665). The second criterion put forth is that glass ceiling inequality is greater at higher status levels than at lower status levels. It assumes that the job limits of women in the middle to higher levels of a hierarchy are worse than for job limits at lower levels.

Despite the gradual increase in the number of women in managerial roles, women in senior management positions are still somewhat under-represented in 'Western' societies. For example, women are estimated to fill only 25 per cent of managerial positions in Germany, 28 per cent in Switzerland and 33 per cent in the United Kingdom. These numbers are significantly reduced at higher levels where women only represent 10 per cent of senior-level management positions in the United States and 5 per cent in Germany (Gardiner & Tiggemann, 1999).

This notion of the 'glass ceiling' was reflected in some of the interviewees' responses regarding the difficulties they had encountered. As mentioned earlier, one respondent had difficulty, initially, when she joined a management consultancy. She had to work twice as hard as the men before her efforts were realised and given due acknowledgement. Another respondent mentioned the great difficulty she had in promoting some of her ideas as they were being sabotaged by her male colleagues.

Hence, though the women interviewed for this study have had to work within the constraints of their culture, gender codification of professions and the discrimination of their sex in the context of job opportunities and male and societal perceptions, it seems that women in the United States are no less plagued and are facing similar gender coding where their professions are still dictated by societal perceptions of gender.

The women in this study were chosen for several reasons. Among them is that they arguably represent Arab professional female role models. It has been argued that female role models can help break glass ceilings by providing mentors. Their image as female role models for other women in their communities directly affects and encourages self-confidence building. Building self-confidence includes 'trusting in one's own competence, knowing one's strengths and weaknesses, taking risks ... and learning to be successful' (Lemons, 2003, p. 251). Women in positions of leadership are few and far between in the Arab world. The women interviewed for this study are part of the first generation who are representative of such a group. Yet this is not simply the case in the Arab world. In fact, there are not many women in leadership positions in the USA:

> The number of women who serve as presidents of American
> colleges and universities has increased by 65 percent since 1978,
> the actual number has only moved from 154 to 253 out of 3200
> institutions. (Moore, 1987, p. 31)

In engendering change and leadership within one's own community, there is a need to redefine assumed and accepted perceptions by gradually leading by example. In the case of the respondents, this is precisely how they have managed to promote changes and redefine their identities as professional Arab Muslim women whilst working within the constraints of their respective patriarchal societies and using their status as a tool for change. Their successes in being accepted and respected by their society and their male co-workers whilst working in male-dominated industries cannot be undermined, underestimated or overlooked.

These are women who have become precursors to change; a change that will take time. Nevertheless, change is inevitable and will come as a result of women themselves stepping forward and identifying themselves as role models and living examples of the possible synergy between tradition and modern. This first generation of Arab professional women is setting a new precedent that will have an impact on their children and their societies. With awareness of women of this type who are making the system work for them by bridging their identity within a modern context, more women will look to follow in redefining the terms their way.

Feminism and female empowerment have different connotations in different contexts. My case studies are all of women who see themselves as empowered, professional and ambitious; however, there is no one way to manifest such empowerment or feminism. Different contexts call for different behaviour. Amongst the women there is diversity regarding levels of liberalism, religious affiliation, familial responsibilities and societal expectations. Nonetheless, all these women have managed to integrate their respective cultural identity, tradition and heritage with professional success. Their educational achievement, among other salient factors, is what has enabled these women to be amongst the few Arab Muslim women who have successfully and simultaneously positioned themselves within both the local and global arenas. Today, Arab Muslim women continue to define and redefine their identities and their place within particular communities and within the international community. The key to deal with what lies ahead is in the relationship between tradition and modernity, the pivotal role of education in this interface, and what role they play in change.

Very often, analysis pertaining to Arab women suffers from the naivety of perceiving another culture through the prism of 'Western' consciousness; such that the fact that women in different cultures might have a somewhat different agenda or methods of achieving their objectives is rarely considered. These women very much subscribe to the philosophy that ancient cultures, like their own, cannot always be judged by the same yardstick employed to judge progress in women's issues in the Western hemisphere. Whilst 'Westerners' view discrimination against women as a product of a male-dominating culture, women in the Arab world and in the developing world believe that their struggles cannot be considered outside regional, political and developmental issues. 'Western' feminism is grounded in 'Western' ideology and values; the plight and struggles of Arab women are equally grounded in the religious, cultural and political norms of the Arab Muslim world. To lose sight of this would result in nothing but false conclusions. Nonetheless, perhaps the differences between the equivalently educated, high-achieving professional Arab woman and the American professional woman are not as distinct and profound as so commonly assumed.

The experiences and insights of select educated, high-achieving Arab women only serve to highlight the pre-eminent role and purpose of education, and the ailing educational systems in the Arab world that have been dysfunctional in respect of serving all its citizens. The current systems throughout the different countries of the region have superficially adopted the 'Western' edifice of a system. But they have been averse to teaching cognitive skill-building and creativity, and encouraging self-expression and self-awareness amongst the younger generations. Indeed, it is the educational systems that have been the apparatus used to reinforce dogmatic beliefs and perpetuate gender stereotyping. The women's personal experiences with such a system were a reason why their 'Western' schooling was that much more illuminating and challenging. Educational reconstruction is what is needed in the Arab countries in order to promote values that integrate and blend cultural identity and tradition with an education for understanding, cognitive skill-building, fostering creativity and competitive efficacy. What is suggested is a system built from the grass roots that aims to unite culture and cognitive learning. It is this combination that will ameliorate the economic and political environment and give true freedom and empowerment to the individual, whether they are male or female. What the Arab world needs is change, yet a change that preserves Islamic values and related traditions; it calls for modernisation but without total 'Westernisation'.

This is no mission impossible. One need not look too far beyond the women who have used their educational experiences to redefine their own identities and engender changes within their own domains. Perhaps what they have achieved is not beyond the reach of others in the region. The intention is to draw attention to these educated high-achieving Arab women role models who have successfully used their education and cross-cultural experiences to break their respective glass ceilings and become leaders in their fields whilst not abandoning their respective cultural identities.

At this point it is important to highlight what is meant by feminism and the awareness of female empowerment that occurred in the West, namely, in the USA in the 1960s and 1970s. The 1960s feminist writer, Betty Friedan, clearly defined the reality. She picked up on the trend of women who were trapped between their educational attainment and the female nature. Through the process of schooling and increased education girls grow into women and become independent and aware of their own potential. They become cognisant of the career opportunities and choices now available to them and the endless possibilities and options they have as a result of their increased educational qualifications. In unleashing female power they targeted the root cause and homed in on the role and power of education. From the 1960s in the USA the importance of female education became the lynchpin for unleashing female empowerment.

Today history is repeating itself as many Arab women call for female empowerment as they graduate in astonishing numbers from some of the most prestigious universities around the world. I personally met with over a dozen women who are precursors to massive change in the Arab world. These women are among the first generation of professional Arab women who are making a change and setting a precedent at the local and international level. They are renegotiating their roles as women and professionals in predominantly male domains and have done so as a direct result of this educational empowerment.

However, who is to say that, simply because Western women began the race a couple of decades earlier, they have necessarily found the right formula? Women are struggling to balance their home life and their careers. This is nothing new. But it has been getting harder and more difficult a task over the past decade for all women who are caught between culture, womanhood and modernity.

The 1960s feminism movement mentioned earlier is no longer what is necessarily needed or what works in today's world. It has not managed to succeed in delivering 'happiness' to the Western woman and it has no bearing or relevance on the realities facing the newly emerged educated, high-achieving Arab women. Professional women of the Arab world are calling for equal rights, in law and in practice. They are fighting to establish their own legacies as women, wives, mothers and professionals, believing that they do not need to forgo their feminine roles in doing so. It is a choice they do not believe needs to be made as they merge profession with womanhood.

It is a contextualised feminism that has begun to emerge among women who are neither 'Western' nor 'Eastern'. They are among globalised Arab women from countries such as Saudi Arabia, Egypt, Morocco, Bahrain and Jordan. In setting a new precedent, a new benchmark, they have unearthed and concocted a blending of the profession with the woman that until today, has escaped many Western, professionally driven women. Could it be possible that they are living proof – indeed – inspirational role models of the feasibility and possibility of both? They represent a new female empowerment that no longer takes the blame for the desperate lonely woman who must sacrifice her quest for family and womanhood for the sake of career, financial independence and equality. It is women like them who are setting a new movement that has chosen to embrace the culture and to work within the given system – they have not rejected the system but have made it and continue to make it work for them. It is not an easy endeavour, but it is work in progress that will take time.

One of the women who is setting the stage for change is the first Arab Muslim Olympic gold medal winner. Because of her, more and more women from the region are today competing in sports and adding their names to halls of fame. This particular woman became Minister for Sports in Morocco and is now actively involved with using sports as a way to bring boys and girls together and to unite society at large. Even she has faced countless obstacles along her road to success. She mentioned that in one instance:

> men I worked with tried to sabotage, destroy and go against the
> projects and initiatives I was trying to implement. The men did

not like the idea that the project was being launched by me or by a woman but this is something I have had to grow accustomed to in my work. There were times when I wanted to quit but it was my husband who pushed me to go back and continue my fight. (Interviewee)

A managing partner at a Jordanian management consultancy stated that:

when I returned to my country after finishing my education abroad, I was expected to conform to social expectations. I found myself caught between what society dictated and who I wanted to be and how I wanted to live. After standing firm for what I believed in, society accepted and actually respected me! (Interviewee)

And the irony of it all is that the very men who have tried to throw them off course, in the end, have become their staunchest supporters.

Since the 1960s emergence of feminism in the USA there has been a revaluing of women's voices. We call this the new liberated feminism, which was the counter-feminist movement to that of the 1960s. It was a call to a revision of feminism that is essentially engrained in femininity and in celebrating female values and the differences between women and men. In the Arab context, the women I met with are living examples of what the West still needs. These women are in fact the representatives of celebrating womanhood whilst stepping into the public domain. They straddle the two worlds; one foot in the private and one foot in the public. They have redefined and continue to redefine these spheres to suit their own agendas, potentials and ambitions as women, professionals, leaders, mothers, wives and partners. Have these women found the balance that has so far escaped their Western female counterparts? Could they be the precursors to change and to the next wave of celebrating liberated feminism? Perhaps what is needed is a revision of the original feminist movement which caused a backlash against motherhood, womanhood, domesticity and the virtues of femininity.

Even Western feminists who rejected these virtues and values are now re-evaluating and amending their stance. They realise they have missed out on the essence of their femininity and acknowledge there was no need to go to extremes. The solution is the discovery of a new middle ground between the extreme Western feminism of the 1960s on the one hand and the extreme subjugation and suppression of women in some Arab Islamic countries on the other.

What is needed is a closer look at the new emerging middle ground that is being initiated by educated, high-achieving, and powerful first-generation professional Arab women from different countries. There is no quintessential notion of empowerment but rather an amalgamation of many new and different interpretations. There exist Arab women today who have found a new feminist approach. They ardently support women's equal rights; strongly believe women should pursue a professional career and have never even contemplated stepping aside for men to lead. In fact, one of the women's rationale to wear the hijab was because she did not want to be objectified as a sex object within her community. She said that because she works alongside men and in most cases is the only woman, she felt that it would allow her to get on with her work and be taken seriously as a professional. The other woman who started wearing the hijab while a student in Canada is now one of the first women Ministers in Bahrain.

For that very reason, it is imperative to erase the erroneous belief that the subjugation of women in the Arab world is a result of Islam. These women do not see Islam as the source of the persistence of inequality. They and their more liberal Arab sisters are all calling and pushing for change. But it is change their way, not necessarily the Western way. Whether their heads are covered with a scarf or not should not and does not take away from the fact that these educated, high-achieving women are demanding change and empowerment, even in the most conservative countries. The women interviewed for this study are women who have gained recognition within their respective professions, within their communities and in the international arena. They are in academia, business, sports, biotechnology, consultancy and education. They have created their own formula that has resulted in their empowerment and leadership. They have charted new professional territories, even those traditionally regarded as 'male' domains. Expertise gained at higher levels in their fields has put them at the forefront of achievement among their male co-workers and has made dreams more realisable. As a result, they are self-confident and aware of their potential. They have felt a sense of empowerment to pursue new ideas and initiatives and go after what they believe in, irrespective of their gender, their religion or their nationality.

There is no one quintessential role model of a woman. These women believe that women in general have different qualities from men and have additional responsibilities. Not only is education and opportunities resulting from it linked to changes and progress in the financial and professional worlds. There is more these women feel passionate about. They have used their positions of power and influence to create greater awareness of women's issues and the vital and instrumental role of education – for everyone. They have accepted a leadership role through example and have become the role models so previously lacking in their traditional cultures.

I wanted to understand how certain first-generation professional women from different Arab countries have managed to forge that much-wanted balance that women all over the world are searching for. It is to understand how these women have managed to redefine their identities within a 'global-cultural' dynamic where they have kept their cultural identities but have renegotiated who they are on their own terms in the globalised world. In fact, one interviewee who heads the leading biotechnology company in Egypt said,

> even though I didn't like certain things in my culture, I never
> believed in going against the system. Actually, I learned to accept
> the system and work within its boundaries; I did not rebel.

Where she worked within the system, others have redefined the system according to what suits them. In either case, they have embraced their femininity and have used certain situations to their advantage.

Of course, as the first real generation of professional women in the Arab world, the women have no doubt found it challenging to combine the more traditional and conventional role of women with the professional. But because of them and others like them, there now exist many women's networks that encourage and support working women who learn to divide their responsibilities between family obligations and work. The women I met with have very demanding jobs and commitments that include a great deal of travelling. Of course, they juggle between their commitments – their roles as mothers, wives, partners and career professionals – yet each one of them has managed in her own way to find her own balance and acknowledge the merit in both. Today, many Arab Muslim women continue to define and redefine their identities and their places within particular communities and within the international community. Where they have had to battle with local social expectations, they too have found it challenging and yet necessary to dispel many misconceptions and wrongly construed stereotypes that the international and Western world have. The challenges they face to redefine and renegotiate their identities are all around, East and West. The answer in dealing with the future is in the nature of the relationship between a woman's tradition and the ever-changing modern world. The Olympic champion reinforced this need to break down misconceptions in the West when:

> at my press conference in Los Angeles [when she won the 1984
> Gold Medal] the press was so taken back that I was a Muslim
> woman wearing shorts and a T-shirt! They were more fascinated
> about who I was than why I was there and what I had just
> achieved! I felt compelled to explain my identity and that my
> beliefs and culture did not stop or prevent me from achieving my
> success and fame. (Interviewee)

Many of the young educated generations of women who have joined the Islamic movement have done so because they see religion as the solution for dealing with the temptations of modernisation. For them, religion gives them a way to choose what they like from modernisation without jeopardising the cultural and religious legacy of their societies. Whether this is the 'right' way to go about embracing modernity is immaterial. For them, they are making it work. What we must do is understand the cultural context in which such women operate. Without understanding their environment and immediate needs and challenges, it is impossible and indeed foolish for us to truly make sense of or pass judgement on their movement of female empowerment. They have found a working balance which, though not applicable to everyone, does allow them to take part and play key roles in their society without forgoing their traditions and beliefs. They have sought to redefine their identity in ways to accommodate modernity within the contexts of their interpretation of their religion and culture. They are similar to many of the men in their communities who are part of a newly emerging Islamist movement of young, educated intellectuals who are Western educated and modern, yet the women are formally more Islamically oriented than their mothers. It is because of the shifting self-perceptions of women themselves that many Muslim women are redefining and renegotiating their identities and places in society. This shift is a direct result of their educational and professional aspirations – regardless of their religious observance.

Perhaps the wearing of the hijab in such instances by a growing number of women is an overtly formal interpretation and compliance with tradition. Nevertheless, it does not necessarily mean a blind commitment to all Islamic ideology as there are quite a few women who are wearing the hijab for reasons that go beyond pure religious observance. For many, it has proven to give them a sense of peace and belongingness. The problems facing the Arab world today can arguably be summed up in three words – women, freedom and knowledge. Focusing on women's empowerment driven by female role models from the region will create a domino effect. By empowering women through education, professional opportunities and awareness of existing role models as featured in this study, society will be eventually transformed, and men and women can draw their own conclusions and recipes for how they wish to live instead of merely depending on the status quo. Why not encourage an informed society who know their rights as well as their religion and tradition? Knowledge is key; not many people, Muslim or otherwise, know that Islam does in effect give marriage and divine rights to women. It gives women the power to divorce. But it is a right that she must know of if she is to ask for it. This is why educating women and making sure they are aware of their religion and their rights will result in their own empowerment. No longer will they need to depend on the existing patriarchal interpretation of religion, which some argue is only a fusion of tribalism and culture with only traces of religious doctrine! In fact, as branded by Irshad Manji, the author of *The Trouble with Islam*, it is nothing more than 'Desert Islam'!

The point made by many Muslim women today is that it may not necessarily be the answer to write religion and culture out of the solution. The interviewees, amongst other women, are working role models of how to strike that balance between personal identity, religio-cultural affinity and professionalism. There is no need to adopt an approach that favours alienation or antagonism. By the same token, neither does the educated Arab woman feel particularly compelled to subscribe to dogmatic secularism.

There is a select group of women who have managed to redefine the concept of feminism by adjusting it to their own personal contexts. They have incorporated only the appropriate elements that form their own personalised brand of feminism and empowerment. This is true for even those who may appear more visibly religious or who seem to be keeping within the boundaries and constraints of their traditional patriarchal societies. The bottom line is to make sure one understands that there is no one definition of what it is to be a 'traditional' woman, and nor is there one meaning of the 'modern' woman; what may seem to be an oppressive situation for women in some contexts may, in other contexts, be seen as providing a certain status. There is no one yardstick by which to measure female empowerment. To do so would be unjust and would be a disservice to bridging the information gap that still separates the Western world from its neighbours.

The research conducted yielded a number of empirical findings that are not simply relevant at the local level, but, in fact, address widely-held concerns regarding cultural identity, the role and purpose of education and the possible ways of creating a synergy between one's tradition and empowerment. The major finding ensuing from the research is that the women sampled benefited from their cultural identity and their dual educational experiences. Though they certainly encountered challenges, there was no conflict within themselves with regard to their self-identity and their educational and professional success. It was this dual educational experience, in the Arab and 'Western' worlds, that served to give them a balance. Exposure to the two distinctly different educational paradigms had a twofold outcome; it reinforced their self-awareness and identity as 'the other' while providing the forum in which to challenge the status quo; it built their cognitive skills, promoted creativity, self-expression, self-confidence and competitive efficacy. It is their educational exposure that facilitated their personal and professional success by imbuing in them distinguishable qualifications and qualities necessary to succeed as leaders within their respective societies.

The intent of this chapter is to elucidate new realities that may not be widely known. There are Arab Muslim women who are making a difference and who are striking a balance between Islam and modernity and between womanhood and professional success. It is women like them who are setting the stage for change and it is women who will be held responsible for engendering change and setting a precedent for such changes in their favour. The women interviewed are amongst the first generation of such women. They are not only making historical changes at this moment, but are also setting a precedent for younger generations of educated Arab Muslim women to push the barriers further.

Perhaps such female empowerment and 'liberation' could in turn ultimately result in the liberation of men, who themselves are in shackles. This point is very much in keeping with Richard Haas's comment in 2002 (US State Department Policy Director): 'patriarchal societies in which women play a subservient role to men are also societies in which men play subservient roles to men'. Change and reform start with the people. These women are living examples and precursors to such reform and change.

Change wears multiple garbs, as demonstrated by this emerging echelon of prominent Arab women. To date, they are breaking the glass ceiling and are role models for the future generation. They have set the precedents and set new benchmarks. They personify women who are proud of their heritage, culture and religion yet who seem to have no qualms or reservations about renegotiating and reformulating their new identities as leaders and precursors to change. They are female entrepreneurs who have embraced Islam their way, according to what suits them, and have benefited from education that is a bastion of this change; in doing so they have shown how to observe Islam by complementing pluralism rather than suffocating it. Today they are amongst a select group of high-achieving women who have successfully broken the glass ceiling in their professions. The survival of globalisation as a system will depend to a large degree on the efficacy of education to achieve such balance; the role of educational systems to lead the way is now, more than ever, the lynchpin in this endeavour (Friedman, 2000). The Arab women sampled used their educational experiences to redefine their own identities and engender changes within their own domains. Perhaps what they have achieved is not beyond the reach of others in the region?

References

Chu, J. & Radwan, A. (2004) Raising Their Voices, *Time Magazine*, 163(8), 42-46.

Cotter, D., Hermsen, J., Ovadia, S. & Vanneman, R. (2001) The Glass Ceiling Effect, *Social Forces*, 80(2), 665.

Esposito.J. & Haddad, Y. (1998) *Islam, Gender and Social Change*. Oxford: Oxford University Press.

Friedman, T. (2000) *The Lexus and the Olive Tree*. New York: Anchor Books.

Gardiner, M. & Tiggemann, M. (1999) Gender Differences in Leadership Style, Job Stress and Mental Health in Male and Female Dominated Industries, *Journal of Occupational and Organizational Studies*, 72(3), 2.

Jeddah Economic Forum (2004) A Saudi Vision for Growth. http://www.saudi-us-relations.org

Kirdar, S. (1997) The Path to Choice: the growth of women's education in the Arab world. Unpublished BA dissertation, University of Oxford.

Kirdar, S. (2004) Education, Gender, and Cross-cultural Experience with Reference to Elite Arab Women. Unpublished D.Phil. thesis, University of Oxford.

Kirdar, S. (2006) The Development of Women's Education in the Arab World, in R. Griffin (Ed.) *Education in the Muslim World: different perspectives*, 191-210. Oxford: Symposium Books.

Lemons, M. (2003) Contextual and Cognitive Determinants of Procedural Justice Perceptions in Promotion Barriers for Women, *Sex Roles*, 49(5/6), 251.

Moore, K. (1987) Women's Access and Opportunity in Higher Education: toward the twenty-first century, *Comparative Education*, 23(1), 31.

Roudi-Fahimi, F. & Moghadam, V. (2003) Empowering Women in Developing Society: female education in the Middle East and North Africa, *MENA Policy Brief: Population Reference Bureau*, 7.

Seikaly, M. (1998) Women and Religion in Bahrain, in J. Esposito & Y. Haddad (Eds) *Islam, Gender and Social Change*. Oxford: Oxford University Press.

United Nations (2000) The World's Women: trend and statistics. http://www.unstats.un.org

Women, Higher Education and Social Transformation in the Arab Gulf

SALLY FINDLOW

Introduction

Western stereotypes depict Arab women as downtrodden. It is still the case that local traditional expectations and employment options can be constraining of these women's ambitions. Yet official rhetoric in favour of women as 'global leaders' and the increasing visibility of women in non-traditional roles combine to underscore the reality that women students and graduates are actually emerging as key players in the cultural and socio-economic transformation of these countries. This chapter looks at aspects of policy in an exceptionally dynamic Arab Gulf society, for insights into the role of higher education in collective transformation of that society. First-hand accounts of local women then capture some of the lived dimensions of this process.

This chapter is broadly informed by my experience of working since the 1980s in the higher and adult education sectors of Egypt, Kuwait, Bahrain and the United Arab Emirates (UAE). It draws more directly on fieldwork I have conducted since the late 1990s. Between 1998 and 1999, a historical and ethnographic study of UAE higher education included a survey of 300 students and interviews with students at each of the state higher education institutions (HEIs), their teachers, administrators and consultants, as well as document and archive analysis.

Most recently, a series of in-depth interviews with UAE women students and graduates has sought to explore the complex 'gendered contours' (Gadd, 2004, p. 158) of these women's lives. Loosely structured, the interviews adopt an inter-subjective approach that engages respondents critically and collaboratively, allowing authentic voices to emerge. Authenticity is especially important in a context where women can feel doubly marginalised, resentful of the assumptions made by non-Arab women who imagine they are speaking up for a lesser category of women who cannot speak for themselves.

The second half of this chapter draws largely on the accounts of two of these women, called here Ghada and Fatima.[1] They are both undertaking graduate studies overseas in Europe, but otherwise representing quite distinct perspectives. Ghada is in her twenties, a member of one of the country's ruling tribes. Fatima is a second-generation immigrant, older, married with children and sponsored in her graduate studies by the HEI for whom she works. In our interview and conversations, Fatima's balanced reflections are informed by her experience of working with male colleagues, while Ghada's more limited 'woman's perspective' comes from social constraints that have restricted her conversations to women. Fatima's answers reflect a view of her engagement with higher education as one of public service, while Ghada's are coloured by a preoccupation with her own personal development and what the system has to offer her. Both tell stories of aspiration, empowerment and tension produced in response to contradictory public messages around themes of tradition, modernity, religion and family.

Women and Marginalisation in Higher Education

Economic arguments for increasing female participation in higher education are well rehearsed, and are generally reproduced so far as developing countries are concerned as if increased access alone, regardless of the equality of actual experience, would solve a plethora of problems (Wagoner & Cook, 1999). For women themselves, access to schooling and the workforce is seen as the key to status, social and economic autonomy, and health. For governments, the advantage is a larger pool of indigenous workers and a reduced drain on national resources (Swantz, 1985; United Nations, 1986; Parpart et al, 2002).

But there are also powerful articulations of benefit in wider terms. The concept of democratic citizenship is grounded in the notion of educated, not merely economically skilled, citizens (Marshall, 1950; Gellner, 1983; Turner, 1993). Various models have been suggested for how such a relationship may apply to different groups of citizens: first, one that 'moulds and integrates the citizen into the polity' (Unterhalter, 1999, 113-114), ignoring difference; a second that considers the roles of gender and ethnic differences in shaping relationships between education and citizenship; and a third that sees the relationship between citizenship and difference as critical in enabling and informing education policy (Unterhalter, 1999, 113-114).

Then again, the idea of 'transformation' – with personal, cognitive, social and emancipatory dimensions (Freire, 1970; Mezirow, 1978; Meyer & Land, 2005; Stromquist, 2006) – provides a still deeper level at which to consider the social role of higher education. Mezirow described 'the urgent need to understand and order the meaning of our experience' as 'a defining condition of being human' (Mezirow, 1978). But it also has more instrumental dimensions. For instance, this kind of transformation is identified as an important element of politicisation or radicalisation through higher education, providing awareness and tools to challenge hegemony (Gellner, 1983; Bourdieu & Passeron, 1990). Freire saw this process, which he called 'conscientisation', as especially important for marginalised peoples and developing countries (Freire, 1970).

In a developing country context, it is argued that public preoccupation with access and economic productivity conflicts with the private motivations of actual women, and detracts from the more important issue of how the experience of higher education can transform the lives of individuals and communities (Heward & Bunwaree, 1999; Stromquist, 2006). Radical transformation through higher education is thought to be most prevalent among groups familiarly unaccustomed to going to university. In many societies, this is mainly a 'class' phenomenon. But where women are belatedly emerging from relative invisibility and under-representation it can, at least hypothetically, be seen as a female one.

In UK policy-oriented work, women tend to be positioned as one of several marginalised categories along with those of ethnicity, class and age (Archer et al, 2003; Reay et al, 2005). Recently, joined-up efforts have been made to increase representation and equality of experience among all these groups. The value placed by the knowledge economy on flexible modes of learning and transferable skills has seen a re-evaluation of women's potential to contribute to society through higher education (Egerton & Halsey, 1993). Nonetheless, gendered inequalities are still judged to be thriving in UK universities – in terms of disproportionate representation among high and low status institutions and across subject areas, career expectations, and conditions of employment for staff (Morley & Walsh, 1996; Morley, 1997, 1999, 2002; Brooks & Mackinnon, 2001). Culturally, universities are still seen as sites for the reproduction of gendered and unequal ideologies, practices and expectations (Apple, 1996; Stromquist, 2006).

In the Arab World

Across the Arab world, women's engagement with higher education in any numbers was initiated at points of dramatic change in ideas about its social function. In common with other models, higher education in the region now reflects two distinct collective and individual visions: the production of knowledge and learnedness, and the creation of economically productive citizens. But national workforce capacity building was only really incorporated into the higher education machinery when changed economic capabilities and political independence enabled those needs to be identified. In some cases, such as Egypt, this happened relatively early in the twentieth century. Elsewhere, the process is much more recent. In both cases, women's access became an issue when higher education moved away from its earlier exclusive concern with the production of religiously oriented or informed higher learning.

Egypt, often looked to for both inspiration and manpower across the Arab world, provides a classic and accessible illustration of this. Cairo University was established in 1908 as a nationalist, secularist, market-oriented answer to the medieval al-Azhar that had produced for Egypt as part of the Islamic Ottoman empire a male elite: clergy, lawyers, scientists, politicians, doctors and philosophers. The new university had foreign teachers, taught foreign languages, and provided frameworks and tools through which students could challenge received ideas and consider ways in which they were – both collectively and individually – unique. In this manner, it presaged the subsequent dual role of many Arab universities as both arms of government and hotbeds of radicalism (Reid, 1990; Said, 1991). This radical ferment saw women fighting for and gaining access to the new national university by 1928. Although this was limited to certain faculties, the idea of schooling at all for girls was only introduced in the 1933 Egyptian Constitution (Reid, 1990). Moreover, in the United Kingdom women had not gained access to higher education until well into the nineteenth century, with women still struggling to be awarded the degrees for which they had studied by the time of the First World War and only admitted to full membership of Cambridge University in 1948 when it was still entitled to limit their numbers.

Gender and Higher Educational Expansion in One Arab Gulf Country

Half a century ago, the small Arab Gulf countries were far behind other Arab states in development terms. But in the 1960s and 1970s, recently independent national governments equipped with new oil wealth established higher educational institutions designed to provide a range of support: symbolic as cultural repositories and emblems of statehood; infrastructural in their workforce training function. Unlike earlier Egyptian and British women, Gulf women were granted immediate access, which they took up in large numbers. Throughout the region since, it has been a public priority to give girls the same educational opportunities as boys, and here as elsewhere women are outperforming men at tertiary level.

In the United Arab Emirates (UAE), higher education has been central to the nation-building project from the start in 1971. Here, the shift from elite to mass higher education has been even more pronounced than in the United Kingdom. It has helped to unite a formerly disparate population, to provide an indigenous national workforce, and to furnish tools and framework for the construction of individual and collective identities (Findlow, 2001). The status and expectations of women have been transformed dramatically through access since 1977 to free state higher education. Prior to federation, students (almost exclusively male) were sent abroad to study while few women even worked outside the home. Yet this convention began to be challenged upon federation via a system of overseas scholarships for women. The 1971 constitution emphasised the right of free education to *all* citizens. The high-profile Women's Federation was set up in 1975 to concentrate initially on eradicating illiteracy and social seclusion among women. There has since been a disproportionate rise in female literacy rates, there are now many more female than male students in the country, and women are also noted to perform better and be more focused on career goals. In 1997, women became eligible to join the UAE Federal National Council, and the first woman joined the cabinet in 2004.

Public rhetoric about the importance of higher education is matched by that extolling the social roles of women. Education has been seen as key to eradicating what the Education Minister in 1980 reportedly called, 'backward and inhuman ideas about women in the home' (*The Emirates* magazine, 1980). While the former ruler Sheikh Zayed's pronouncements about the national importance of educating women are, in fact, very cautiously phrased to avoid offending traditionalists, they are reproduced to illustrate what is said to be his wholehearted support for women: 'Women should be respected and encouraged in whatever work they might do' (uaeinteract, 2006, attributed to Sheikh Zayed, 2002). Press coverage traces female success with pride, publicly congratulating the first women graduates and the first female PhD holder in 1983.

There are now over thirty HEIs in the country, and women's access has been the main theme behind the planning of the three federal institutions. The decision to locate UAE University in 1977 at one of the furthest points inland, al-Ain, was informed according to those involved at the time by considerations of suitability for young women from conservative families. Both institution and location were to accommodate potential female students, whom social restrictions had by and large prevented from going abroad to study. A highly publicised policy of strict segregation helped further to overcome conservative reservations and is widely held accountable for the higher than expected initial intake of female students (205 from a total of 535) (Findlow, 2001). In 1981, new female enrolments exceeded those of men (UAEU, 1987). The following year, distance learning ('*al-Intisab al-muwajjah*') was introduced for women whose family responsibilities prevented them from travelling to al-Ain to study. By 1999, the student body consisted of approximately 80% women (UAEU, 1998).

It had been proposed during planning to restrict female admission to the Faculty of Education. However, thoughts had changed by the time of inauguration and women were admitted to all courses that were considered suitable, on the basis of whether women could take up professions in the relevant fields. The policy was approached not as a matter of exclusion, but as an effort to link higher education provision to market needs. The primary mission of UAE University in relation to women had originally been limited to training indigenous schoolteachers. Teaching was seen as an acceptable job for women, akin to their roles as mothers in terms of 'bringing up' the next generation. A pool of indigenous teachers was seen as key to creating a 'national' culture and to reducing reliance on an expatriate workforce (Findlow, 2001).

In 1988, the Higher Colleges of Technology (HCT) linked higher education even more directly to workforce provision. Gender segregated sites were opened across the emirates to teach technology, business, health sciences and applied arts. Genders at HCT have been more balanced than at UAE University. Female enrolments overtook male ones in the HCT's sixth year, in 1993. In 2002, there were 1402 men compared to 2528 women (HCT, 2002). Against a local context in which technical work is both residually unpopular and considered unsuitable for women, the extent to which the glamour of the HCT has helped to overturn this pattern of prestige, and to attract large numbers of women to technical education and work, is impressive. It also compares favourably to the wider context of male-dominated technical education (Webster, 1996; Venkatesh & Morris, 2000; Martin et al, 2004).

The third federal HEI, Zayed University, was opened in 1998 in Dubai and Abu Dhabi for women only; demand was judged to have exceeded capacity at UAE University in al-Ain. Zayed University's mission combines dual goals: local manpower provision with 'advancing the UAE as a participant in a modern, global society' (Zayed University, 1998). Emphasising applied science and technology, the university has offered courses in Arts and Sciences, Business Sciences, Communications and Media Studies, Education, Family Sciences, and Information Sciences. The rhetoric accompanying its high, even international, profile ('Women as Global Leaders' conference, 14-16 March 2005, Dubai, advertised in the *Times Higher Education Supplement*, 21 January 2005, p. 20) does not portray women as a marginalised category. Students' femininity is de-emphasised in favour of their potential roles as future leaders:

> Zayed University was founded to prepare leaders who will foresee
> the possibilities to capture the opportunities that will create the
> future of the United Arab Emirates. ... The curriculum reflects the
> UAE's need for graduates well prepared to enter the workforce
> and to assume their place of responsibility and leadership in
> family, community and nation. (Zayed University, 2005)

It is possible to see these three distinct institutional approaches together as reflecting a feminist-internationalist policy orientation, constrained only by residual social conservatism. But a simultaneous, distinct narrative emphasises localism, continuity and conservatism. Talk about workforce nationalisation being in the hands of the women moves from positioning these women as entrepreneurs and leaders to mothers and teachers. A cultural residue sees the point of women's education helping them to bring up the nation's children. Policy emphasises both equality of opportunities and the importance of motherhood and family. In 1995, the UAE delegation to the United Nations sponsored International Women's Conference in

Beijing vetoed the draft conference declaration, arguing that, 'its [the UAE's] stand demonstrates its firm commitment to the reality that the family is the foundation of a sound community' (UAE Ministry of Information and Culture, 1995, p. 106). And a closer look at Sheikh Zayed's pronouncements on women reveals diplomatic balance rather than wholehearted support for women's rights:

> Women have the right to work everywhere. Islam affords to
> women their rightful status, and encourages them to work in all
> sectors, as long as they are afforded the appropriate respect. The
> basic role of women is the upbringing of children, but, over and
> above that, we must offer opportunities to a woman who chooses
> to perform other functions. (uaeinteract, 2006, p. 20, speech
> attributed to Sheikh Zayed)

The ambiguity can be seen as representing different messages for different audiences. UAE University's strict segregation policy, for instance, set out in the founding decree, proclaimed on a banner displayed at the inauguration and detailed in subsequent university publications, is described in publications intended for overseas readerships as only a temporary measure to placate conservative local society (*The Emirates*, 1978). Alternatively, the ambiguity can be viewed as flexible interpretation in line with changing public opinion, in the alleged regional style (Doumato, 1995). Beyond the rhetoric, more reliable indicators of policy intent might lie in the extent to which women have access to equal experience of higher education, and in their public visibility.

Segregation, across campuses and institutions, can be viewed as an example of gendered inequality in terms of differentially prestigious institutions attended. For example, male–female proportions have tended to be reversed at the fee-paying, co-educational, English-medium, modernist American University of Sharjah (AUS, 1998). Conservative parents' refusal to send their daughters here, despite being offered scholarships, is rumoured to be the reason for the establishment of its sister HEI, the segregated University of Sharjah where approximately 60% of students are female.

But increased levels of female visibility, in the forms of both public and self-representation, are evident. Official education-related websites and publications feature pictures of girls and women in contexts of academic and career success, looking happy, serious and professional (careersuae, 2005). Examples of girls' outperformance of boys at school level are presented as successes (UAE Ministry of Education, 2006). The Women's Federation is no longer women's only means of formal self-representation. Over the past decade, higher education has provided public venues at which women students have spoken, and which are beginning to be reported internationally. Female students' greater accessibility is another way in which public knowledge about their views and needs is increasing. UK researchers' experience that British female students are more willing than their male counterparts to participate in research (David et al, 2003) is replicated in the UAE. Illustrating the sort of experience encountered by both female and male researchers in this particular field, four-fifths of the 300 students I managed to access in 1999 were women.

Local Women's Aspirations

The economic rationale's assumption of a reasonably direct relationship between higher education and employment is challenged by the reasons UAE women themselves give for going to university or college. Like women elsewhere (Heward & Bunwaree, 1999), UAE women cite reasons other than career, economic or narrow instrumental ones. In 1999, I found that career-governed choice of degree subject was less prevalent among the women I surveyed (35%) than among the men (77%); 22.8% of the women cited self-improvement in terms of gaining knowledge and/or skills as the main desired outcome of higher education, compared to only 7% of the men.

Another measure of the economic rationale lies in the numbers of women graduates actually working. In1995, the HCT published the fact that 56.6% of their female graduates were working (HCT, 1995). That an employment rate of just over half is published as a success highlights the problem that the UAE Yearbook of five years later describes as follows:

> despite the major advances in emancipation of women in the UAE, more needs to be done. For example, there is increasing focus on the inability of some well-educated women to take up employment. In 1980 females constituted 3.4 per cent of the labour force. By 1995 this figure had only risen to 13 per cent, despite the fact that the majority of HCT and university graduates are women. ... the low female participation in the workforce is partly due to custom and tradition, while economic prosperity also means that employment is a matter of choice, rather than of necessity. There are also indications that the educational qualifications obtained by many UAE women are not always those most in demand in the job market .... Another problem that has been identified is the failure of women to take up employment in a wider range of professions. Although barriers have begun to crumble in recent years, there is still a strong emphasis on the government, health and education sectors. The majority of women have chosen to work in government establishments ... 15 per cent of working women are professors [lecturers] in higher education institutions. (UAE Ministry of Information and Culture, 2001)

My own survey found that of those women who gave a specific career goal, the largest proportion (45%) cited teaching. Although teaching is not seen as a prestigious career, education is still the most heavily subscribed subject at UAE University, for reasons including social conservatism, patriotism, parenting, and the fact that education has one of the lowest entry requirements. But the women students I surveyed also anticipated careers in business, banking, information technology, hospital/office/library work, medicine, social science, food and nutrition, special education, interior design, and management. More women than men talked about having entrepreneurial and private sector careers.

Still, these students identified a lack of economic imperative, which was endorsed by both Fatima and Ghada. Ghada talks about employment in terms of, 'self-development ... the general attitude is about getting a job for the sake of getting a job. Not many people have that long-term view of what they want to do. ... It's like the cool thing to do'. This lifestyle approach to employment offers one explanation for the growing acceptance among UAE women of traditionally disdained low-paying jobs (*Gulf News*, 2005a).

The same approach seems to govern decisions to enter higher education. Fatima and Ghada agree that women's decisions to become students are seldom connected to considerations of finance and employment. Fatima believes that higher education is seen as a more productive way of spending time that also usefully keeps options open:

> What other options do these women have? They finish high
> school. Some of them do get married, or ... some of them decide
> to stay at home. But what other options do they have? I mean,
> even a fixed term job these days requires to have certain
> competencies, at least computer and language, which they don't
> have coming from high school. So really, I think it is seen as a way
> out for them really. It's not like, ... in Sri Lanka people see higher
> education as a way out of poverty, but for our women, I think they
> see higher education as a way out to bigger and better things. ...
> They see this as the only way out if, for example they never get
> married or they do get married, they have something there.
> Otherwise ... Most of our women they move from parents to
> husbands. They don't have a transition of really finding out where
> they are themselves. So I think it's time at college, it gives them
> that little bit of time to just reflect on their own identity, on who
> they are as people. ... Whereas with men it's very very different,
> they have more options.

Barriers to Achievement

Barriers to higher education and graduate employment for UAE women are found more in external factors – family resistance, cultural expectations – than in discriminatory aspects of the system itself. Marriage is the theme that crops up most in this context. In the 1960s and 1970s, Betty Friedan urged women to enter higher education as a means of escaping what has been called the 'baby trap' (Peck, 1971). There were two dimensions to this freedom: a non-domestic role, and financial autonomy (Friedan, [1963] 1983).

In the UAE, a degree can be seen as insurance against not finding a husband, or against poverty in the event of divorce. While the female students I surveyed in 1999 reproduced government rhetoric about education making better mothers and wives, using phrases such as, 'A girl with no education is of no use', the increasing proportion of women in higher education is creating problems for the marriageability of local women. Everyone I spoke to endorsed the conventional wisdom that men are reluctant to take wives who are more highly educated than themselves. Fatima says, 'I hear from some of my students ... Oh I have to quit my course. Why? ... I'm getting married and my husband, you know, doesn't want it ... One of my students, she'll say, my husband, he didn't finish high school and he's in the military, and he doesn't want me to have a higher status than him'. Although my informants were reluctant to commit themselves on whether this was always a matter of men's wishes or women's perceptions of those wishes, the issue is perceived as problematic from the point of view of sociocultural stability. Fatima: 'The fact that they're going into higher education would be a big influence, it might mean that they'll never get married. Because in the UAE as you know, if you're past 20 then it's over to get married'. Government legislation in 1994 set out to address the increase in foreign brides by offering financial incentives to men to take UAE national brides.

Economics, lifestyle and status are all involved in this mismatch. The more highly educated a woman is, the higher her bride-price. Fatima described prevalent male attitudes to their wives working with: 'What kind of man would agree to their wife just setting off for meetings? Or working till six in the evening?' But fear of having traditional ideas of status challenged and disrupted are major themes. Ghada, herself struggling to find a husband who 'ticks the right boxes', says that the current politico-religious climate is making men keener than ever to find 'a traditional woman' to marry, not one who is going to challenge them and society. I asked her, 'And is being highly educated part of that?' She said, 'Yes, that's it. That's what traditional means. You would accept a traditional view, you know, being obedient to your husband'.

The female students I surveyed in 1999 provided conflicting pictures of the relative status of husband/family and academic career success. They were unanimous that marriage was less central to their life goals than it had been for their mothers. On the other hand, several said that, should marriage and children intervene, any academic and career plans were subject to their husband allowing them to continue. However, a few emphasised that they would not want a husband who would not let them continue their study.

For UAE women, extended families and plentiful domestic labour help to meet the challenge of balancing family, study and work commitments, although such arrangements are not without acknowledged problems (UAE

Ministry of Information and Culture, 2001). However, the integration of family, study and work has been central to UAE higher education from the start. UAE University's early distance learning programme, for instance, can be seen as a local model of the sort of lifelong and flexible learning provision called for by UNESCO, which it pessimistically predicted would remain both irrelevant and unhelpful for developing countries (UNESCO, 1978, p. 16). Institutional attitudes are also relatively accommodating. When I taught at UAE University in the 1990s, it was usual for women to bring their young children into class with them if childcare arrangements had fallen through. Fatima described the way she and her husband take turns in prioritising their academic careers over caring for their children as somewhat exceptional. She thinks that expectations about such gender roles are definitely changing: 'I think the whole culture, in terms of family culture, is going to change'. But she feels that that this change will meet resistance from men and from the forces of traditionalism.

Government commitment to increasing graduate employment is compromised by social constraints of different kinds. Fatima sees an element of disingenuousness in assumed cultural limits to the kinds of work women will do: 'I mean, they'll say, "I'm not going to do a night shift, I'm a woman!" ... And if someone questions that, "Oh, my husband won't allow it, or because I don't *want* to work at nights, it's not acceptable for me to work at night"'. There is a perception that opportunities for graduate career advancement are additionally curtailed by UAE women's nationality. Fatima recounts one of her very highly qualified friends laughing off a suggestion that she apply for a director's post with: 'Please, I'm a woman, and a *national* woman' ('National' in this context means 'local', as opposed to expatriate.) Linked to this is a perception among women that local men find it very difficult to be in professionally junior positions to local women, especially young, highly qualified women. Fatima describes what she calls, 'national male syndrome': 'Oh you know "I can't take orders from a woman", you know, "How dare you tell me what to do and what not to do!" ... I think the men they'd rather take orders from an expatriate woman, especially if she is older'. There are also real religious barriers, such as interpretations of Islamic law, that prohibit confidential discussion behind closed doors between a man and a woman. 'That', says Fatima, 'is why a lot of women don't want to work in an environment which is male and female'. She interprets her own husband's concern at the prospect of her travelling alone as a feeling of responsibility and a religious duty. It is a problem she sees as unavoidable, and central to what it means to be female, Muslim, and professionally or academically aspiring today.

Transformation through Higher Education

The female students I taught in the mid 1990s and those I surveyed in 1999 mostly attributed their attendance to their mothers. While elsewhere the highest rates of maternal influence on such decisions are found to be from those mothers who had been to university themselves (David et al, 2003), a rather different process has been evident in the UAE. Here, the emerging sense of national identity that shared experience of state-provided higher education has helped foster has been linked, for the women, to awareness that they are experiencing opportunities unknown to their mothers and grandmothers, many of whom were/are illiterate (Findlow, 2001). Nor did their mothers and grandmothers have freedom from the imperative of marriage. It appears to be mothers' low level of education that is a motivating factor behind daughters' academic aspirations, in so far as higher education holds out the promise of choice, security and autonomy they did not have. How then to explain Fatima's mother's reaction to her academic ambition: 'How much education do you need?! You need to settle down. You will regret it when you're old and grey'? Actually, what unites both stories is the theme of maternal influence driven by concern for security. Thus, a degree is seen as insurance – against having to marry, against not finding a husband, against divorce, husbands getting new wives. But the added security is only up to a point – the point at which other competing routes to security begin to be closed.

Fatima and Ghada both say that higher education's main impact on UAE women's lives, in conjunction with information and communication technology (ICT), has been to introduce the possibility of challenging tradition. Fatima: 'Just the fact that they have access to higher education, their generation is very different from my Mom's or my grandparents' generation. Just, I think, they *choose* the husband they are gonna marry, for one … . In terms of traditionally things that were a given, another issue is, you know, *I'll* finish my education before *I* get married'. But Ghada warns that there are two sides to this kind of change: 'The whole ICT thing definitely makes you more aware generally of what is going on in the world. And then that also intensifies the reactive tendency'.

In relation to raised awareness of social injustice and of an individual's place in the scheme of things (Freire, 1970; Stromquist, 2006, p. 149), I found women students in 1999, unlike the men I surveyed, preoccupied with the idea of duty. Some 65% of women gave their primary higher educational goal as helping their country through transmitting knowledge to their fellow citizens. Fatima and Ghada are equally critical of social inequities and duplicity. Fatima reports a widespread perception of lip-service in public campaigns for nationalisation of the UAE workforce. She argues that the cause is undermined by a system that forces graduate women, via unfavourable terms for maternity leave and inadequate childcare provision, to go into low-skilled or temporary jobs. Ghada and Fatima both identify a gap between government rhetoric and women's experience, which they attribute partly to a lack of female clout on the Federal National Council. Fatima says, 'the women they do have are really puppets'. Ghada says, 'The things happening in our society claiming to give women more rights are mostly just cosmetic things, you know, we have a couple of female ministers and, there's all this rhetoric about women's leadership ... but when you come to the actual mentality, what people believe in, there's gross gender stereotypes among the people that are at the highest level of society I think'.

HEIs are identified both as mechanisms for bringing about this sort of critical awareness, and as spaces in which you can see such tensions and duplicities writ large. Single-sex institutions and campuses are a case in point. On the plus side they are spaces for young women to develop a sense of self and society. Women at single-sex HEIs enjoy opportunities to be open in a way that the constant presence of men in a family setting otherwise prohibits. Ghada is concerned that mooted plans to admit men to Zayed University will remove such 'social spaces for girls to interact and to explore what it means to be a woman without the insecurity of ... men'. On the negative side, my informants feel that these institutions attempt uncomfortably to yoke together conflicting ideologies. 'For example', says Ghada, 'in Zayed University you'll find an emphasis on family, family sciences and ...there's still an emphasis on women as domestic'. As for the other visions Zayed University is promoting, of ICT competence and women as leaders, she says: 'Exactly, there's a contradiction. ... On one hand you're told to be *global* leaders and on the other hand you're not allowed to leave the campus unless you have permission from your parents. ... But what kinds of messages are you sending to these girls?' Measures such as these, introduced at Zayed University to 'reflect local custom', would not, argue Fatima and Ghada, have been introduced at an institution for male students.

Ghada believes that critical transformation in the UAE case is largely a religious matter, and that exposure to foreign ideas through the positive regulatory framework of higher education introduces a 'more liberal interpretation of Islam'. She thinks that the large numbers of young people travelling abroad to attend university are central to the collective critical transformation of her society. Her time overseas, she feels, has given her a more 'nuanced' perspective than that of her sheltered compatriots, especially women: 'I think most girls of my generation really are not aware of the different discourses that exist within Islam. ... how religion is ... influenced by the particular social context. ... This whole dynamic view of Islam is quite new to me, you know. That was part of the transformation that I went through'. Yet, she says, the power of social conservatism is strong: 'People that have been exposed, that went to study abroad but are very careful about expressing their views. ... there's still a great fear of passing a certain limit in their minds'.

The theme of caution, or fear, echoes Fatima's account of her conversations with her mother. It is such fear, Ghada says, which is currently governing her own relations with her parents: 'They're very concerned that I'm going to come and want to start a revolution ... they think that my ideas are just too Westernised and too anti-Islam and everything'.

Self-representation, Feminism
and Women as Political Actors

Increased critical awareness of self within a wider scheme has involved engagement with what would elsewhere be called 'feminist' ideas. It has also promoted consciousness of the ethics of taking a position, for instance, in relation to the meaning of the veil.

Ghada describes herself, in common with other UAE women she knows, as a feminist in her personal life. But she thinks the term has no currency as a public, political, cause:

> The cause of feminism back home is very stigmatised. I think
> people relate it to people like Nawal al-Sa'adawi [2] and, you
> know, radical things .... Feminism as such is not something you
> would want to use as a term in the Emirates because it has
> negative connotations, anti religious, anti everything and Western
> connotations.

Fatima condemns what she sees as misinterpretations by non-Arabs of social conventions that Arab and UAE women *choose* to conform to. Even among her Western colleagues, she says, people assume that, 'as an Arab woman you are kept in a locked room, harem ...: "You are an educated woman. Why, for example, did you let your parents choose a husband for you?" And so, I think [there's this view] among the expatriate women, "I'll come and save the women of the UAE. How come you cover yourself, you go to America ..."'. Fatima is emphatic that educated UAE women are making their own choices, and working hard to deal with structural relics that limit their freedom.

The complex symbolism of the veil interacts with higher education as another tool for the current generation of highly educated UAE women to represent themselves in relation to things like tradition, modernity, religion and gender. Fatima's and Ghada's dress codes embody their contrasting approaches to challenging society. Fatima wears the hejab to cover her hair – at first sight a discrete signifier of, if not traditionalism, then possibly conformity. But conversation with her soon reveals this to be merely outward conformity, an acquired invisibility that allows her to challenge issues she thinks are more important than dress. While her ideas may be challenging, her approach to bringing them about is to work subtley within existing strictures. Ghada is self-consciously unveiled, tight jeans pointing up her combative position on everything. She has the confidence of privilege to rebel and challenge openly.

The meaning of the veil in a higher educational context has changed over the years. Higher educational publicity brochures and the media have almost always shown female students veiled. In the early days, they helped male policy makers reassure conservative families and moral guardians that higher education was not dangerous (Findlow, 2001). Now the veil is mobilised to support a rather different message: 'Our culture, religion and the *abaya* should give us a boost. ... Globalisation and open-mindedness should urge the UAE woman to join the train of development', a prominent Zayed University student leader studying media and communications is quoted as saying (*Gulf News*, 2005b).

It is now less likely to be men in paternal roles than young women themselves, empowered through higher education, who are now providing the public rationale. Ghada attributes the way she makes reflective, almost experimental, choices about when and where to wear the hejab to her transformative experience of higher education, which helped her realise that there are choices in everything:

> Now, what it means to me is very different from what it used to
> mean to me .... I went through a transformation. My whole
> perspective on life and religion changed a lot over the past two
> years. Before, I just took it for granted that that's something you
> have to do as a Muslim. Just you know, you don't ... argue with
> that. And, and then with time gradually ...I realised that that's
> probably not the case. It's just, that there's lots of interpretations
> out there, that religion is not as defined as we think it is.

These are some of the ways in which both veil and hejab acquire both flexibility and ambiguity. If 'feminism' has limited currency as a slogan and a historical set of ideas, the veil might actually be seen as a subversive tool in these women's 'feminist' (Nicholson, 1992) move from private to public domain. This works in several ways. While women like Fatima wear it so that they might be left alone to deal with more important things, for others it is a definite statement, a claim to a particular heritage and collective identity and simultaneous demand not to be taken less seriously because of this. Taking the veil can be one of the strategies young educated women adopt to fill the 'need to express their culture, their identity' (Ghada), particularly in the face of higher education's internationalism.

To date, there does not appear to be a really direct route between women's experience of higher education, changed outlook and actually becoming empowered to act in a focused way. Ghada says that among the women students she knows, novel rhetoric is adopted eagerly, but at the expense of engagement with underlying ideas:

> They've been given these opportunities and ... especially among
> some of the students that are going to the more liberal universities,
> I think they're starting to feel like they want to make a difference.
> It's more than just rhetoric, it's a real desire, and commitment to
> do something. But in terms of practice, I think they still haven't
> hit reality yet.

But several phenomena do underline women's involvement in the reshaping of national culture through higher education in a way that is far removed from rhetoric about national identity being in the hands of women as mothers and teachers. Local newspapers this year reported Dubai Women's College (Higher College of Technology)'s first student elections, held, according to its American Director, 'to help students understand the "democratic process"'(*Gulf News*, 2006). More radically still, HCT's own website recently announced that eight named and pictured female students had been sent to Qatar to represent the colleges in the BBC's World Doha Debates in May. The motion of the debate they took part in was entitled, 'This house believes that the family is a major obstacle to reform in the Arab world'. The debates, we are told, are, 'a public forum for dialogue and freedom of speech in Qatar' (home of the al-Jazeera news agency), attended by speakers from around the Arab and Islamic worlds and chaired by a BBC broadcaster renowned for bringing to air controversial views from around the world, including women's rights in the Arab Gulf (HCT website, 2006). This is in a region where women are still campaigning, in some cases with the support of governments but in opposition to conservative lobbies, for the right to vote.

Conclusions

The UAE higher education system, founded thirty years ago amid an ill-defined set of objectives and anticipating only marginal rates of female involvement, was initially surprised by the large female take-up but has since striven enthusiastically to accommodate it in a diverse range of ways. Justification for this running-to-catch-up provision has intermittently mobilised economic arguments about the need for a highly skilled indigenous workforce, in which the role of national, mostly female teachers was portrayed as central. But the economic rationale has been undermined by two interrelated things: the gap between numbers of female graduates and rates of graduate employment, and evidence suggesting that the other things women get from their higher education might be more significant.

On a structural level, increasing numbers of highly educated and able women in the region means that there will inevitably be more cases of what Fatima described as a recently almost unimaginable scenario: 'national men reporting to a national woman as director?!' If one standard measure of social class is level of education, then UAE women's recent mass ascent to degree level and beyond is surely contributing to a restructuring of the 'class' structure of this country. It is possible to see this illustrated in the way that the elements of risk accompanying UAE women's conscious choice to become students mirror the experiences of working-class youngsters in the United Kingdom (Archer & Hutchins, 2000; Reay et al, 2005).

On a more direct policy level, the role of these visible, and audible, women in informing policy is likely to increase. Women students and graduates are already engaging in public dialogue that challenges the status quo, with apparent government sanction. The same women are also criticising the 'token' nature of female representation in government. The process feeds into classic paradigms of the relationship between an educated citizenry and democracy (Marshall, 1950; Gellner, 1983; Turner, 1993).

Women students' strong social conscience and the emphatically patriotic tone of those who have exercised their voices in public is interesting in relation to what difference their influence might make to political direction. It remains to be seen, for instance, how far increased female representation will see an integrative approach in which differences are accommodated on an ad hoc level, as opposed to one that promotes a general awareness of the needs of marginal groups, or one that is formally framed around the needs of women and/or other marginal groups (Unterhalter, 1999).

It is important to remember that Arab and Arab Gulf societies are not *one* society. Across the Gulf and the wider Arab world there are of course many discontinuities, but also continuities, in terms of the issues I have outlined here. It has been suggested that governments region-wide may favour greater equality between men and women, but that they are constrained by public opinion (Doumato, 1995). In these terms, the exponential increase over a generation in numbers of informed and publicly engaged women might be seen as a process in which the scope of such 'public opinion' was being redefined.

Note

[1] Identifying details have been changed, but I have tried not to compromise analytical significance.

[2] The celebrated Egyptian dissident feminist writer.

References

American University of Sharjah (AUS) (1998) National Distribution of Students. Internal memo, 20 April 1998.

Apple, M. (1996) *Cultural Politics and Education*. New York: Teachers College Press.

Archer, L. & Hutchings, M. (2000) 'Bettering Yourself'? Discourses of Risk, Cost and Benefit in Ethnically Diverse, Young Working-Class Non-participants' Constructions of Higher Education, *British Journal of Sociology of Education*, 21(4), 555-575.

Archer, L., Hutchings, M. & Ross, A. (Eds) (2003) *Social Class and Higher Education: issues of exclusion and inclusion*. London: RoutledgeFalmer

Bourdieu, P. & Passeron, J. (1990) *Reproduction: education, society and culture*. London: Sage.

Brooks, A. & Mackinnon, A. (Eds) (2001) *Gender and the Restructured University: changing management and culture in higher education*. London: Society for Research into Higher Education.

careersuae (2005) http://www.careersuae.ae/news/050518.html (accessed 15 August 2005).

David, M., Ball, S., Davies, J. & Reay, D. (2003) Gender Issues in Parental Involvement in Student Choices of Higher Education, *Gender and Education,* 15(1), 21-37.

Doumato, E.A. (1995) The Ambiguity of Shari'a and the Politics of 'Rights' in Saudi Arabia, in Mahnaz Afkhami (Ed.) *Faith and Freedom: women's human rights in the Muslim world,* chapter 8. Syracuse: Syracuse University Press.

Egerton, M. & Halsey, A.H. (1993) Trends by Social Class and Gender in Access to Higher Education in Britain, *Oxford Review of Education,* 19(2), 183-196.

Emirates, The (1980) New Educational Policy under Discussion, 39. London: UAE Embassy.

Emirates, The (1978) Feb/March. London: UAE Embassy.

Findlow, S. (2001) Higher Education and National Identity in the United Arab Emirates. Unpublished PhD thesis, University of Cambridge.

Freire, P. (1970) *Pedagogy of the Oppressed.* New York: Herder & Herder.

Friedan, B. ([1963] 1983) *The Feminine Mystique.* New York: Dell.

Gadd, D. (2004) Biographical Reflections on the Problem of Changing Violent Men, in P. Chamberlayne, J. Bornat & U. Apitzisch (Eds) *Biographical Methods and Professional Practice: an international perspective,* 149-163. Bristol: Policy Press.

Gellner, E. (1983) *Nations and Nationalism.* Oxford: Basil Blackwell.

Gulf News (2005a) National Women Willing to Work as Public Relations Officers for Dh4,000. http://www.gulfnews.com/articles/nation (accessed 15 August 2005).

Gulf News (2005b) Religion and Abaya Should Give Us a Boost. http://www.gulfnews.com/articles/nation (accessed 15 August 2005).

Gulf News (2006) Dubai Women's College Holds Its First Student Elections, posted on UAEInteract: http://uaeinteract.com/news (accessed 19 May 2006).

Higher Colleges of Technology (HCT) (1995) What Female Graduates are Doing, HCT Central Services, Abu Dhabi.

Higher Colleges of Technology (HCT) (2002) Demographics and Statistics: student data. http://www.hct.ac.ae (accessed 12 October 2002).

Higher Colleges of Technology (HCT) (2006) SWC to Doha for BBC Debates. http://www.hct.ac.ae (accessed 24 August 2006).

Heward, C. & Bunwaree, S.S. (1999) *Gender, Education and Development: beyond access to empowerment.* London: Zed Books.

Marshall, T.H. (1950) *Citizenship and Social Class* (1949 lecture). Cambridge: Cambridge University Press.

Martin, U., Liff, S., Dutton W. & Light, A. (2004) *Rocket Science or Social Science? Involving Women in the Creation of Computing.* Oxford: Oxford Internet Institute.

Meyer, J.H.F. & Land R. (2005) Threshold Concepts and Troublesome Knowledge (2): epistemological considerations and a conceptual framework for teaching and learning, *Higher Education,* 49, 373-388.

Mezirow, J. (1978) Perspective Transformation, *Adult Education,* 28(2), 100-109.

Morley, L. (1997) Change and Equity in Higher Education, *British Journal of Sociology of Education,* 18(2), 231-242.

Morley, L. (1999) *Organising Feminisms: the micropolitics of the academy*. London: Macmillan.

Morley, L. (2002) Widening Access to Higher Education: challenging elitism. Paper presented at policy research seminar: 'Widening Access to Higher Education – new culture of change or changing cultures?', Institute of Education, University of London, 17 May 2002.

Morley, L. & Walsh, V. (1996) *Breaking Boundaries: women in higher education*. London: Taylor & Francis.

Nicholson, Linda J. (1992) Feminist Theory: the private and the public, Article 1:3 in L. McDowell & R. Pringle (Eds) *Defining Women: social institutions and gender divisions*, 36-43. Cambridge: Polity Press in association with the Open University.

Parpart, J., Rai, S. & Staudt, K. (Eds) (2002) *Rethinking Empowerment: gender and development in a global/local world*. London: Routledge.

Peck, E. (1971) The Baby Trap, *Cosmopolitan*, 170(6), 82.

Reay, D., David, M. & Ball, S. (2005) *Degrees of Choice: social class, race and gender in higher education*. Stoke-on-Trent: Trentham Books.

Reid, D.M. (1990) *Cairo University and the Making of Modern Egypt*. Cambridge: Cambridge University Press.

Said, E. (1991) Identity, Authority and Freedom: the potentate and the traveler. T.B. Davie Academic Freedom Lecture, University of Cape Town, 22 May 1991.

Stromquist, N.P. (2006) Gender, Education and the Possibility of Transformative Knowledge, *Compare*, 36(2), 145-161.

Swantz, M. (1985) *Women in Development: a creative role denied?* London: Hurst & Company.

Turner, B.S. (Ed.) (1993) *Citizenship and Social Theory*. London: Sage.

UAE Ministry of Education (2006) UAE Education. http://www.uae.gov.ae/education.htm (accessed 1 March 2006).

UAE Ministry of Information and Culture (1995) *The United Arab Emirates Yearbook 1995*. London: Planet Publishing and Ministry of Information and Culture, UAE.

UAE Ministry of Information and Culture (2001) *The United Arab Emirates Yearbook 2000-2001*, 'Women's Federation'. http://www.uaeinteract.com/uaeint_main/yearbook/yr_soc_dev. Also: London: Trident Press.

uaeinteract (2006) A Special Tribute. http://www.uaeinteract.com/uaeint_misc/pdf_2005/zayed_tribute (accessed May 2006).

UAEU (UAE University) (1987) al-jami'a fi ashara sanawat [The University in ten years]. UAE: UAEU Publications.

UAEU (1998) UAE University General Catalogue 1996-1998. UAE: UAEU Publications.

UNESCO (1978) *Trends and Issues in Technical and Vocational Education*, vol. 1, *Lifelong Education and University Resources*. Paris: UNESCO.

United Nations (1986) *World Survey on the Role of Women in Development.* New York: United Nations Publications E86.

Unterhalter, E. (1999) Citizenship, Difference and Education: reflections inspired by the South African transition, in P. Werbner & N. Yuval-Davis (Eds) *Shaping Women's Work: gender, employment and information technology,* 100-117. London: Zed Books.

Venkatesh, V. & Morris, M.G. (2000) Why Don't Men Ever Stop to Ask Directions?, *Management Information Systems Quarterly,* 24(1), 115-139.

Webster, J. (1996) *Shaping Women's Work: gender, employment and information technology.* Harlow: Longman.

Werbner, P. & Yuval-Davis, N. (1999) *Women, Citizenship and Difference.* London: Zed Books.

Wagoner, H.T. & Cook, A.S. (1999) Enhancing the Economic Contributions of International Women through Education and Training, *International Education,* 29(1), 71.

Zayed University (1998) Draft Plans, March.

Zayed University (2005) Vision. http://www.zu.ac.ae (accessed 15 August 2005).

Besieging the King's Tower? En/Gendering Academic Opportunities in the Gulf Arab States

ANDRÉ ELIAS MAZAWI

Introduction

Two of the more striking contrasts associated with higher education in the Gulf Arab states pertain to the 'inconsistency' or 'mismatch' between women's educational achievements and their limited occupational and social mobility opportunities.[1] Official Gulf Cooperation Council (GCC) statistics published for 2003 place the total number of higher education students at about 661,000, of whom at least 60 per cent are women, and the total number of faculty members at over 30,000, of whom around 40 per cent are women (see also, Bahry & Marr, 2005, p. 106; Abdalla, 2006).[2] Women's representation among faculty members varies between 20 and 40 per cent depending on the GCC state concerned.[3] Yet, in universities, women's share in faculty positions is lower, and insignificant in some disciplinary fields such as engineering and technology.

Gulf Arab women also outperform men in terms of graduation rates (Bosbait & Wilson, 2005, p. 535). Yet, their power to exchange educational credentials (degrees) for occupational and social mobility remains severely hampered by a complex web of laws, policies and practices. Despite significant variations between Gulf Arab states, women are marginally represented in the labour force, as shown in Appendix 1. Mellahi & Al-Hinai (2000) observe that 'the extreme degree of occupational segregation limits women's chances to obtain work' (p. 180). Women's representation among power elites is symbolic and when their presence in the labour market starts to be visible, as in Kuwait, it is challenged and deemed to be threatening by some groups (Tétreault, 1999, pp. 244-245; 2000).

The mismatch between women's achievements and their limited social opportunities raises critical questions regarding the interrelations between gender, educational resources and the negotiation of social and political

77

power. It also calls for an examination of the mechanisms which position women in Gulf academe as a subordinate social group. These questions stand at the forefront of the present chapter, which aims to illustrate tentatively how these mechanisms operate within increasingly differentiated and restructured Gulf higher education institutions. Sadly, a review of the literature highlights the paucity of analytic and critical research on Gulf women academics and on Arab women academics generally. Based on the few studies available, it is possible to identify two broad explanatory frameworks that account for the mismatch between women's achievements and their limited social opportunities.

The first explanatory framework, labelled by Longva (1993, p. 446) as the 'modernization-hampered-by-religious-norms' approach, draws on modernisation theory and its variants. The inconsistency in the status of Gulf women is explained in terms of the 'contradiction between "modernization" and "cultural/religious authenticity"' (Seikaly, 1994, p. 416). This perspective considers 'change as coming into conflict with the traditional cultural value-systems tied to religion that control social behavior' (p. 416). Extended to Gulf academe, proponents of this approach would probably argue that the 'mismatch' between women's achievement and their marginal location in academe (as in the broader society) reflects a conflict between 'modern' forms of social organisation and the traditional 'mentality and attitudes of Gulf citizens' which seem 'to have changed very little' (Bahgat, 1999, p. 129). Proponents of this view claim that 'educational policies pursued in the last several decades have contributed to a number of social distortions', generating a 'mismatch' between 'traditional' and 'modern' values (p. 129). A major shortcoming of this approach is that it disregards how power plays out within Gulf Arab societies as part of processes of change. Nor does this approach clarify how local configurations of power pervade academic institutions, ultimately determining women's opportunities and institutional location.

The second framework, of which two variants are discussed here, capitalises on the intersection of state structure, market economies and culture. More specifically, it focuses on the impact of the Gulf's 'rentier' [4] economies and patriarchal mode of social organisation on women's academic opportunities. According to Joseph (1996), patriarchal social structures are 'woven throughout Arab society partly because of the fluidity between civil society and state, public and private domains, family and government' (p. 16). Central to the first variant is Sharabi's (1988) thesis on 'neopatriarchy'. Developed partly from within a Marxist perspective and partly from within a modernisation perspective, this thesis posits that when traditional culture and modernity collide within a context of economies dependent on oil rents, the collision gives rise to 'a conservative, relentless male-oriented ideology, which tend[s] to assign privilege and power to the male at the expense of the female, keeping the latter under crippling legal and social constraints' (p. 33). Proponents of this variant would argue that the expansion of Gulf higher education, initially financed from surpluses in oil rents (revenues), re-inscribes the broader patriarchal order within higher education institutions in ways which 'disguise' tribal and economic clientelism, domination and subordination under the attributes of the 'modern' scholar and university professor. As one former Gulf university chancellor candidly acknowledges, the university he presided over reflects the 'patriarchal tilt in the society' (Zabalawi, 2000). As Shaw (1993) further observes, unless Gulf Arab universities 'exhibit cultural authenticity' through the development of critical reflexivity and a vibrant research agenda, they will continue to be characterised by 'coercion, patron/client, ascriptive relationships, what Sharabi has called "neopatriarchy"' and 'overshadow the public good'.

A second variant, inspired by Bourdieu's (1985, 1988) conceptualisation of the social space, may be identified too. In a pioneering study undertaken in the 1980s, Sabour (2001) examines how different forms of capital – cultural, educational, symbolic and social – determine the respective location of Arab men and women faculty across the academic field, within the larger context of 'the Arab society's specific games, stakes, conflicts and strategies' (p. 23).[5] Central to Sabour's approach is the spatial lens projected on the academic field. By reconstructing the social location of Arab faculty, qua actors, in relation to their gender, habitus and the forms of capital they accumulate, Sabour shows how marginalisation places the Arab academic woman 'socially, intellectually and psychologically in a contradictory position in a society experiencing ambivalent dialectical and historical transformations' (p. 70). He concludes that Arab women academics are subject to a 'double' marginalisation. First, as academics they depend on the good will of the state. As women, they are located in a space regulated by men's habitus as the driving rationality, making academe 'an almost entirely man-molded, man-minded, and man-oriented institution and place' (Sabour, 1996, p. 82).

Significant differences notwithstanding, the above two variants assume that a 'correspondence principle' links the patriarchal mode of social organisation and its institutional manifestations within academe in terms of gendered opportunities. With regard to the Gulf Arab states, this assumption is challenging. First, there are important differences among Gulf Arab states in terms of population size and demographic composition, the structure of their higher education systems, state policies, the forms and types of capital valued, and patterns of women's resistance.

Secondly, the patriarchal mode of social organisation is not monolithic. It exhibits internal tensions and stimultaneously, contradictions, between competing patriarchal social and political formations which vie for legitimacy and power. These contradictions have been amplified in the aftermath of the Gulf war, from 1990 onward.[6] The political crises triggered by the war sharpened ideological differences over the role of culture, religion and state within Gulf Arab societies and 'brought issues surrounding democratization to the forefront' (Rizzo et al, 2002, p. 647). Within this broader context, debates around the role of women in society – and around gender roles in general – emerge as critical junctures for the organisation of the state and the economy in relation to the field of culture. Tétreault (1999) points out that in a Gulf Arab society like Kuwait, 'conflicts over the construction of gender and family are embedded in and around conflicts over the construction of political authority' (p. 238) because 'women so frequently are implicated in practical strategies for community self-definition and governance' (p. 251).

Thirdly, in the aftermath the Gulf war, governments in the Gulf embarked on extensive projects of restructuring, privatisation and Americanisation of higher education institutions. International organisations, semi-government agencies and Western private and public universities became overwhelmingly involved in the provision and expansion of academic opportunities across the Gulf Arab states (Coffman, 2003; Mazawi, 2003, pp. 237-238). These processes are indicative of the greater reliance of Gulf governments on private markets in their attempts to boost the employability of their citizens and their integration into the national labour force. This is particularly the case in the United Arab Emirates, Oman, Qatar and Bahrain, and Kuwait (less so in Saudi Arabia), where the role of the private sector in operating post-secondary institutions is dominant (for Oman, see Al-Lamki, 2006). Gulf governments and policy makers hoped that the private sector would help lessen the overwhelming dependence of their economies on imported expatriate workers and on oil revenues, thus diversifying the economy and shielding it from global fluctuations (Kapiszewski, 2001; Al-Sayegh, 2004, pp. 111-112).

Several questions arise at this point. How does the expansion of higher education and the growing importance of educational credentials (degrees) for social mobility impact on women's location and access to positions of power and influence within academe? With a greater emphasis placed on the employability of nationals, how does the restructuring and privatisation of Gulf higher education shape discourses around women's career opportunities and their integration into the labour market? Not least, how do conflicts over the construction of political authority, in the aftermath of the Gulf war, affect women's ability to forge alliances and networks that reposition them in relation to men within academe?

To address these questions, this chapter zooms in on three Gulf academic contexts. The aim is to tentatively illustrate some of the mechanisms involved in determining women's academic opportunities. The first illustration, entitled 'A Spatial Political Economy of Academic Opportunities', focuses on Saudi Arabia. This part examines how the territorialisation of the academic space by contending patriarchal elites genders access opportunities to higher education and to educational credentials, ultimately allocating faculty positions along a gendered 'matrix' of social cleavages. The second illustration, entitled 'Globalising Opportunities, Privatising Emancipation', focuses on the United Arab

Emirates (UAE). It illustrates how local representations of privatisation and internationalisation operate as a 'discursive mechanism' which recasts the gendered epistemic and social foundations of patriarchal power relations within academe in novel institutional forms. The third illustration, entitled 'Academic Opportunities as Topographies of Struggle', focuses on the dialectic contradictions underpinning academic women's attempts to carve new institutional and political spaces as part of their political enfranchisement, as equal Gulf citizens. Here, the focus on women's agency helps offer, in the words of Mahmood (2001), 'a crucial corrective to scholarship on the Middle East that had portrayed Arab and Muslim women for decades as passive and submissive beings, shackled by structures of male authority' (p. 205).

A caveat is in order here. The mechanisms illustrated in the present chapter should not be viewed as mutually exclusive. Nor should they be viewed as characterising one particular Gulf context to the exclusion of others. Rather, as heuristic devices, these mechanisms operate simultaneously and in multifaceted configurations which reflect the complex imbrication of contexts of power in which Gulf women act and work.

A Spatial Political Economy of Academic Opportunities: the case of Saudi Arabia

The Saudi Arabian higher education system is the largest in the Arabian Peninsula, employing in 2002-03 almost 77 per cent of all GCC faculty members and enrolling about 80 per cent of all GCC students. This system expanded dramatically, from a single higher education institution in the 1960s, to a fully-fledged national system with well over a hundred tertiary institutions of different types by the early 2000s. Post-secondary institutions include teachers' institutes, technological institutes, women's and community colleges, privately funded undergraduate liberal-arts colleges, military colleges and academies, and state universities.[7] During that same period, the number of students increased from a few thousand to well over half a million and the number of faculty members employed in all post-secondary institutions reached about 25,000 (of whom about 40 per cent were women).[8]

Access to educational credentials and academic positions is tightly controlled by the state, through the Council of Higher Education (CHE) and other state ministries and agencies. Alkhazim (2003) observes that, in universities, 'any created position, promotion, or salary has to be approved first by the Ministry of Employment and must be based on the unified rules of employment and faculties' (p. 482). Those seeking academic careers are screened, appointed and distributed over the space of academic opportunities based on an elaborate 'classification scheme' organised according to degree type and level, and according to the holder's nationality and gender. Until its integration into the Ministry of Education in 2002, the '*ulama* – or religious clerics – supervised and controlled all educational settings for girls and women (schools and colleges) through the then General Presidency for Girls' Education (GPGE). At the same time, the state directly oversees institutions serving men through the CHE, particularly in state universities.

With the expansion and differentiation of the Saudi Arabian academic field, educational credentials (degrees) have come to assume a greater social and political role.[9] From the late 1970s onward, credentials created new forms of authority and legitimised new positions of power, circumventing or weakening established ones. Educational degrees also undermine the principles on which the religious hierarchy is organised. This holds particularly true for the doctorate, which became a major status symbol, facilitating access to positions of power associated with appointments to 'consultative bodies' and to ministerial and other senior positions in the public service. Moreover, existing bodies of knowledge witnessed a process of 'academisation' through the extension of the degree system. For instance, Al-Rasheed (2007) observes that the extension of the doctorate to include Islamic studies 'was a novelty which accompanied the establishment of religious universities' in Saudi Arabia (p. 61). It symbolises 'the transformation of the consolidation and transmission of [religious] knowledge' (p. 62). Al-Rasheed further observes that this innovation produced not only the 'religious scholar' but also 'the Islamic intellectual', 'who has enough understanding of the tradition to articulate opinions and offer interpretations' to a wide audience (p. 63). Moreover, Rugh (2002, p. 52) points out that the status of the granting university reproduces within the public service social distinctions and divisions of power between distinct degree holders.

One of the doxas re-enacted across the Saudi Arabian academic field (as in other social fields) pertains to the segregation of women and men within distinct institutional settings (Abukhalil, 2004, pp. 69-70, 146-149). A closer look reveals that segregation is differentially structured for men and women. Women's academic opportunities represent disjointed spaces. Effectively, the way institutions serving women are positioned in relation to each other, and the extent to which women can or cannot move across types of institutions, establishes what El-Sanabary calls 'spatial barriers' (El-Sanabary, 1994) that impede women's autonomy. These barriers not only restrict women's movements between distinct types of institutions, but further territorialise their horizon of opportunities by bringing it under the control of competing power elites, those aligned with the GPGE-entrenched *'ulama* or those aligned with competing branches within the ruling kinship groups.[10] Thus, different elites control different segments of the space of women's academic opportunities. Each elite group promotes institutional settings differentiated by contents, educational aims and types of educational credentials granted to graduates. In contradistinction, men's academic opportunities offer a relatively more 'coherent' space, one which allows much more movement across institutional types of higher education institutions, either within or outside Saudi Arabia for those who wish to pursue their studies abroad. That space is also more directly located under the jurisdiction of the ruling elites. In this sense, men have significantly less 'spatial barriers' determining their horizon of opportunities. This said, the lines demarcating the control of the 'ulama and the royal establishment over the academic field have not remained fixed over time. Quite the contrary, since the introduction of schools for girls in the 1950s by the ruling family, constant power struggles with the 'ulama and tribal leaders take place over the education of women (AlMunajjed, 1997). Lines of demarcation controlling women's opportunities shifted significantly over the years along with the expansion and differentiation of the higher education system.

First, the opening of 'women campuses', affiliated with state-controlled universities from the 1970s onward, carved new gender-specific spaces for women (Altorki & Cole, 1989, p. 191). Initiated and controlled by the ruling elites, these campuses created a new category of women academics which bypasses the GPGE-entrenched 'ulama. This process was further intensified from the 1990s onward through the creation of 'private', 'non-profit' 'community' undergraduate colleges and universities, organised along the model of the American liberal-arts college. Some serve women exclusively (e.g., Effat College in Jeddah); others operate separate campuses for men and women (e.g. Prince Sultan University in Al-Riyadh and Prince Muhammad bin Fahd University in Al-Khabr). Sponsored or effectively operated by different branches associated with the ruling elites, these new foundations signal yet another round in the struggle over the boundaries controlling women's horizon of academic opportunities, either among contending groups within the ruling elites or in relation to the religious establishment.

These processes of expansion and differentiation stratify women academics vertically and horizontally. Vertically, women working within the universities are perceived as located at the 'apex' of the higher education system located in the large urban universities of Riyadh and Jeddah. Their social status contrasts significantly with that of Saudi Arabian women academics of rural background, or with that of expatriate women who are hired on renewable contracts and who work in women's colleges. This spatial stratification of women academics not only differentiates between women employed in rural colleges and those employed in urban universities. It also reproduces within the academic field the differential statuses of kinship (tribal) groups prevalent within Saudi Arabian society, reproducing the social and spatial relations of power which undergird the state.

Horizontally, women academics are further differentiated between those who work within the humanities, social sciences and education and those working in the sciences and medicine. Educational credentials play an important role in this regard (see Mazawi, 2003, 2005, 2006): Saudi Arabian men holding 'local' degrees are more likely to be located in Islamic universities, while those holding Western (mainly American) degrees are more likely to be located in the humanities and the social sciences in the non-

Islamic universities. Expatriates with Western degrees are more likely to be found in science and medicine. In contradistinction, women, who have access mainly to local degrees due to restrictions on their travel abroad, are more likely to be found in women's colleges and in disciplinary fields such as education and the humanities. Women are virtually absent from disciplinary fields which are associated with Saudi Arabia's industry and technology. Their presence in fields associated with the production of religious knowledge remains confined. In sum, the matrix of policies, practices and power which controls access to academic degrees intersects powerfully with gender, reproducing within the Saudi Arabian higher education institutions highly gendered disciplinary spaces.

A second example which illustrates shifts in the boundaries that control women's academic opportunities pertains to the merger of the GPGE with the Ministry of Education in 2002. Under the pressure generated by a mediatised public campaign, which pointed to 'negligent' GPGE policies towards girls and women, a royal decision merged GPGE institutions as a directorate within the state Ministry of Education.[11] This measure effectively restructured the space of academic opportunities available to women. It also strengthened the 'benevolent' image underpinning the educational initiatives supported by the royal establishment and its allies. The merger brought the education of all Saudi Arabian students under the jurisdiction of the same state ministry, about six decades following the introduction of education for girls, while continuing to maintain strict gender segregation.

In sum, the expansion of women's opportunities is associated with the continued and intensifying competition between male power elites embedded within the Saudi Arabian state, each vying to enhance its positions over the broader domain of state politics. In this competition, claims purporting to promote women's dignity and status according to the *Shari'a* (Islamic law) serve as forms of symbolic capital mobilised to consolidate a party's claim or effective control over the spatial structures which determine women's opportunities. According to Doumato (2003), competing textual and discursive representations of the ideal Saudi Arabian woman are constructed in order to garner support for and legitimise distinct moral orders.

Globalising Opportunities, Privatising Emancipation: the case of the United Arab Emirates

From the mid-1990s onwards, the number of private foreign higher education institutions – operated among others by universities based in New York, London, Paris, and Wollongong – surpassed the number of their public Gulf counterparts.[12] Offering undergraduate and sometimes graduate programmes of study, several of these campuses operate as fully-fledged Gulf-based universities accredited locally and abroad.

The expansion of private higher education opportunities transformed the Gulf Arab states, and particularly the UAE and Qatar, into what is perceived by many observers as a hi-tech and globally oriented society (Al-Sayegh, 2004, p. 113). Colleges – where faculty recruited in Western countries teach in English – offer programmes of study in areas such as communications and media, information technology, alongside other internationally benchmarked programmes in health care, business administration, education and languages. One American consultant, involved in programme accreditation, described the flurry of economic activity around the foundation of private universities in the UAE in the following words:

> Just as I observed bankers and sales forces from Russia, Pakistan, and the Netherlands doing business in Dubai and Abu Dhabi, I saw teachers and consultants from a number of countries sharing their expertise and ideas with faculty and administrators. (Banta, 2003, p. 3)

Public universities are coming under increasing pressures to accommodate constantly growing cohorts of applicants. Some contend that these pressures are exacerbated by admissions policies implemented in private universities. Moreover, Gulf Arab governments are seeking to reconfigure the interface between higher education and the labour market, as part of the restructuring of the economy. One Assistant Secretary General for Political Affairs in the Gulf Cooperation Council (GCC) General Secretariat stated that GCC governments must 'review the existing "open door" admission policy' into publicly funded academic institutions. Governments, he added, must 'strike a balance between the need to prepare professionals such as engineers, doctors and lawyers, and the need for middle-level workers such as technicians and semi-skilled workers' by shifting 'their emphasis from universities to lower-cost training colleges and polytechnics in order to enhance their capabilities of providing better quality training for larger numbers' (Al-Sulayti, 1999, p. 275).

Within this context, the occupational integration of women is perceived as a way through which the private sector could be strengthened, the diversification of the national economy pursued, and reliance on oil rents and imported labour lessened. One senior male administrator, working in a university for women in the UAE, explained why Emirati women should study and contribute to the country's economy:

> We can't afford not to have women in the work force any longer. When we give young women a chance for education, they don't want to stay at home any longer. They choose to work, to improve themselves, to use their skills. Their country needs this. (Cited in Zoepe, 2006)

The self-driven vitality and vision of women towards emancipation is thus politically constructed (*'their* country needs ...') and discursively 'objectified'

('... this') as a worthy individual/ised choice, associated with the building of a work career. Yet, if women's careers are endorsed, they are carved in a fashion which does not challenge local cultural mores. One female professor, teaching at the same university in the UAE, captured the nuances and tensions underpinning the university's 'progressive' role in facilitating women's emancipation in the following words:

> When I say that these institutions are free and progressive, I don't want to insinuate that they are like Western universities ...
> 'Progressive' in this case means better, but those universities are progressive without breaking with the customs, culture, and traditions of the UAE. (Cited in Zoepe, 2006)

The discourses cited above suggest that women's academic opportunities are locally 'assembled' by policy makers, faculty members and consultants, through a network of private international higher education institutions. The latter are perceived as 'modern' and 'global' in terms of their facilitation of women's professional careers. At the centre of this 'assemblage' stands the political construction of ideal-typical 'modern-yet-authentic-Gulf-woman' who represents a cultural project of modernity and renaissance endorsed and promoted by a benevolent state (see, for example, the description by Salloum, 2003, p. 104).

Academic Opportunities as Topographies of Struggle

While Gulf governments promote personalised emancipatory projects for women, they appear less inclined to accommodate women's movements which operate outside the realm of state hegemony. According to Chatty (2000), 'there exists a resistance and a hesitancy on the part of governments to allow women to come together in formal groups'. Governments 'seem to share a hostility to formal, independent women's groups' (p. 241). If women's groups nonetheless exist, they 'are most often created and tightly organized by men for women' (p. 241), or they operate as charitable organisations which provide women with outlets 'to express their creative capacities in a well-contained as well as culturally appropriate environment' (Pharaon, 2004, p. 363). Women's associations in the Gulf are, 'like all voluntary associations ... under the aegis of the state' (al-Mughni, 1997, p. 195).

In most Gulf states the political struggle of women is concerned with civil and political rights, given that until recently Gulf women were politically disenfranchised (Rizzo et al, 2002).[13] In the aftermath of the Gulf war, women academics became increasingly involved in public protest, demonstrations and the signing of petitions calling for democratisation and political reforms, perhaps more than ever before.[14] For instance, in Bahrain (Human Rights Watch, 1997; Fakhro, 1997) and Saudi Arabia (Yamani, 1996, p. 272; Al-Rasheed, 2002, pp. 166-168), women academics who participated in diverse forms of political protest were dismissed from their university positions or subjected to public criticism in some newspapers.[15] While some women were reinstated shortly afterwards, others, for instance in Saudi Arabia, were reportedly boycotted by some of their (female) students. In the heated political debates that followed, the controversies surrounding the social and political visibility of Gulf women academics were further exacerbated by 'divisive' rivalries among women's associations over 'practical and strategic gender needs'. In Kuwait, leaders of women's professional associations 'overwhelmingly saw the lack of political rights as the main problem', while leaders of service-oriented women's associations 'tended to target divorce and education as areas that needed improvement' (Rizzo, 2004, p. 15). Al-Mughni (2001) reports that disagreements among women's movements 'were seized upon by the state to weaken the women's rights movement'. The alliance of elite women with Islamists 'made it possible for the state to maintain control over women's lives and prevent female disobedience to social norms' (p. 171). Rivalries among women's associations were also fuelled by social class, religious traditions and regional cleavages. In Saudi Arabia, the battle over women's rights witnessed the emergence of what Yamani (1996, p. 278) calls 'the New Islamist Feminists', 'a new phenomenon that has emerged at the women's sections of the universities in the 1980s, and intensified following the [1990-1991] Gulf War' (p. 279). By 'going back to the basics of the *shari'a*', Yamani (1996) observes, these women 'seem to derive a liberating force', thus 'creating a forum with a cultural context or idiom in which they are able to negotiate power' in a patriarchal society (p. 280).

Women's growing political and civic activism in the post-war period, and the support extended to women's movements by some liberal groups across the Gulf, catapulted gender issues into the focus of political conflict. This process fuelled debates between contending tribal, religious and liberal (male) elites regarding the role of academe in relation to issues of identity, culture and religion. The case of Kuwait is indicative in this respect. Al-Mughni (2001) observes that, after the Gulf war, as Kuwaiti women became occupationally more mobile and politically active, a 'battle has ensued between the Islamists and their liberal opponents, a battle – as one put it – "over the character of society"' (p. 158). Tétreault (2000) explains that this battle was partly fuelled by the weakness of the post-war economy, as 'Islamists sought to reduce women's access to high status and high-income degrees in such fields as medicine and engineering and to limit their job prospects following graduation' (p. 29).[16] As women gained greater social and political visibility, the Islamist bloc in Kuwait's National Assembly sought to regulate Kuwait University, given that it was serving simultaneously as 'a site and an object of contestation' (Tétreault, 1999, p. 246). The Islamic bloc ultimately succeeded in adding a clause to a government-sponsored bill on private universities, effectively instituting gender segregation in public tertiary institutions. Referring to the confrontation between liberal urbanised elites and their Bedouin-backed Islamist counterparts, one Kuwait University dean observed that 'this is all about the imposing of tribal values through Islam' (cited in Del Castillo, 2003). The battle over academic (and other social institutions) has not abated, despite the fact that Kuwaiti women were ultimately granted the right to vote and stand for election by the National Assembly in May 2005.[17]

With the exception of Saudi Arabia, the first appointments of women to senior positions within Gulf higher education institutions occurred after the war. In 1994, the appointment by Kuwait's ruler of a woman academic to preside over Kuwait's national university was labelled as 'the Arab world's first' (Bollag, 1994). Since then, women academics have been appointed to lead universities in Bahrain and Qatar. In these and other Gulf states (like Kuwait and Oman), other appointments have consolidated women's access to ministerial positions in education, higher education and scientific research. Notwithstanding, Tétreault (1999, p. 243) argues that these appointments represent a 'class strategy', whereas women from the ruling families are used as 'place holders' to shore up the positions of ruling elites. The incorporation of women into senior academic, management and executive positions within (and outside) academe emphasise differences between Saudi Arabia and the other five GCC states in terms of the impact of women's social and tribal affiliation on their academic careers and paths.

Conclusion

This chapter examines the factors affecting the location of women within Gulf academe. It illustrates the ways in which women's academic opportunities can be accounted for while avoiding the linear normative trappings of modernisation approaches and the determinism of theories built around reified notions of patriarchy and power. The chapter suggests that Gulf women's academic and occupational opportunities are imbricated within multifaceted processes that affect the foundations of power on which the Gulf state rests, as a rentier state and as a patriarchal mode of social organisation operating at the juncture of dynamic regional and global sociocultural, economic and political transformations.

Some of the patterns documented in this chapter resonate with findings generated by studies concerned with the location of women in academe and which were undertaken in academic settings worldwide. These studies consistently report that women's representation in higher education expands much more rapidly among students than it does among faculty members (Bradley, 2000). Moreover, professional-organisational and institutional barriers continue to confine and limit women's visibility and access to senior ranks within higher education worldwide (Bain & Cummings, 2000). For instance, in the United Kingdom, the largest proportion of women is found 'in the most junior positions', 'while the proportion of women professors remains around 10% on average, and is considerably less in some institutions' (Finch, 2003, p. 133). With regard to the United Kingdom and Canada respectively, Finch (2003) and Andres & Adamuti-Trache (2007) conclude that gender segregation in academe reproduces gender inequities in the larger labour market, both vertically (within professions) and horizontally (across professions). Rees (2001) shows that, in the European Union, women drop out of scientific careers in disproportionate numbers 'at every stage', particularly at the post-doctoral level. Approached from this particular angle, it may be argued that the barriers impacting women's location within Gulf academe reflect the challenges faced worldwide by women who access positions associated with social and political power, and with social status and prestige. These challenges also highlight the linkages operating between the internal structure of academic institutions and the broader 'field of power' (politics), much along Bourdieu's (1988) conceptualisation of the academic field as a social space of differences. For Bourdieu, 'it is in and through its functioning as a space of differences between positions' that the academic field reproduces 'the space of the different positions which constitute the field of power' (pp. 40-41).

Notwithstanding, this chapter also documents significant differences among the Gulf Arab states regarding the configuration of women's opportunities in relation to the broader field of power. To start with, in the aftermath of the Gulf war, the 'woman question' has become hyper-politicised, as Gulf ruling elites seek to regenerate the political legitimacy of the state. Moreover, ruling elites are eagerly seeking to reposition the state in relation to both civic society and the economy in order to negotiate both regional geopolitical developments, as well as rising domestic resistance and protest (Ehteshami, 2003). Within this context, the enfranchising of Gulf women in the post-war period is seen by some as a strategy deployed by ruling elites to accommodate a patriarchal 'bargain' or 'contract' which preserves the hegemony of established elites and tribal mode of social organisation over the distribution of social opportunities.[18] For others, these policies are part of 'nation-building' strategies which aim to bolster women's role as a 'reserve force' brought forward to endorse conceptions of citizenship which aim to mitigate the overwhelming reliance of Gulf economies on imported labour. These processes assume different dynamics in different Gulf Arab states. For instance, in the case of the UAE, the official discourse on nation-building and citizenship constructs women's subjectivities as part of salutary notions of a 'benevolent' nation state, and as part of a deeply rooted 'national identity' and 'cultural authenticity'. In this discourse, women are framed as culturally authorised or 'culturally devolved' individuals who can (freely) pursue autonomous careers, as productive agents of the nation, by virtue of their degrees, the academic and professional opportunities they are provided with, and by virtue of their international education. To expand the words of Meyer & Jepperson (2000), it may be argued that Emirati women 'are constructed as having the capacity and responsibility to act as an 'other' to themselves, to each other, and indeed for the wider cultural frame itself', ultimately enacting 'a highly standardized individualism' (pp. 102 & 111). In the process, the patriarchal state – initially functioning as an allocative mechanism of rent revenues – 're-invents' itself as an interpreter of culture and as an agent which seeks to control the field of cultural production to ensure its political viability. The construction of the 'modernised Gulf woman' (see, Salloum, 2003, p. 104) – in which state elites, policy makers, expatriate consultants, foreign universities and academics are all fervently engaged – re-inscribes within higher education the prevailing hegemony of power rooted in patriarchy, yet cushioned within notions of citizenship and participation that attempt to reconcile the tensions undergirding the various elements of these manufactured subjectivities of modernity.

In the case of Saudi Arabia, the discourse on women's location in academe is framed in terms of 'social opportunities' and less so in terms of 'citizenship'. The gendering of educational opportunities – through differential access to local versus foreign credentials, to different types of higher education institutions, and to different disciplinary fields – institutes unequal and gendered academic paths which construct within the academic field a 'matrix of correspondences'. The latter partitions control over women's and men's opportunities among contending elites. Within this context, compared to men, women have significantly less mobility opportunities in a heavily disjointed space. Moreover, forms of capital accumulated by women cannot be easily transferred or exchanged across academic or occupational 'territories'. As the Saudi Arabian case further reveals, the shifting boundaries determining women's 'spatial barriers' express the consolidation of the political centrality of educational credentials in enabling ruling elites to exercise, in the words of Bourdieu (1985), their 'monopoly over legitimate naming' by deploying 'instituted taxonomies' of educational credentials as 'symbolic strategies'. Credentials are used to impose the ruling elites' 'vision of the divisions of the social world' and their 'position within it' (p. 732). One may therefore argue that the expansion of Saudi Arabia's credentialing mechanisms – as regulative devices controlled by the state – has played a role in reconfiguring the power of the *'ulama* and of tribal leaders in their 'struggle over classifications' and in their bid to exert control 'over the power of knowledge' and the naming of the 'correct classification, the correct order' (p. 734).

The discussion of the academic opportunities of Gulf women highlights, therefore, significant differences among Gulf Arab states in terms of how women are 'called upon' into academe, and how they are distributed across disciplinary fields and positions of power (either within academe or within the state bureaucracy). Yet, despite these differences, the multifaceted processes associated with women's access to Gulf academe suggest that the patriarchal mode of social organisation is relatively more fragmented and diffused than is otherwise acknowledged, being itself caught within larger – regional and global – relations of power. Hence, despite its social pervasiveness, the Gulf patriarchal mode of social organisation is nonetheless underpinned by contradictions and tensions and by political divisions and competing interests. These are further exacerbated by global processes associated with the fluctuations of oil markets and their national, regional and global political ramifications. At the juncture of these power fractures, the patriarchal foundations of the Gulf Arab state and of academic institutions more specifically, have become more complex and subtle in terms of their accommodation of women. At the same time that Gulf women 'have come to be seen as political and economic actors who fend for themselves and struggle' (Chatty, 2000, p. 241), they have also become more vulnerable at the juncture of socio-political and economic processes in which local male elites, expanding cohorts of expatriate experts and consultants, and massive labour imports all vie for economic and political opportunities. Gulf women are therefore challenged to carve their spaces of opportunities and participation not only in relation to local ruling elites, but also in relation to a myriad of individual and corporate actors situated at the interface of global and local processes. Within this context, Gulf academe is no exception. To expand Marginson & Rhoades's (2002) argument, it 'takes us beyond nation states, national markets, and national systems and institutions of higher education to consider organizational agencies and human agency ... [which] operate simultaneously in the three domains or planes of existence – global, national, local – amid multiple and reciprocal flows of activity' (p. 305).

Acknowledgement

I am extremely grateful to Dawn Chatty for her constructive and incisive comments on an earlier draft of this chapter. I bear exclusive responsibility for the chapter's contents and for any errors therein.

Notes

[1] The Arab Gulf states, currently organised within the Gulf Cooperation Council (GCC), include the kingdoms of Bahrain and Saudi Arabia, the Sultanate of Oman, and the states (emirates) of Kuwait, Qatar and the United Arab Emirates (UAE).

[2] See the statistics section on the website of the GCC General Secretariat: http://www.gcc-sg.org. With regard to the population size of the six GCC member states, see Appendix 1.

[3] In the UAE, the majority of faculty are women, either nationals or expatriates.

[4] In 'rentier' economies, ruling elites depend on revenues (or rents) which are not derived from taxation on productive work but are generated, for instance, through the export of oil. Elites in rentier states draw their political legitimacy from the redistribution of acquired rents to citizens, making citizenship 'a source of economic benefit' rather than a source for political participation (Moaddel, 2002, p. 377). Ruling Gulf Arab elites derive their legitimacy not

from proportional political representation but from their monopoly over the redistribution of oil revenues to citizens (Okruhlik, 1999, p. 297).

[5] In his study, Sabour does not focus exclusively on academe in the GCC states. However, he includes academics who work in the Gulf Arab region in his sample drawn from several Arab states.

[6] Throughout this chapter the terms 'Gulf war' and 'war' refer to Iraq's invasion of Kuwait in summer 1990 and to the subsequent US military intervention in winter 1991. The terms 'aftermath of the war' or 'post-war' refer to the political and economic ramifications of this event, from early 1991 up to and including the US-British-led military occupation of Iraq in 2003.

[7] Saudi Arabia operates three universities which specialise in religious knowledge and traditions (the Islamic University, Al-Imam University and Um Al-Qura University). Five other universities are named for kings (Abdel-Aziz, Fahd, Saud, Faisal and Khalid). These eight universities were all founded prior to 2000 (for details, see Mazawi, 2005). The second half of the 2000s witnessed the foundation of regional universities at Al Jouf, Al Taif, Al Qassim, Jazan, Hail, and Taibah. Before obtaining their status as universities, many of these new foundations operated as regional branches of the more veteran eight universities.

[8] In the eight public universities founded prior to 2000 (see note 7), women represented around 16 per cent of all faculty members in the late 1990s (Mazawi, 2003, 2005).

[9] In 2002, 14.6 per cent of all men and 9.5 per cent of all women aged 15 years (*sic*) and above held a post-secondary degree (ranging from an undergraduate diploma to a postgraduate degree). Between 1975 and 2002, the enrolment ratio narrowed from 1.95 boys for every girl to 1.11:1 in elementary school, from 3.2:1 to 1.06:1 in secondary school and from 4.43:1 to 1.14:1 in tertiary education. On average, the gender gap narrowed from 2.16:1 to 1.06:1 (United Nations Development Programme, 2003, pp. 77 & 106).

[10] At the same time, women's movements are restricted by limitations imposed on their travel, leaving them with access to whatever post-secondary institution is locally available.

[11] The incident which triggered this 'merger' is associated with a fire that broke out in Intermediate School No. 31 in the city of Mecca. At least fourteen young girls perished, reportedly because the 'religious police' prevented the rescue services from entering the enflamed building out of fear that the girls would be improperly dressed. See, Human Rights Watch (2002, March 15) and Abukhalil (2004, pp. 151-152).

[12] In 2006, 2 out of 11 universities in the UAE were public. In Kuwait, 1 out of 8 universities and colleges was public. In Oman, 1 out of 4 universities was public. Saudi Arabia is an exception with 8 public universities and 6 new public universities under consideration. Two 'private' universities are operated by branches affiliated with the ruling family. In addition, there are two regional Gulf universities: the Arabian Gulf University (founded in 1982 in Bahrain) and the Arab Open University (founded in 2002 in Kuwait). It bears noting that Gulf governments are involved in the creation of semi-

public foundations, such as the Qatar Foundation (in Qatar), to promote the reforming and the privatisation of education and higher education in their countries. In the Sultanate of Oman, the state relies on the direct involvement of for-profit groups such as the Nuaimi Group and Oman Education and Training Investment Groups in establishing for-profit partnerships with foreign higher education providers.

[13] Women's right to vote and run for office was granted in 2002 in Bahrain and in 2005 in Kuwait. In Saudi Arabia, women's right to vote in the newly introduced municipal elections triggered heated debates regarding its feasibility.

[14] Women's involvement in public protest is part of the broader disillusionment of Gulf societies with their governments, following the Gulf war.

[15] For instance, in April 1995, Munira Fakhro, a professor at Bahrain University and a political activist, was suspended with over 90 other government employees, following protests and the signing of a petition by 310 women, calling for political reforms in Bahrain. See Fakhro (1997).

[16] Tétreault (2001) points out that Kuwaiti 'working mothers especially are favorite scapegoats for such social problems as rising rates of delinquency, alcoholism, drug addiction, and divorce' (p. 210). See also, al-Mughni (2001, pp. 157-158).

[17] Shortly afterwards, in June 2005, the first woman, a Kuwait University political science professor affiliated to one of Kuwait's ruling families, joined the Kuwaiti cabinet as minister of planning and as minister of state for administrative development affairs (*New York Times*, 2005).

[18] For a review of these concepts, and how they are used, see, for instance, Moghadam (1993), Fakhro (1997), Olmsted (2005) and Zuhur (2003, p. 19).

References

Abdalla, F. (2006) Education and Employment among Women in the UAE, *International Higher Education*, 45, 9-10.

Abukhalil, A. (2004) *The Battle for Saudi Arabia: royalty, fundamentalism and global power*. New York: Seven Stories Press.

Alkhazim, M.A. (2003) Higher Education in Saudi Arabia: challenges, solutions, and opportunities missed, *Higher Education Policy*, 16(4), 479-486.

Al-Lamki, S. (2006) The Development of Private Higher Education in Oman: perception and analysis, *International Journal of Private Education*, 1, 55-77.

al-Mughni, H. (1997) From Gender Equality to Female Subjugation: the changing agendas of women's groups in Kuwait, in D. Chatty & A. Rabo (Eds) *Organizing Women: formal and informal women's groups in the Middle East*, 195-209. Oxford and New York: Berg.

al-Mughni, H. (2001) *Women in Kuwait: the politics of gender*. London: Saqi Books.

AlMunajjed, M. (1997) *Women in Saudi Arabia*. London: Macmillan.

Al-Rasheed, M. (2002) *A History of Saudi Arabia*. Cambridge: Cambridge University Press.

Al-Rasheed, M. (2007) *Contesting the Saudi State: Islamic voices from a new generation*. Cambridge: Cambridge University Press.

Al-Sayegh, F. (2004) Post 9/11 Changes in the Gulf: the case of the UAE, *Middle East Policy*, 11(2), 107-124.

Al-Sulayti, H. (1999) Education and Training in the GCC Countries: some issues of concern, in Emirates Center for Strategic Studies and Research *Education and the Arab World: challenges of the next millennium*, 271-278. Abu Dhabi: The Emirates Center for Strategic Studies and Research.

Altorki, S. & Cole, D.P. (1989) *Arabian Oasis City: the transformation of 'Unayzah*. Austin: University of Texas Press.

Andres, L. & Adamuti-Trache, M. (2007) You've Come a Long Way, Baby? Persistent Gender Inequality in University Enrolment and Competition in Canada, 1979-2004, *Canadian Public Policy*, 33(1), 93-116.

Bahgat, G. (1999) Education in the Gulf Monarchies: retrospect and prospect, *International Review of Education*, 45(2), 127-136.

Bahry, L. & Marr, P. (2005) Qatari Women: a new generation of leaders? *Middle East Policy*, XII(2), 104-119.

Bain, O. & Cummings, W. (2000) Academe's Glass Ceiling: societal, professional-organizational and institutional barriers to the career advancement of academic women, *Comparative Education Review*, 44(4), 493-514.

Banta, T.W. (2003) Assessment at the United Arab Emirates University, *Assessment Update*, 15(1), 3 & 11.

Bollag, B. (1994) There is No Glass Ceiling: a female president, the Arab world's first, guides the restoration of Kuwait U, *Chronicle of Higher Education*, 16 February, p. A45.

Bosbait, M. & Wilson, R. (2005) Education, School to Work Transitions and Unemployment in Saudi Arabia, *Middle Eastern Studies*, 41(4), 533-545.

Bourdieu, P. (1985) The Social Space and the Genesis of Groups, *Theory and Society*, 14(6), 723-744.

Bourdieu, P. (1988) *Homo Academicus*. Trans. Peter Collier. Cambridge: Polity Press.

Bradley, K. (2000) The Incorporation of Women into Higher Education: paradoxical outcomes, *Sociology of Education*, 73, 1-18.

Chatty, D. (2000) Women Working in Oman: individual choice and cultural constraints, *International Journal of Middle East Studies*, 32, 241-254.

Coffman, J. (2003) Higher Education in the Gulf: privatization and Americanization, *International Higher Education*, 33, 17-19.

Del Castillo, D. (2003) Kuwaiti Universities Return to Separating Men and Women, *Chronicle of Higher Education*, 49(17), 3 January, A44.

Doumato, E.A. (2003) Education in Saudi Arabia: gender, jobs, and the price of religion, in E.A. Doumato & M.P. Posusney (Eds) *Women and Globalization in the Arab Middle East*, 239-257. Boulder: Lynne Reinner.

Ehteshami, A. (2003) Reform from Above: the politics of participation in the oil monarchies, *International Affairs*, 79(1), 53-75.

El-Sanabary, N. (1994) Female Education in Saudi Arabia and the Reproduction of Gender Division, *Gender and Education*, 6(2), 141-150.

Fakhro, M.A. (1997) The Uprising in Bahrain: an assessment, in G.G. Sick & L.G. Potter (Eds) *The Persian Gulf at the Millennium: essays in politics, economy, security, and religion*, 167-188. New York: Palgrave Macmillan.

Finch, J. (2003) Foreword: Why Be Interested in Women's Position in Academe? *Gender, Work & Organization*, 10(2), 133-136.

Gulf Cooperation Council, General Secretariat (2005) *Statistical Yearbook 14*. Riyadh: Gulf Cooperation Council.

Human Rights Watch (1997) *Routine Abuse, Routine Denial: civil rights and the political crisis in Bahrain*. New York: Human Rights Watch. http://www.hrw.org/reports/1997/bahrain/#P347_76924

Human Rights Watch (2002, March 15) Saudi Arabia: religious police role in school fire criticized. New York: Human Rights Watch. http://www.hrw.org/press/2002/03/saudischool.htm

Joseph, S. (1996) Patriarchy and Development in the Arab World, *Gender and Development*, 4(2), 14-19.

Kapiszewski, A. (2001) *Nationals and Expatriates: population and labour dilemmas of the Gulf Cooperation Council states*. Reading: Ithaca Press.

Longva, A.N. (1993) Kuwaiti Women at a Crossroads: privileged development and the constraints of ethnic stratification, *International Journal of Middle East Studies*, 25(3), 443-456.

Mahmood, S. (2001) Feminist Theory, Embodiment, and the Docile Agent: some reflections on the Egyptian Islamic revival, *Cultural Anthropology*, 16(2), 202-236.

Marginson, S. & Rhoades, G. (2002) Beyond National States, Markets, and Systems of Higher Education: a glonacal agency heuristic, *Higher Education*, 43, 281-309.

Mazawi, A.E. (2003) The Academic Workplace in Public Arab Gulf Universities, in P.G. Altbach (Ed.) *The Decline of the Guru: the academic profession in developing and middle-income countries*, 231-269. New York: Palgrave Macmillan.

Mazawi, A.E. (2005) The Academic Profession in a Rentier State: the professoriate in Saudi Arabia, *Minerva*, 43, 221-244.

Mazawi, A.E. (2006) State Power, Faculty Recruitment and the Emergence of Political Constituencies in Saudi Arabia, in R. Griffin (Ed.) *Education in the Muslim World: different perspectives*, 55-76. Oxford: Symposium Books.

Mellahi, K. & Al-Hinai, S. (2000) Local Workers in Gulf Co-Operation Countries: assets or liabilities? *Middle Eastern Study*, 36(3), 177-190.

Meyer, J.W. & Jepperson, R.L. (2000) The 'Actors' of Modern Society: the cultural construction of social agency, *Sociological Theory*, 18(1), 100-120.

Moaddel, M. (2002) The Study of Islamic Culture and Politics: an overview and assessment, *Annual Review of Sociology*, 28, 359-386.

Moghadam, V. (1993) *Modernizing Women: gender and social change in the Middle East*. Boulder: Lynne Rienner

New York Times (2005) Woman to Join Kuwait Cabinet, 13 June, 8.

Okruhlik, G. (1999) Rentier Wealth, Unruly Law, and the Rise of Opposition: the political economy of oil states, *Comparative Politics*, 31(3), 295-315.

Olmsted, J.C. (2005) Gender, Aging, and the Evolving Arab Patriarchal Contract, *Feminist Economics*, 11(2), 53-78.

Pharaon, N.A. (2004) Saudi Women and the Muslim State in the Twenty-first Century, *Sex Roles*, 51(5-6), 349-366.

Rees, T. (2001) Mainstreaming Gender Equality in Science in the European Union: the 'ETAN Report', *Gender and Education*, 13(3), 243-260.

Rizzo, H. (2004) Divisions among Women's Groups: implications for feminism in Kuwait, *The MIT Electronic Journal of Middle East Studies*, 4, 6-25.

Rizzo, H., Meyer, K. & Ali, Y. (2002) Women's Political Rights: Islam, status and networks in Kuwait, *Sociology*, 26(3), 639-662.

Rugh, W.A. (2002) Education in Saudi Arabia: choices and constraints, *Middle East Policy*, IX(2), 40-55.

Sabour, M. (1996) Women in the Moroccan Academic Field: respectability and power, *Mediterranean Journal of Educational Studies*, 1(1), 75-92.

Sabour, M. (2001) *The Ontology and Status of Intellectuals in Arab Academia and Society*. Aldershot: Ashgate.

Salloum, H. (2003) Women in the United Arab Emirates, *Contemporary Review*, 283 (Issue 1651), 101-104.

Seikaly, M. (1994) Women and Social Change in Bahrain, *International Journal of Middle East Studies*, 26(3), 415-426.

Sharabi, H. (1988) *Neopatriarchy: a theory of distorted change in Arab society*. Oxford: Oxford University Press.

Shaw, K.E. (1993) Development Tasks for Arab Gulf Universities, *Arab Studies Quarterly*, 15(4), 83-90.

Tétreault, M. (1999) Sex and Violence: social reactions to economic restructuring in Kuwait, *International Feminist Journal of Politics*, 1(2), 237-255.

Tétreault, M. (2000) Women's Rights in Kuwait: bringing in the last Bedouins? *Current History*, January, 27-32.

Tétreault, M. (2001) A State of Two Minds: state cultures, women, and politics in Kuwait, *International Journal of Middle East Studies*, 33, 203-220.

United Nations Development Programme (2003) *Human Development Report: Saudi Arabia*. Riyadh: UNDP.

Yamani, M. (1996) Some Observations on Women in Saudi Arabia, in M. Yamani (Ed.) *Feminism and Islam: legal and literary perspectives*, 263-281. New York: New York University Press.

Zabalawi, I.H. (2000) Academic Freedom and Gender Equities. Paper presented at the International Conference on Higher Education in Asian Universities: Challenges and Future Trends. Sharjah, UAE, University of Sharjah, 25-26 November.

Zoepe, K. (2006 April 14) Universities for Women Push Borders in Persian Gulf, *Chronicle of Higher Education*, 52(32), pp. A45-A47.

Zuhur, S. (2003) Women and Empowerment in the Arab World, *Arab Studies Quarterly*, 25(4), 17-38.

APPENDIX 1

GCC State	Area ('000s Km^2)	Population (estimate in millions)	Expatriates in population (%)	Nationals in total labour force (%)	National women in total labour force (%)	Oil production ('000s barrels/ day)
Bahrain	0.7	0.7	38	41	11	38
Kuwait	17.8	2.5	63	19	7	2108
Oman	309.5	2.3	24	29	7	820
Qatar	11.5	0.7	-	45	19	721
UAE	83.6	4.0	-	-	15*	2601
S. Arabia	2250.0	22.0	27	50**	8	8410

Notes:

Adapted from: GCC General Secretariat (2005).

Figures are rounded to the nearest decimal or digit.

- Figure not available. However, expatriates represent the overwhelming majority of residents or workers

*The figure includes both national and expatriate women active in the national workforce.

**Figure for 2002.

Table AI. Select Official Statistics of Gulf Cooperation Council Member States for 2003.

Religious Education of Muslim and Non-Muslim Schoolchildren in the Islamic Republic of Iran

GOLNAR MEHRAN

Introduction

Iran is a multi-faith society composed of a predominantly Muslim population, the majority of which are Shi'i. Judaism, Christianity and Zoroastrianism are the only other 'officially recognised' religions in the country. Iran was declared an Islamic Republic in 1979 and Iranian schools have ever since aimed at creating pious and politicised schoolchildren. Separate religious education textbooks have been compiled for Muslim and non-Muslim students. A content and pictorial analysis of religious textbooks compiled by the Iranian Ministry of Education for majority (Muslim) and minority (Jewish, Christian, Zoroastrian) students reveals that state religious education aims at bringing about unity rather than division by emphasising commonalities and ignoring dissimilarities among monotheist religions. Religious education in Iranian schools is marked by a policy of silence that deliberately avoids potentially divisive issues. However, acknowledging and addressing religious diversity, especially in contemporary Iran, is also ignored. The guiding policy of religious education in Iran, therefore, aims at unity in commonality rather than unity in diversity.

Iran is a multi-faith society composed of Muslims (99.5 per cent) – the majority of whom are Shi'i, Christians (0.13 per cent), Zoroastrians (0.04 per cent), Jews (0.02 per cent), and the remainder are followers of other faiths.[1] Despite the existence of other faiths, Judaism, Christianity and Zoroastrianism are the only other officially recognised religions in the country, whose followers have their own representatives in the Iranian parliament. According to Article 13 of the Constitution of the Islamic Republic of Iran:

> Zoroastrian, Jewish, and Christian Iranians are the recognized religious minorities, who, within the limits of the law, are free to perform their religious rites and ceremonies, and to act according

to their own canons in matters of personal affairs and religious education.[2]

The name of the country points to the conscious effort to Islamise the society and bring about the rule of Islam in the public and private lives of individuals. However, what does it mean to Islamise Iran, that is, a country that is predominantly Muslim and has been governed by Muslim rulers since the downfall of the Persian Empire in the seventh century? Is there a difference between an Islamic society and an Islamised state? The answer is that in this chapter, an Islamic society is referred to as one characterised by a predominantly Muslim population and the prevalence of Islamic beliefs and practices in the private lives of its inhabitants. An Islamised state, on the other hand, is marked by politicised Islam, governing both the private and public lives of individuals. What distinguishes Islamised Iran from other Islamic societies is the rule of religio-political authorities and the strict enforcement of religious laws in all spheres of life.[3] It may be said that it is the politicised version of Islam and the close intertwinement of religion and politics that distinguishes Iran as an Islamised state. Subsequently, there has been an open and deliberate effort on the part of Iranian schools to create pious Muslims who are loyal to the dictates of the ruling religio-political ideology. The rule of politicised Islam led to the exodus of an unprecedented number of Iranians from the country, many of whom were members of religious minority groups.

The multicultural nature of the Iranian society, marked by ethnic and linguistic diversity, is not reflected in its schools. The system of education in the Islamic Republic of Iran is highly centralised, using a standard curriculum throughout the country. Teachers are trained in state-sponsored teacher training centres that offer the same courses. Uniform textbooks are used throughout the nation with the exception of religious education books that take the multi-faith nature of society into consideration. Consequently, the Ministry of Education prepares separate textbooks for Muslim and non-Muslim students (Jews, Christians, Zoroastrians) with the aim of 'attracting them to religion, developing their faith, and bringing about piety'.[4] An in-depth study of religious textbooks would provide insight into the similarities and differences that may exist in terms of religious instruction and educational values provided for members of the majority and minority religions.

The purpose of this chapter is twofold: to identify the goals of state religious education for Muslim and non-Muslim alike and to determine whether religious instruction in schools aims at unity or division among members of different faiths. So this study seeks to answer the following questions:

- What are the main themes discussed in state religious education textbooks?
- How is religious diversity addressed in school books?

- What are the messages conveyed to students from diverse religious backgrounds? and
- What are the similarities and differences in religious education for majority and minority students?

The chapter is based on the content and pictorial analysis of religious education textbooks used throughout the period of formal compulsory schooling (age 7-16) during the 2004-05 academic year by both Muslim and non-Muslim students.

Religious Education in Iran

The study of religion and education has long been the focus of research among scholars. Among the topics discussed have been the relationships between religion and the state in education [5], religious instruction and values education [6], the relationship between religion, and educational aspirations [7], religion and school attainment [8], and the role of religious education in promoting dialogue and tolerance [9], especially in pluralist societies.[10] Most studies conclude that religious instruction plays an important role in the transfer of culture and transmission of values among the youth, and Iran is no exception.

Religion has a strong presence in Iranian education, reflecting the dominance of religious ideology in the country since the establishment of the Islamic Republic in 1979.[11] In fact, Iran ranks fifth among fifty-four countries studied in terms of percentage of teaching time allotted to religious education during the first six years of formal schooling. Iranian schools spend an average of 13.9 per cent of time teaching religion, following Saudi Arabia (31 per cent), Yemen (28.2 per cent), Qatar (15.5 per cent) and Libya (14.3 per cent).[12]

Iranian education is openly and avowedly religious with clear emphasis on Islam as the majority religion. In fact, religious instruction provided for Muslim schoolchildren is none other than Islamic education. In 1987, the Ministry of Education (MOE) stated that the fundamental goal of Iranian schooling is to 'strengthen the spiritual beliefs of schoolchildren through the explanation and instruction of principles ... of Islam and Shi'ism on the basis of reason, the Qur'an, and the traditions of the Innocent Ones' [13], referring to the Prophet Mohammad, his daughter Fatemeh, and the twelve Shi'i Imams. To reach the above goal, Iranian schools were asked to:

- develop moral and ethical virtues among schoolchildren and purify their souls according to the teachings of Islam;
- explain Islamic values and educate schoolchildren accordingly;
- strengthen the spirit of reliance on God;
- create the spirit of religious devotion and obedience along with practical undertaking of Islamic commandments;

- promote political insight based on the principle of *velayat-e faqih* (governance of the religious jurisprudence) in various fields, aimed at informed participation in the political destiny of the country.[14]

Eleven years later in 1998, the Ministry of Education presented a more detailed classification of educational goals emphasising faith in God, belief in the fundamentals of Islam on the basis of the Qur'an and the traditions of the Prophet and the Shi'i Imams, obedience to Islamic rules and regulations, and acceptance of the rule of *velayat-e faqih* in society.[15] Such goals not only illustrate the religious nature of Iranian education, but also point to the predominance of Islam and the link between religion and politics in formal schooling.

The key role of religion in Iranian schooling is illustrated in the following statement: 'the mission of education is the overall development of schoolchildren based on the teachings and orders of Islam'.[16] The above applies to all Iranian pupils with the exception of officially recognised minorities, including Christians, Jews and Zoroastrians. Based on the Constitution of the Islamic Republic of Iran, religious minorities are free in the compilation and teaching of their own religious textbooks, based on their holy book, customs and traditions under the supervision of the Ministry of Education. According to Article 12 of the Constitution, the Ministry of Education is obliged to ensure that the religious education of non-Shi'i followers of Islam is in accordance with their own jurisprudence.[17] In addition, religious minorities have to pass their own religious education examinations based on the textbooks compiled for non-Muslims. The latter are also exempt from taking examinations on the Qur'an. The entire student population is exempt from taking examinations during the times of Shi'i mourning, during the months of Ramadan (coinciding with the martyrdom of Imam Ali) and Muharram (coinciding with the commemoration of 'Ashura and the martyrdom of Imam Hossein in the battle of Karbala). Armenian schools can also close during Christian holidays.[18]

In accordance with the Constitution regarding the preparation of separate religious education books for religious minorities, there are two sets of textbooks compiled for Muslim and non-Muslim schoolchildren aged 7 to 16. Both sets are prepared by the Religion Team of the Office of Planning and Compilation of School Textbooks at the Ministry of Education. The set compiled for Muslim students consists of ten books that are accompanied by four workbooks at the primary education level. The title of textbooks used in grades two, three and four of primary school (age 7-10) is *Gifts from Heaven (Islamic Education)* (Hadiyehha-ye Aseman [Ta'lim va Tarbiyat-e Islami]). They have been compiled in recent years and are filled with stories, activities and colourful paintings. The fifth-grade textbook is named *Religious Education* (Ta'limat-e Dini) and has been in use for many years. The title of textbooks changes to *Islamic Culture and Religious Education* (Farhang-e Islami va Ta'limat-e Dini) at the guidance cycle level (age 11-13). There have been minor revisions in these books over the years but they remain fundamentally unaltered. The textbooks used at the secondary education level (age 14-16) are titled *Religion and Life (Qur'an and Religious Education)* (Din va Zendegi [Qur'an va Ta'limat-e Dini]) for the first two years of high school and *Islamic Insight* (Binesh-e Islami) in the third and final year. The two recently compiled *Religion and Life* books are aesthetically beautiful with a totally new and engaging approach to teaching morality and religion. *Islamic Insight* is a strictly ideological textbook and a remnant of the spirit prevailing during the early years of the revolution.

The religious education textbooks compiled for non-Muslim students are written for the officially recognised religious minorities – Jews, Christians and Zoroastrians. The same textbook is used for all three groups from age 7 to 16, the title of which is *Teaching Divine Religions and Ethics (for Religious Minorities)* (Ta'limat-e Adyan-e Elahi va Akhlaq [vizheh Aqalliyatha-ye Mazhabi]). The total number of textbooks is ten, used from grade two to the end of high school. The books follow the same pattern as the ones prepared for Muslim students. They are filled with stories conveying simple religious messages at the primary school level and gradually become more complex with in-depth discussions about the fundamentals of religion as the grades progress.

The Teachings of Religious Education Textbooks

A study of state religious education textbooks used in Iranian schools for the Muslim majority and the officially recognised religious minority groups indicates that all students are presented with a strictly dichotomous image of the world divided between good and evil and comprised of believers and non-believers. The Islamisation of society, formation of a strong Shi'i identity, and presentation of Muslim role models, mainly Shi'i and male, comprise the major bulk of textbooks compiled for Muslim students. Textbooks for religious minorities, on the other hand, emphasise the commonalities of the major religions of the world, mainly Judaism and Christianity, and deliberately avoid any mention of dissimilarity and difference. Religious education textbooks in general focus on the historical presentation of non-Muslims with minimum attention to the contemporary scene. Religious groups in Iran other than Jews and Christians are basically ignored in the school books. The messages conveyed in textbooks compiled for Muslim and non-Muslim Iranian schoolchildren emphasise unity of religions without any mention of division or conflict.

The following sections discusses ten themes that were identified in religious education textbooks in Iran, an in-depth analysis of which will shed further light on the messages conveyed to Iranian schoolchildren.

Dichotomous Image of the World

The image of the world presented to Iranian schoolchildren is a strictly dichotomous one. According to the religious education textbooks for Muslim and non-Muslim students, the world is divided into two camps: good (*kheir*) and evil (*sharr*) [19], or right (*haqq*) and wrong (*batel*).[20] Schoolchildren are also taught that the world is divided into two groups of people: the pious (*dindar*) and the irreligious (*bidin*), who are not equal in the eyes of God.[21] The different types of good and evil are as follows.

Presentation of good in religion textbooks in Iran:
Believers, Chaste, Clean, Devout, Faithful, Followers of the Divine, Prophets, Friends of God, Inhabitants of Heaven, Monotheist, Moral, Obedient to the Commandments of God, Pious, Pure, Religious, Righteous, Servants of God, Virtuous, Worshippers of God. (Source: Religious Education Textbooks for Muslim and Non-Muslim Students, Islamic Republic of Iran, 2004-2005 Academic Year)

Presentation of evil in religion textbooks in Iran:
Apostates, Atheists, Blasphemers, Defiled, Deniers of God, Dwellers of Hell, Enemies of God, Evil, Doers, Heathens, Heretics, Idol, Worshippers, Immoral, Impious, Impure, Infidels, Insubordinate to the Will of God, Irreligious, Materialists, Non-Believers, Pagans, Polytheists, Secular, Sinners, Unclean, Unfaithful, Worshippers of Satan. (Source: Religious Education Textbooks for Muslim and Non-Muslim Students, Islamic Republic of Iran, 2004-2005 Academic Year)

Believers (*mo'menan*) belong to the good camp [22] while the evil camp is filled with non-believers and infidels (*kafaran/koffar*).[23] The definition of *kafar* or infidel presented to Muslim students is 'one who denies God, believes God has a partner, or does not accept the prophethood of prophets.[24] Such a definition does not include followers of other religions. In fact, the same textbook teaches Muslim students that 'all believers are brothers'.[25] Non-Muslim students are told that the determining factor is faith in God (*iman beh khoda*) regardless of the religion one adheres to, and a believer (*mo'men*) is anyone 'who has accepted to serve and worship God'.[26]

In the black and white image of the world portrayed for students from different religious backgrounds, the pious (*mottaqi*) are virtuous (*parhizgar*), pure and chaste (*pak*), righteous (*nikukar*) and devout (*parsa*) and will be rewarded in heaven (*behesht*). On the other hand, the impious and irreligious are sinners (*gonahkar*), impure (*aludeh*) and evil doers (*badkar*) and will be punished in hell (*jahannam/duzakh*).[27] The dichotomy is clear in the following statement: 'The inhabitants of heaven (*beheshtian*) are worshippers of God, pious, and righteous ... and the dwellers of hell (*jahannamian*) are infidels, evil doers, and oppressors'.[28] Stated more simply, fifth graders are told that 'the pious go to heaven and the irreligious go to hell'.[29]

The symbol of goodness and light (*nur*) presented to Muslim and non-Muslim students alike is the monotheist (*movahhed/yeganeh parast/yekta parast*) while the atheist (*molhed*), polytheist (*moshrek*), idolater (*bot parast*), apostate (*mortad*), and the materialist (*maddeh gara*) personify evil and darkness (*zolmat*). The ultimate evil, however, lies in Marxism. An entire chapter is dedicated to introducing the Marxist world-view on creation and life, education, and the role of the human being as an 'economic animal' (*heyvan-e eqtesadi*) for non-Muslim secondary school students.[30] It is interesting to note that Marxism is dealt with in detail solely in the textbook for religious minorities, with passing reference to it in books for Muslim students.

Religious education textbooks for Muslim and non-Muslim schoolchildren state that there is one God and all monotheists are equal.[31] It is also noted that the main yardstick is faith in God and following the orders and decrees of the divine prophets. This, however, does not mean that the Islamisation of the Iranian society is undermined and that clear circles of inclusion and exclusion composed of 'us' and 'them' do not exist. Such themes will be further explored in the following sections.

Diversity in Iran

A content analysis of religious education textbooks for schoolchildren indicates that Iranian society is introduced first and foremost as Islamic, with a more or less homogeneous population marked by minimum diversity. In fact, diversity in Iran is mentioned only twice in the twenty-four textbooks analysed. Muslim students read about ethnic variety in the country in a paragraph in which they are told that Islam accepts variety, and Muslims throughout the world are composed of various national and ethnic groups who have their own customs and traditions, especially with regard to covering (*pushesh*) for men and women.[32] In another instance, they are told that

> We Muslims have faith in all divine prophets and respect them all.
> We know that they have been sent by God and we are grateful for
> their efforts and sacrifices. On the basis of Islamic laws, it is our
> duty to treat the followers of Moses and Jesus, (known as Jews and
> Christians), and Zoroastrians well and respect their rights.[33]

The above statement is the most direct one regarding the officially recognised religious minorities in contemporary Iran and the only one that mentions Zoroastrians.

Diversity is treated in more general terms for non-Muslim students, who are told that human worth and respect is not restricted to any race, colour, or sect. They learn that divine religions 'do not consider any human being as superior due to his/her race, tribe, color, wealth, and power'.[34] Students are taught that there is one God and all humans are equal.[35] They read about Prophet Mohammad's statement that

all humans are created by God and should be treated fairly: black
and white, yellow and red, man and woman, Arab and non-Arab;
all humans have the right to freedom and life; and the most
cherished by God is the most pious one.[36]

The above statements convey two important messages to Iranian students.
First, there is an emphasis on monotheism and the equality of monotheists.
Second, while all humans have rights regardless of their race, colour, sex and
nationality, the cherished ones are the believers and the pious. Various circles
of inclusion and exclusion are thus made clear for schoolchildren, who are
taught that there are indeed qualitative differences as between people.

Religious versus National Identity

The emphasis on the Islamic nature of Iranian society in religious education
textbooks has also led to the undermining of Iranian identity. It seems that
there is every effort to introduce Iranians as members of the Islamic nation
(*umma*) and de-emphasise a sense of belonging to the Iranian nation, mainly
to avoid separation from other Muslims on the basis of nationality or
language. Schoolchildren rarely encounter symbols of Iranianness. The two
exceptions are the picture of the national flag raised by Iranian soldiers in the
battleground during the 1980-88 Iran–Iraq war [37] and the passages about
the necessity of fighting against aggression in 'our country' and the
importance of helping 'our homeland' flourish through cooperation and
work.[38] The above constitute the rare references to Iranianness in the
school books in an attempt to present the religious as opposed to the national
identity of Iranians.

The fact that Muslimhood (*Islamiyyat*) is deemed more important than
Iranianness (*Iraniyyat*) is evident in the choice of names in religious
education textbooks. The majority of male and female names appearing in
school books are Arabic/Islamic names, most of which are the names of the
prophet of Islam and Shi'i Imams. Examples are Mohammad, Ali, Hassan,
Baqer, Sa'id, Sadeq, Morteza, Mohsen, Abbas, Reza, Majid, Javad, Mehdi,
Mas'ud, Vahid, Ahmad and Taqi for boys. The single non-Islamic female
name mentioned is Maryam, the Persian version of Mary, the mother of
Jesus Christ.[39]

Arabic/Islamic names are also used in textbooks for religious minorities,
such as Majid, Mas'ud, Sa'id and Hamed for boys and Kowkab, Zohreh and
Sa'ideh for girls. There are two instances in which the female name Maryam
and the male name Davud – the Persian version of David – are
mentioned.[40] Unlike textbooks for Muslims, there are a number of Persian
names in school books for religious minorities. Examples are Fereshteh and
Mahin for girls and historical Persian names, such as Jamshid, Bizhan,
Manuchehr and Hushang, for boys.[41]

Islamisation of the Iranian Society

There has been a conscious and deliberate effort to Islamise Iranian society since the 1979 revolution. In fact, the post-revolutionary name of the country – the Islamic Republic of Iran – is a clear manifestation of the existing priorities and the dominance of the majority religion, Islam. Undermining religious diversity and national identity are examples of the attempt by the Iranian educational authorities to present schoolchildren with an image of the country as first and foremost an Islamic one.

Adding the word Islamic to almost everything in the public and private realms (illustrated in the Appendix) symbolises the serious attempt to Islamise various layers of life in the country. The introduction of such terms as Islamic science, Islamic economics, Islamic banking, Islamic education, Islamic psychology, Islamic universities, and even Islamic human rights has been a major task undertaken by the ruling authorities since they took power in 1979. The Appendix also illustrates the attempts to Islamise beyond the Iranian borders through the use of such terms as Islamic territories, the great Islamic civilisation, the great Islamic nation, Islamic solidarity, and universal Islamic rule.[42]

Religion and Politics

The political nature of Islam practised in post-revolutionary Iran is made clear in the following statement by the founder of the Islamic Republic of Iran. According to Ayatollah Khomeini, 'political activity and struggle is an important part of religious responsibilities.[43] The aim of the educational system is thus creating politically and ideologically committed (*mote'ahhed*) Muslims whose mission transcends national borders and includes 'spreading the Islamic revolution throughout the world ... helping the oppressed, fighting against the oppressors, and mobilising the deprived and dispossessed of the world against injustice and oppression.[44]

Students are constantly reminded that Islam is a 'multidimensional religion' with a 'comprehensive' plan for the personal, political, social and economic lives of Muslims.[45] Yet the political nature of Islam depicted in textbook pictures is a militant one, with Muslim men and women carrying guns and wearing headbands and flags with the words 'God is Great' (*Allah-o Akbar*) written on them.[46]

Politicised Islam in Iran is described in detail for Muslim secondary school students. They read about the necessity of Islamic rule and the creation of an Islamised society, governed by religio-political leaders and led by the religious jurisprudent (*vali-ye faqih*), who is characterised by knowledge, justice, prudence, merit and courage.[47] They also read the remarks by Ayatollah Khomeini that helped pave the ground for establishing the governance of the religious jurisprudence (*velayat-e faqih*) and Islamising the Iranian society: 'Since any non-Islamic political order is a polytheist one governed by an idol (*taghut*), it is our duty to eliminate the signs of polytheism from the lives of the Muslims'.[48]

Muslim schoolchildren learn more about the intertwinement of religion and politics in Iran through the study of the writings of the two religio-political leaders governing the country since 1979 – namely, Ayatollah Khomeini and Ayatollah Khamene'i – from primary school until the end of secondary education.[49]

The political nature of Islam in Iran transcends national borders when two kinds of Islam are introduced to secondary school students: 'pure Islam' and 'American Islam'. According to Ayatollah Khomeini, 'the pure Islam of Prophet Mohammad' (*Islam-e nab-e Mohammadi*) is the religion of the poor, oppressed, dispossessed, and those who have suffered throughout history, while 'American Islam' (*Islam-e Amerika-yi*) is the religion of the oppressors, opportunists, capitalists, hypocrites, infidels and atheists. 'American Islam' is led by the West and 'war mongering America' and the East, headed by the 'criminal Soviet Union'.[50] The above classification portrays a politicised religion that does not take into consideration differences in religious faith but rather deals with friends and enemies in the political arena.

Islamic Unity

Undermining diversity among Iranians is accompanied by emphasising unity among Muslims in religious education textbooks in Iran. Such themes as Islamic unity and brotherhood, mutual responsibility among Muslims, protecting Islam, and defending Islamic lands permeate school books compiled for Muslim students in a conscious effort to place Iranian schoolchildren among members of the Islamic nation (*umma*). While acknowledging diversity among Muslims throughout the world based on nationality, race, ethnicity and language, school books emphasise the sheer number of Muslims throughout the world and the responsibility of the strong and wealthy ones to help the poor, weak and hungry regardless of geographic borders. Furthermore, Muslims living in free and advanced Islamic countries are asked to assist those who are colonised and imprisoned.[51] Brotherhood/sisterhood among Muslims is also emphasised, stating that Islam regards Muslim men and women as brothers and sisters in faith (*khaharan va baradaran-e imani*). Muslims are asked to be kind, helpful and forgiving towards each other, avoiding cruelty and oppression in their relations.[52]

The ultimate symbol of Islamic unity and strength depicted for schoolchildren is the annual pilgrimage to Mecca (*hajj*). It portrays the 'faith, power, glory, and unity of the great Islamic nation' and provides an opportunity for Muslims to 'shake their hands in brotherhood' and 'yell against the enemies and foreigners and their mercenaries', cutting their hands from the 'great land of Islam'.[53] Muslim students are told that Muslims throughout the world are a unified nation who should be kind to each other and help one another; that aggression against one Islamic territory is aggression against Islam, the Islamic world, and the unified nation of Islam, and it is, therefore, the obligation of all Muslims to free the Islamic land from the aggressive enemy; and that the Islamic world should avoid friction and conflict and not allow foreigners and infidels to interfere in the affairs of Muslims or gain dominance over them.[54] 'Self' and 'other' is thus clearly portrayed in terms of Muslims and their enemies – namely, foreigners (*biganegan*) and infidels (*koffar*).

Protecting Islam from the Enemy

The need for unity and solidarity among Muslims to protect Islamic territories and defend the religion from the 'enemies of Islam' is an important theme in Iranian education. The concept of the 'enemy' (*doshman*) is an ever-present one in religious education textbooks. Students are told that 'the enemies of Islam are always plotting to defeat Islam and Muslims' [55] and it is their religious duty (*farizeh*) to defend their 'land, honor, and faith'. They read that an important lesson taught by Ayatollah Khomeini is knowing the enemy (*doshman shenasi*) and fighting the enemy (*doshman setizi*).[56]

Who is the enemy? The enemy includes foreigners, aggressors, infidels, colonialists, the East and the West – usually referred to as the 'army of infidelity' (*lashkar-e kofr*). The latter continuously seeks to defeat the 'army of Islam' (*lashkar-e Islam*) through direct aggression (military action) or indirect conspiracy (political, economic, or cultural infiltration). According to school books, the enemy is not always an outsider; it can be domestic 'agents or mercenaries' who can help the foreigners in their cultural and spiritual colonialism by importing 'alien' values and culture. Trained by the East (the former Soviet Union) or the West (Europe and the USA), such agents are referred to as Eastoxicated (*sharqzadeh*) and Westoxicated (*gharbzadeh*) individuals who continue to serve the hostile 'other'.[57]

Schoolchildren are told that the symbol of constant alert against the ever-present enemy is the Friday prayer in which the prayer leader (*imam jom'eh*) holds a gun at all times to let foreign and domestic enemies know that Muslims are always prepared to defend the land of Islam.[58] Mosques are yet another symbol of Muslim unity against the enemy. Young Iranians learn that mosques are 'trenches' which must be filled to create fear in the enemy. The call for unity and struggle against the enemy is loud and clear in the following statement by Ayatollah Khomeini:

> Muslims of the world, rise and free yourself from the claws of the
> criminal oppressors. Muslims of the world, wake up and liberate
> Islam and Islamic lands from the colonialists and their
> affiliates.[59]

The ultimate form of defending and protecting Islam against the enemy is presented as holy war (*jihad*). Twelve-year-old Iranian schoolchildren learn that holy war is 'armed struggle against the enemies of Islam and Muslims'.[60] They are taught that Islam is the 'religion of peace and tranquility', that believes in logic and reasoning instead of force and aggression. Yet holy war becomes a religious duty when Muslims are attacked by internal or external enemies. Both foreign aggression and domestic threat render holy war a compulsory act for all Muslims. According to Ayatollah Khomeini, 'the defense of Islam and Islamic lands is a religious, divine, and national duty and compulsory for all strata and groups'.[61]

It is important to note that throughout religious education textbooks, the enemy is never presented as a member of another religious faith. In other words, it is political stance vis-à-vis Iran as opposed to religious affiliation that determines who is an enemy. This applies to both domestic and foreign enemies. Thus, the frequently mentioned enemies such as Israel, the United States (the West), and the Soviet Union (the East), no longer existing in reality but still mentioned in Iranian school books, are introduced as such due to their hostile relationships with the Islamic Republic and not for being Jewish or Christian.

A close study of the ever-present enemy in Iranian textbooks leads one to conclude that the main purpose of intensive focus on the enemy is to better define the 'self'. Only by providing a clear definition of the 'other', especially a hostile one, can the educational system instil a strong sense of what the 'self' is and is not. In other words, 'us' is made clear when schoolchildren learn about 'them'; the insider is understood only after the outsider is defined.

The notion of 'self' and 'other' is further reinforced by such statements as 'we Muslims', 'our Islam', and 'our holy book Qur'an'.[62] While a significant number of passages exist in textbooks compiled for Muslims regarding the need to honour and respect all divine religions, specifically mentioning Judaism and Christianity, Muslim students are still taught that Islam is the last and best divine religion.[63] Islam is introduced as the eternal religion and the best way of life, the Qur'an as the last holy book, and Prophet Mohammad as the final messenger of God and the best human being.[64]

Muslim/non-Muslim dichotomy and the need to give priority to the former group is clearly illustrated in discussions about the importance of cultural, political, military and economic independence in an Islamic society. Secondary school students learn that 'any transaction or relationship that leads to the domination of non-Muslims over Muslims is wrong *(batel)* and prohibited *(haram)*.[65] In addition, Ayatollah Khomeini is quoted as stating that

> if in commercial or non-commercial relations there is fear of
> political or non-political domination of aliens over Islam and
> Islamic territories that would lead to colonization [of Muslims]
> and the colonization of their lands, even if it is spiritual

colonization, it is compulsory for all Muslims to refrain from it
and these relations are prohibited.[66]

The fact that unequal economic and political relations between Muslims and
non-Muslims in both domestic and international affairs is forbidden points to
clear preference for 'us' Muslims over 'them' non-Muslims. Religious
education textbooks play an important role in creating an Islamic identity
among schoolchildren.

Formation of an Islamic Identity

Identity formation is an important goal of systems of education throughout
the world and Iran is no exception. Religious education books in Iran make
every attempt to create a strong Muslim identity with well-defined religious
and political values. The fundamentals of Islam are taught through simple
stories in early grades, followed by in-depth discussions about complex
religious themes in the final years of formal schooling. Faith in God; the
characteristics of an ideal Muslim and his/her relations with members of the
family and society; performance of religious rituals such as daily prayers
(*namaz*), fasting (*ruzeh*), attending mosque, visiting holy shrines (*ziyarat*)
and pilgrimage (*hajj*); attending mourning ceremonies; reading the Qur'an;
and stories about the prophets and Imams comprise the bulk of themes
discussed for younger schoolchildren. Older students, on the other hand,
read about monotheism (*towhid*), prophethood (*nabovvat*), life after death
(*ma'ad*), Islamic decrees (*ahkam*), the social and political teachings of Islam,
Muslim community (*umma*), Islamic ethics and Islamic governance. Verses
of the Qur'an along with their Persian translation abound in textbooks.

Textbook pictures also instil a strong Islamic identity by portraying
various symbols of Muslimhood. School books are filled with pictures of
mosques, prayer leaders, boys performing ablution (*vozu*) before prayers, and
men and women reading the Qur'an and praying.[67] Men have beards in
every picture and girls and women are always covered with scarves or the
long veil (*chador*), portraying the officially sanctioned image of Muslim men
and women in Iran. Interestingly, textbooks for non-Muslim students also
portray bearded men and veiled women. There are pictures of Iran's religio-
political leaders, Ayatollah Khomeini and Ayatollah Khamene'i – the present
religious jurisprudent ruling the country at the time of writing. Every single
textbook for Muslim and non-Muslim students begins with a picture of
Ayatollah Khomeini and a selected statement from him, mainly about Islam
and Islamic teachings.

The introduction of religious role models is yet another attempt to
create a strong Islamic identity among schoolchildren. The religious figures
introduced include Prophet Mohammad and the members of his family, the
Imams, historical figures who played an important role in the early years of
Islam, contemporary religious scholars and religio-political leaders in Iran.
The life and teachings of Prophet Mohammad along with anecdotes about

his relations with members of his family (*ahl-e beyt*) and leadership of the Islamic community abound in religious education textbooks for all ages. He is referred to as 'our prophet', the symbol of kindness, purity and honesty, and the 'perfect model' for 'us'.[68]

Historical figures who aided Prophet Mohammad in the early years (*Abu Zar Ghaffari*), fought for Islam (*Hamzeh and Malek-e Ashtar*) or became martyrs (*shahid*) while defending Islam (*Yasser*) are also introduced as role models in terms of their faith and devotion. Schoolchildren also learn about religious scholars (*ulama*), such as 'Allameh Tabataba'i and Motahhari, as well as religio-political leaders such as Beheshti, Dastgheib-e Shirazi, Sadr and Mirza-ye Shirazi. The ruling religious jurisprudent at the time of writing in Iran, Ayatollah Khamene'i, is introduced as a role model and referred to as the 'grand leader of the Islamic revolution' as well as the 'honorable leader of the Islamic umma'.[69]

The ultimate religio-political role model introduced to schoolchildren is the ever-present Ayatollah Khomeini. He is referred to as a 'pious and conscious jurisprudent', the 'great leader of the Islamic revolution', and the 'glorious' founder of the Islamic Republic'. 'Acquaintance with the Thoughts of the Founder of the Islamic Republic of Iran' is the title of a chapter entirely devoted to Ayatollah Khomeini, introduced as 'a free revolutionary, a maker of history, and an incomparable leader of the world of Islam'.[70] Secondary school students read that 'our dear Imam was the true example and the perfect model of an Islamic leader'.[71] In fact, Ayatollah Khomeini is kept alive via his pictures and statements on religion and politics in the minds of schoolchildren who may not have even been born when he ruled Iran.

The role models presented to young Iranians are not all male. Female symbols of Islamic faith and devotion are historical figures and members of Prophet Mohammad's family. None of the female role models are Iranian and none live in contemporary times. The first female role model presented is Khadijeh, introduced as the 'loyal wife' of Prophet Mohammad, the 'grand lady of Islam', and a 'true devotee of Islam' who spent her wealth to propagate the religion and help the Muslims.[72] Religious education textbooks compiled for Muslim students also include a number of anecdotes about Fatemeh, the daughter of Prophet Mohammad. Introduced as pious and godly, Fatemeh is referred to as the 'most faithful wife', the 'kindest mother' and the 'most meritorious woman in the world'.[73]

The label 'heroine' is reserved for Zeynab, the granddaughter of Prophet Mohammad, who is introduced as the 'manifestation of courage and dignity'.[74] High school students learn about her brave statements against the oppressive rulers of her time and her fearless efforts to raise the consciousness of Muslims regarding tyranny and injustice.[75] The only female role model not related to Prophet Mohammad is Somayyeh, introduced as the first female martyr in the history of Islam who was brutally murdered due to her conversion to Islam and loyalty to the Prophet.[76]

112

Piety, devotion to Islam, and loyalty to Prophet Mohammad are some of the characteristics of the historical female role models presented in textbooks for Muslim students. The ideal Muslim woman of today, however, is cherished for her Islamic covering (*hejab*). All students, even non-Muslims whose religious teachings do not require special clothing for women, read about the importance of proper and modest covering for women to avoid 'social and moral deviation, debauchery, and decadent behavior', and protect women from becoming 'toys' and mere 'playthings'.[77] Both men and women are asked to have proper clothing and textbooks emphasise the importance of modesty and decency (*haya*) for everyone regardless of gender. Nonetheless, the words Islamic clothing and proper covering (*pushidegi*) are used synonymously with chastity (*effat*), sanctity (*qedasat*), honour (*ezzat*), purity (*paki*) and modesty (*hojb*) specifically for women.[78]

What is considered proper clothing for women in the Islamic Republic of Iran? Female students are told that they should cover their body and hair from men who are not members of the immediate family and thus considered strangers (*na-mahram*). Secondary school students are given specific information as to what is considered proper clothing for women. They should cover their entire body, except their face and hands up to the wrist, and avoid wearing tight clothing.[79] They are told that the long veil (*chador*) meets the above criteria and is considered to be 'superior covering' (*hejab-e bartar*). It should be noted that Islamic clothing (*pushesh-e Islami*) is obligatory for all women in Iran, including non-Muslim Iranians and non-Iranians.

The contemporary female role model presented to Iranian schoolchildren is a pious and politicised woman who 'protects the Qur'an and defends the land of Islam'.[80] The ideal Muslim woman portrayed in textbooks is pious, modest, veiled, familiar with martial arts, and active in the revolutionary institutions that seek to bring freedom and development for the Islamic country. She is, in short, religious, committed to the cause of the Islamic revolution, and active in the political affairs of her country. The image of veiled women who carry guns symbolises the ideal women of the Islamic Republic of Iran.[81]

Creation of a Pious and Politicised Shi'i

The close intertwinement of religion and politics in Iranian education culminates in the effort to create the ideal citizen of the Islamic Republic – a pious and politicised Shi'i. Formation of a strong Shi'i identity begins during the early years when primary schoolchildren read about the lives and religious teachings of the Shi'i Imams, referred to as the Innocent Ones (*ma'sumin*). Every single religious education textbook is filled with anecdotes about the Imams along with stories about their lives and struggles against the rulers of their time. Pictures of holy shrines where the Imams are buried along with illustrations of Shi'i symbols, rituals, feasts and mourning ceremonies abound in textbooks. Older students are told that 'Imamate is one of the basic principles of Islam' and following the twelve Shi'i Imams will 'guarantee salvation and bliss both in this world and in afterlife'.[82]

The Shi'i Imams are introduced as perfect role models, beginning with Imam Ali and ending in the twelfth Imam Mahdi, who is absent (*gha'eb*) and will return to bring peace and justice for the world. Eleven-year-old students read that Prophet Mohammad chose Imam Ali as his successor and the future leader of the Islamic community. It should be noted that due to the difference is opinion among Shi'is and Sunnis regarding succession to Prophet Mohammad, religious education teachers are told that it is not compulsory for Sunni students to study the textbook chapters on succession after the Prophet's death.[83]

Imam Ali is introduced as the 'ideal human being', the 'leader of the pious' (*amir al-mo'menin*) and the 'model of perfection'. He is presented as pious, committed, brave, and 'in love with holy war (*jihad*) and martyrdom (*shahadat*)'.[84] The above are indeed the characteristics of the ideal Muslim – the perfect role model presented to schoolchildren in Iranian religious education textbooks.

The other Imams are also introduced as role models to be emulated for two reasons: first, for their personal characteristics such as humanity, bravery, kindness, honesty, perseverance and profound knowledge about Islam; second, for their opposition to the tyranny and oppression of their times. Their piety as well as resistance to oppression make them symbols of the ideal Muslim. According to the school books, every single Imam tried to establish a just Islamic rule during his lifetime which led to his imprisonment, murder, or martyrdom. Schoolchildren are told that Shi'i Imams also experienced torture, exile and poisoning as part of their political struggle against oppressors.[85] The close intertwinement of religion and politics is thus clearly reflected in the lives and struggles of Shi'i Imams who embody the ideal Muslim – a pious and politicised Shi'i engaged in holy *jihad* to establish true Islam.

The ultimate symbol of Shi'ism presented in school books is Imam Hossein, Prophet Mohammad's grandson and Imam Ali's son. The life and struggle of Imam Hossein is the true embodiment of the pious and politicised identity instilled in young children. It may be stated that the formation of the Shi'i identity reaches its climax when schoolchildren read about Imam Hossein. The third Imam is introduced as the symbol of Shi'i honour, dignity and sacrifice – one who preferred death to shame and humiliation and welcomed martyrdom instead of surrendering to the enemy. His famous statement appears in the textbook for secondary school students: 'I see death as nothing but bliss and life alongside tyrants as nothing but disgrace and degradation'.[86]

Martyrdom (*shahadat*) and martyrs (*shohada*) are highly esteemed in Iranian school books. Eleven-year-old students learn that martyrdom means 'fighting for God and according to the orders of a godly leader, against infidels and oppressors'.[87] They are told that martyrs dwell in heaven along with the prophets and Imams. The ultimate martyr is Imam Hossein, introduced as the Lord of Martyrs (*seyyed al-shohada*), who sacrificed his life to protect Islam against the corruption and oppression of the Umayyad dynasty on 'Ashura – the tenth day of the month of Muharram. 'Ashura symbolises the spirit of sacrifice and martyrdom-seeking (*shahadat talabi*) among Shi'is. Religious education textbooks are filled with detailed anecdotes about what happened in Karbala (a city in present-day Iraq) on the day of 'Ashura. Furthermore, a significant number of pictures in the textbooks also seek to portray Shi'i symbols, flags, colours and mourning rituals related to the month of Muharram and the martyrdom of Imam Hossein.[88] Imam Hossein, 'Ashura, Muharram, Karbala and martyrdom symbolise the intertwinement of religion and politics for young Iranians who are trained to become pious and politicised Shi'is.

Minority Religions and Religious Minorities

The study of the religious education of non-Muslims in Iran seeks to answer two questions: how are minority religions presented in textbooks for Muslim students, and how is religious diversity treated in school books compiled for minority students?

Both Muslim and non-Muslim students are constantly reminded that all divine religions (*adyan-e elahi*) are based on three principles – namely, monotheism (*towhid*), belief in resurrection day and afterlife (*ma'ad*), and faith in prophethood (*nabovvat*).[89] They are told that all divine prophets had a common mission: guiding humans and inviting them to believe in one God and surrender to the will of God; transmitting the divine decrees and commandments to the people; and struggle against polytheism and idolatry. Textbooks emphasise the common characteristics of divine prophets, such as honesty, trustworthiness, commitment to moral principles, piety, innocence, conviction, determination, persistence, decisiveness, firmness, patience and competence. Schoolchildren are told that all prophets were innocent (*ma'sum*) and infallible, superior human beings who never made a mistake or committed a sin.[90] They were the most favourite creatures of God who were selected to act as teachers, guides and role models for others. The adjectives used for all divine prophets are 'chosen', 'exemplary' and 'perfect'.[91]

As can be seen, there is every effort to focus on the common teachings of different religions and prophets. Emphasis on commonalities rather than differences and the request to respect and honour all divine prophets who have been sent by God and 'thank them for their efforts and sacrifices' [92] is an important feature of religious education textbooks in Iran. Non-Muslim Iranian students are told that all prophets sought one goal and there is no difference among the general teachings of heavenly (*asemani*) religions and divine (*elahi*) prophets. They learn that 'there may have been differences in the minor decrees of various religions ... such differences were, of course, due to the conditions and situation of the time'.[93] It is important to note at this point that only monotheist religions and prophets are recognised by the Islamic Republic and other faiths are completely ignored in textbooks.

Iranian students learn that there have been 124,000 prophets beginning with Adam and ending with Prophet Mohammad. Despite the emphasis on the common message and mission of all divine prophets and the obligation to honour and respect all, students are told that only five had a distinct religion (*din*) with specific religious laws (*shari'at*). The five great (*olol-'azm*) prophets are introduced as Noah, Abraham, Moses, Jesus and Mohammad.[94]

Muslim and non-Muslim students read about the five prophets and the holy books – The Old Testament, Bible and Qur'an – in their religious education textbooks. There are a number of anecdotes about Noah and Abraham; the latter is introduced as an exemplary model and a true leader. Stories about the life, times, and teachings of Moses also abound in textbooks. Students read about his holy book – The Old Testament (*Torat*) – miracles, and struggle against the tyranny and oppression of his time. Nine-year-old children learn about the infancy of Moses and how he was saved and raised by the pharaoh's wife Asiyeh, introduced as a model of faith and courage and 'one of the best women in the world'.[95]

Iranian schoolchildren learn about Jesus Christ by reading about his miracles, and holy book the Bible (*Enjil*). His mother Mary is also mentioned in textbooks compiled for Muslims, where she is introduced as the manifestation of chastity, purity and modesty.[96] Interestingly, Asiyeh and Mary are the only non-Muslim female role models introduced to schoolchildren. As noted before, the Iranian prophet Zoroaster is never mentioned in school books although Zoroastrianism is an officially recognised religion in the Islamic Republic of Iran.

The presentation of Jews and Christians in Iranian textbooks is for the most part limited to historical figures. Schoolchildren read about the early followers of Moses the children of Israel (*bani Israel*) during the times of David and Jesus [97], and the Jews who lived at the same time as Prophet Mohammad and Imam Ali. The present state of Israel is mentioned within a political context where relations between pre-revolutionary Iran and Israel are noted.[98]

The Christians presented are historical figures as well, including Christian scientists living during the time of Prophet Mohammad and various Shi'i Imams; the Christian king of Abyssinia (Ethiopia) who gave refuge to early Muslims fleeing Mecca for fear of their lives; and Christians who converted to Islam after meeting Prophet Mohammad and Imam Ali.[99] In a rare reference to Zoroastrians, it is noted that Zoroastrian women living in pre-Islamic Iran had full covering in public places.[100] The only time contemporary Jews and Christians are mentioned in religious education textbooks is in relation to female covering. It is stated that Christian painters always portray Mary with complete covering (*hejab*) and Christian nuns are totally covered in public. Furthermore, pious Jewish women also cover themselves according to the dictates of Judaism.[101]

Textbooks compiled for Muslims and non-Muslims do not mention Jews, Christians and Zoroastrians living in present-day Iran. The same is true about Sunni Iranians. Sunnism is discussed in historical terms in textbooks compiled for Muslim students. In addition, there are religious studies books compiled specifically for the followers of Sunnism (*ahl-e sonnat*), distributed in the predominantly Sunni provinces of Iran.

The information provided about Sunnism for Iranian schoolchildren in general is centered on the differences of opinion among Shi'is and Sunnis regarding Prophet Mohammad's successor. Utmost respect is paid to both sides of the argument although at one point it is stated that 'it is the rightful belief of us, Shi'is' that Prophet Mohammad would not neglect the need to determine who would succeed him as the leader of the Islamic community.[102] The above statement notwithstanding, schoolchildren are provided with two historical versions of succession. Thirteen-year-old students learn that Muslims are divided into two major groups – Sunni and Shi'i. Sunnis believe that Prophet Mohammad did not appoint a successor for himself and the first caliph, Abu Bakr, was selected to succeed him, followed by 'Omar, 'Osman, and Ali. Shi'is, on the other hand, believed that the Prophet introduced Ali as his successor during his lifetime. According to Shi'is, Ali is the first Imam followed by eleven of his male descendants ending in the twelfth Imam.

After having explained the difference between the two groups, the school books emphasise that although Shi'is and Sunnis have different opinions about the issue of caliphate after the Prophet and some differences regarding certain matters of jurisprudence, 'both are Muslims, they have one religion and one prophet, they pray facing the same direction (*qebleh*). Their holy book is the Qur'an. They are brothers and united and work together for the glory and advancement of Islam and the victory of Islam over infidelity'.[103] Every attempt is made to undermine differences and disputes among Shi'is and Sunnis and emphasise the need for unity and solidarity against the enemies and foreigners in order to bring about dignity and honour for Muslims and grandeur for the world of Islam. Iranian students then read that Ayatollah Khomeini, the 'great forerunner of Islamic unity', has asked Muslims 'from different nations and races to shake hands in brotherhood' and establish the greatest power in the world.[104]

One can see that in the case of Sunnis, just like the Jews and Christians, religious education textbooks prefer to address historical and theoretical issues instead of dealing with the present situation in Iran. The rare occasion in which religious minorities living in contemporary Iran are addressed is the statement by Ayatollah Khomeini appearing on all religious education textbooks compiled for Jews, Christians and Zoroastrians. The statement, 'Islam respects religious minorities; Islam honors religious minorities in our country; this country belongs to all of us' [105], may be found in the ten textbooks prepared for non-Muslim students aged 7 to 16.

In an introductory note to instructors teaching religious studies to non-Muslim students, it is emphasised that they should educate pious believers who are familiar with the fundamentals of religion and actively practise the religious commandments. In fact, faith, piety and practical commitment are the ideals enumerated in textbooks compiled for religious minorities.[106] This returns us to the initial discussion on the Iranian textbooks' division of the world into good and evil, composed of the pious and the infidels. The black and white world divided into believers and non-believers ranks people on the basis of their faith and level of religiosity as opposed to which monotheist religion they adhere to. This is not to say that the circles of inclusion and exclusion are not clear; it is merely a reminder that the ultimate determining factor is whether one is a believer or not.

Concluding Remarks

An in-depth study of state religious education textbooks in Iran points to different approaches undertaken for Muslim (majority) and non-Muslim (minority) students vis-à-vis religion. The main purpose of school books for Muslim students is direct and deliberate instillation of the Islamic world-view and values with minimum reference to religious diversity in contemporary Iran. There is, at the same time, utmost respect paid to two monotheist religions (Judaism and Christianity) along with exclusive reference to the five 'great' prophets (Noah, Abraham, Moses, Jesus, Mohammad) without mentioning any other prophet or religious leader. Non-Muslims presented to schoolchildren are all historical figures, a number of whom either converted to Islam or helped Muslims during difficult times, especially when they were persecuted for their religious beliefs during the early years of Islam. Sunnism is introduced and discussed in textbooks compiled for Muslim students but there is no mention of Sunni Iranians in contemporary Iran.

Emphasising similarities and undermining differences is the guiding philosophy in textbooks compiled for Jews, Christians and Zoroastrians in Iran. Religious minorities are exposed to universal moral themes such as goodness, honesty, truth and kindness at an early age. They also learn about a bipolar world divided into good and evil, comprised of believers and non-believers. More complicated themes such as monotheism, idolatry, atheism, heresy, apostasy and materialism are discussed in textbooks studied by secondary school students.

There is a deliberate emphasis on the common decrees of monotheist religions and the universal teachings of divine prophets. Judaism and Christianity are mentioned in a historical framework without any mention of Iranian Jews or Christians living in contemporary Iranian society. Both religions are discussed mostly in terms of their moral decrees, with various anecdotes about the teachings and miracles of Moses and Jesus. There is no specific mention of the various Christian groups living in Iran or any information about the contribution of Iranian Jews and Christians to social, economic, political, cultural, artistic and intellectual life in their country.

The presentation of Zoroastrianism in Iran raises serious questions in the mind of the textbook analyst. Unlike Judaism, Christianity and Islam, Zoroastrianism is the only officially recognised religion in the country that has Iranian roots. Zoroaster was born in Iran and Zoroastrianism was the state religion in the Persian Empire during the pre-Islamic era. Yet the religion and its followers are mentioned only twice in textbooks for Muslim and non-Muslim students. Zoroastrianism is completely ignored both in historical anecdotes and in the contemporary scene.

One can state that educational authorities in the Islamic Republic of Iran try to avoid in-depth discussion of religious diversity in the country by adopting the following policies: confining themselves to the safer realm of history; totally ignoring specific religious groups; avoiding contemporary and potentially controversial discussions of religion in multicultural education; and focusing on the commonalities instead of pointing to differences among religious groups in Iran. Thus, while there is mention of religious diversity in religious education books, there is never any in-depth discussion of the multi-faith nature of Iranian society. The same is also true in the minimal treatment of ethnic and linguistic diversity in Iran in other parts of the school curriculum.[107] This may reflect the conscious effort of the educational authorities to focus on the Islamic nature of Iran and introduce the country as first and foremost a Muslim one with a deliberate attempt to undermine any kind of variation from the dominant religion and culture.

The original question raised in this chapter was whether state religious education in Islamised Iran unites or divides. In response, one can say that the official policy is to bring about unity instead of division by emphasising commonalities and ignoring dissimilarities. Educational authorities in Iran have made every effort to unite by undermining diversity and avoiding issues that may bring about disunity. A close reading of religious education textbooks by those who may not be aware of the multi-faith nature of the Iranian society may lead to a false image of a totally homogeneous society marked by a uniform population. Such an image has been created through a policy of silence. In other words, potentially divisive issues have been deliberately left out instead of being openly acknowledged and addressed. It may be said that the guiding principle of religious education in Iran is unity in commonality as opposed to unity in diversity.

Notes

[1] A. Hakimi (2004) *A General Overview of Education in the Islamic Republic of Iran*, 23. Tehran: Institute for Educational Research, Ministry of Education.

[2] Ministry of Education (MOE) (2003) *Education in the Islamic Republic of Iran*, 17. Tehran: Bureau of International Scientific Cooperation.

[3] Golnar Mehran (2003) The Paradox of Tradition and Modernity in Female Education in the Islamic Republic of Iran, *Comparative Education Review*, 47, 269-286.

[4] MOE (1988) *A Guide to the Religious Education Curriculum at the Primary School Level* [Rahnema-ye Barnameh-ye Darsi-ye Ta'limat-e Dini-ye Doreh Ebteda'i], 2. Tehran: Office of Textbook Planning and Compilation.

[5] H. Judge (2002) *Faith-Based Schools and the State: Catholics in America, France, and England*. Oxford Symposium Books; G.Z.F. Bereday & J.A. Lauwerys (1966) *The World Year Book of Education, 1966: church and state in education*. London: Evans Brothers.

[6] K. Cummings, S. Gopinathan & Y. Tomoda (Eds) (1988) *The Revival of Values Education in Asia and the West*. Oxford: Pergamon Press; Y.K. Cha, S.K. Wong & J.W. Meyer (1992) Values Education in the Curriculum: some comparative empirical data, in J.W. Meyer, D.H. Kamens & A. Benevot (Eds) *School Knowledge for the Masses: world models and national primary curricular categories in the twentieth century*. Washington, DC: Falmer Press.

[7] M.A. Najmi (1969) Religion, Socioeconomic Status, and Educational Aspirations, *Education and Urban Society*, 1, 453-468.

[8] C.W. Mueller (1980) Evidence on the Relationship between Religion and Educational Attainment, *Sociology of Education*, 53 140-152; W. Sanders (1992) The Effects of Ethnicity and Religion on Educational Attainment, *Economics of Education Review*, 11, 119-135.

[9] J. Wimberly (2003) Education for Intercultural and Interfaith Dialogue: a new initiative by the Council of Europe, *Prospects*, 33, 199-209; M. Zachariah & G. Mehran (1996) Needed: disciplined dialogues on religion and education, *Comparative Education Review*, 40, 1-6.

[10] P.R. Hobson & J.S. Edwards (1999) Religious Education in a Pluralist Society: the key philosophical issues. London: Woburn Press; UNESCO-IBE (2000) Globalization and Living Together: the challenges of educational content. Paris: UNESCO.

[11] MOE (2004) Pathology of Religious Education: interview with Gholam 'Ali Haddad 'Adel, vol. 1 [Asib Shenasi-ye Tarbiyat-e Dini: Goft-o-Gu ba Gholam 'Ali Haddad 'Adel]. Tehran: Madreseh Publications; MOE (2004) Pathology of Religious Education: interview with faculty members at the religious seminaries and universities, vol. 2 [Asib Shenasi-ye Tarbiyat-e Dini: Goft-o-Gu ba Ostadan-e Howzeh va Daneshgah]. Tehran: Madreseh Publications; MOE (2003) The Document and Charter of Reform in the Educational System of Iran [Sanad va Manshur-e Eslah-e Nezam-e Amuzesh va Parvaresh-e Iran]. Tehran: Institute for Educational Research.

[12] J.F. Rivard & M. Amadio (2003) Teaching Time allotted to Religious Education in Official Timetables, Prospects, 33, 211-217.

[13] A. Safi (2000) The Organization, Rules, and Regulations of Education in Iran [Sazman va Qavanin-e Amuzesh va Parvaresh-e Iran], 36. Tehran: Samt Publications.

[14] A. Hajforoosh (1998) A Brief Study of the Duties and the Organizational Structure of the Organization of Research and Educational Planning [Barresi-ye Ejmali-ye Vazayef va Sakhtar-e Tashkilat-e Sazman-e Pazhuhesh va Barnameh Rizi-ye Amuzeshi], 42. Tehran: Ministry of Education.

[15] MOE (2000) Collection of the Ratified Laws of the High Council of Education [Majmu'eh Mosavvabat-e Shora-ye 'Ali-ye Amuzesh va Parvaresh], 3, 4. Tehran: Madreseh Publications.

[16] Ibid., 14.

[17] Hajforoosh, 42.

[18] MOE, Collection, 304, 336, 362, 364, 488.

[19] (2004) Islamic Culture and Religious Education (Guidance Cycle, Third Year) [Farhang-e Islami va Ta'limat-e Dini (Sal-e Sevvom, Doreh-ye Rahnemayi Tahsili) 1383], 28. Tehran: Ministry of Education [for Muslim students].

[20] (2002) Teaching Divine Religions and Ethics: for religious minorities (Secondary Education, Third Year) [Ta'limat-e Adyan-e Elahi va Akhlaq: Vizheh Aqaliyyatha-ye Mazhabi (Sal-e Sevvom, Amuzesh Motevasseteh) 138], 112. Tehran: Ministry of Education [for non-Muslim students].

[21] (2002) Teaching Divine Religions and Ethics: for religious minorities (Primary School, Grade 2 [Ta'limat-e Adyan-e Elahi va Akhlaq: Vizheh Aqaliyyatha-ye Mazhabi (Dovvom-e Dabestan) 1381], 25. Tehran: Ministry of Education [for non-Muslim students].

[22] (2002) Teaching Divine Religions and Ethics: for religious minorities (Secondary Education, First Year) [Ta'lilmat-e Adyan-e Elahi va Akhlaq: Vizheh Aqaliyyatha-ye Mazhabi (Sal-e Avval Dabirestan) 1381], 71. Tehran: Ministry of Education [for non-Muslim students].

[23] (2004) Islamic Culture and Religious Education (Guidance Cycle, First Year) [Farhang-e Islami va Ta'limat-e Dini (Sal-e Avval, Doreh-ye Rahnamayi Tahsili) 1383], 21. Tehran: Ministry of Education [for Muslim students].

[24] (2004) Islamic Culture and Religious Education (Guidance Cycle, Second Year) [Farhang-e Islami va Ta'limat-e Dini (Sal-e Dovvom, Doreh-ye Rahnamayi Tahsili) 1383], 83. Tehran: Ministry of Education [for Muslim students].

[25] Ibid., 67.

[26] (2002) Teaching Divine Religions and Ethics: for religious minorities (Guidance Cycle, Second Year) [Ta'limat-e Adyan-e Elahi va Akhlaq: Vizheh Aqaliyyatha-ye Mazhabi (Sal-e Dovvom, Doreh-ye Rahnamayi Tahsili) 1381], 59. Tehran: Ministry of Education [for non-Muslim students].

[27] (2002) Teaching Divine Religions and Ethics: for religious minorities (Primary School, Grade 3) [Ta'limat-e Adyan-e Elahi va Akhlaq: Vizheh Aqaliyyatha-ye Mazhabi (Sevvom-e Dabestan) 1381], 21. Tehran: Ministry of Education [for non-Muslim students].

[28] Islamic Culture (Guidance Cycle, Third Year), 23 [for Muslim students].

[29] (2004) Religious Education (Primary School, Grade 5) [Ta'limat-e Dini (Panjom-e Dabestan) 1383], 11. Tehran: Ministry of Education [for Muslim students].

[30] Teaching Divine Religions (Secondary Education, Third Year), 16-21 [for non-Muslim students].

[31] Teaching Divine Religions (Guidance Cycle, Second Year), 21 [for non-Muslim students].

[32] (2004) Religion and Life: Qur'an and religious education 2 (Secondary Education, Second Year) [Din va Zendegi: Qur'an va Ta'limat-e Dini 2 (Sal-e Dovvom, Amuzesh Motevasseteh) 1383], 141. Tehran: Ministry of Education [for Muslim students].

[33] Islamic Culture (Guidance Cycle, First Year), 32 [for Muslim students].

[34] (2002) Teaching Divine Religions and Ethics: for religious minorities (Guidance Cycle, Third Year) [Ta'limat-e Adyan-e Elahi va Akhlaq: Vizheh Aqaliyyatha-ye Mazhabi (Sal-e Sevvom, Doreh-ye Rahnamayi Tahsili) 1381], 59. Tehran: Ministry of Education [for non-Muslim students].

[35] Teaching Divine Religions (Guidance Cycle, Second Year), 21 [for non-Muslim students]

[36] (2002) Teaching Divine Religions and Ethics: for religious minorities (Guidance Cycle, First Year) [Ta'limat-e Adyan-e Elahi va Akhlaq: Vizheh Aqaliyyatha-ye Mazhabi (Sal-e Avval, Doreh-ye Rahnamayi Tahsili) 1381], 33. Tehran: Ministry of Education [for non-Muslim students].

[37] (2004) Gifts from Heaven: Islamic education (Primary School, Grade 4) [Hadiyehha-ye Aseman: Ta'lim va Tarbiyat-e Islami (Chaharom-e Dabestan) 1383], 35. Tehran: Ministry of Education [for Muslim students].

[38] Teaching Divine Religions (Primary School, Grade 3), 2 [for non-Muslim students].

[39] Islamic Culture (Guidance Cycle, First Year), 16 [for Muslim students].

[40] Teaching Divine Religions (Primary School, Grade 2), 8 [for non-Muslim students].

[41] (2002) Teaching Divine Religions and Ethics: for religious minorities (Primary School, Grade 5) [Ta'limat-e Adyan-e Elahi va Akhlaq: Vizheh Aqaliyyatha-ye Mazhabi (Panjom-e Dabestan) 1381], 8. (Tehran: Ministry of Education [for non-Muslim students].

[42] Islamic Culture (Guidance Cycle, Second Year), 77 [for Muslim students].

[43] Islamic Culture (Guidance Cycle, Third Year), 96 [for Muslim students].

[44] Religious Education (Primary School, Grade 5), i [for Muslim students].

[45] Islamic Culture (Guidance Cycle, First Year), 104 [for Muslim students].

[46] Religious Education (Primary School, Grade 5), 36, 39; Islamic Culture (Guidance Cycle, Second Year), 60 [for Muslim students].

[47] (2004) Islamic Insight (Secondary Education, Third Year) [Binesh-e Islami (Sal-e Sevvom, Amuzesh Motevasseteh) 1383], 12-15. Tehran: Ministry of Education [for Muslim students].

[48] Ibid., 6.

[49] Religious Education (Primary School, Grade 5), i and 61; Islamic Insight (Secondary Education, Third Year), 25-41 [both for Muslim students].

[50] Islamic Insight (Secondary Education, Third Year), 30 [for Muslim students].

[51] Islamic Culture (Guidance Cycle, Second Year), 63-64 [for Muslim students].

[52] Islamic Insight (Secondary Education, Third Year), 69 [for Muslim students].

[53] Islamic Culture (Guidance Cycle, Second Year), 101-102 [for Muslim students].

[54] Ibid., 67.

[55] Islamic Insight (Secondary Education, Third Year), 14 [for Muslim students].

[56] Ibid., 28.

[57] Ibid., 15, 122.

[58] Religious Education (Primary School, Grade 5), 68 [for Muslim students].

[59] Islamic Culture (Guidance Cycle, Second Year), 65 [for Muslim students].

[60] Islamic Culture (Guidance Cycle, Third Year), 67 [for Muslim students].

[61] Ibid., 70-71.

[62] (2004) Gifts from Heaven: Islamic education (Primary School, Grade 3) [Hadiyehha-ye Aseman: Ta'lim va Tarbiyat-e Islami (Sevvom-e Dabestan) 1383], 18 and 62. Tehran: Ministry of Education [for Muslim students].

[63] Islamic Culture (Guidance Cycle, Third Year), 31 [for Muslim students].

[64] Gifts from Heaven (Primary School, Grade 4), 65 [for Muslim students].

[65] Islamic Insight (Secondary Education, Third Year), 8 [for Muslim students].

[66] Ibid., 8-9.

[67] (2004) Gifts from Heaven, Work Book: Islamic education (Primary School, Grade 4) [Hadiyehha-ye Aseman, Ketab-e Kar: Ta'lim va Tarbiyat-e Islami (Chaharom-e Dabestan) 1383]. Tehran: Ministry of Education [for Muslim students].

[68] Religion and Life: Qur'an and Religious Education 1 (Secondary Education, First Year) [Din va Zendegi: Qur'an va Ta'limat-e Dini 1 (Sal-e Avval Dabirestan) 1383], 105. Tehran: Ministry of Education [for Muslim students].

[69] Religious Education (Primary School, Grade 5), ii, 62 [for Muslim students].

[70] Islamic Insight (Secondary Education, Third Year), 25-41 [for Muslim students].

[71] Ibid., 24.

[72] Gifts from Heaven (Primary School, Grade 4), 66-69 [for Muslim students].

[73] Gifts from Heaven (Primary School, Grade 3), 33 [for Muslim students].

[74] Religion and Life (Secondary Education, Second Year), 156 [for Muslim students].

[75] Ibid., 156-159.

[76] Islamic Culture (Guidance Cycle, Second Year), 38-43 [for Muslim students].

[77] Teaching Divine Religions (Secondary Education, First Year), 61-62 [for non-Muslim students].

[78] Islamic Culture (Guidance Cycle, Third Year), 82 [for Muslim students].

[79] Religion and Life (Secondary Education, Second Year), 142 [for Muslim students].

[80] Religious Education (Primary School, Grade 5), 37 [for Muslim students].

[81] Ibid., 36.

[82] Islamic Culture (Guidance Cycle, Third Year), 91 [for Muslim students].

[83] Islamic Culture (Guidance Cycle, First Year), 44 [for Muslim students].

[84] Ibid., 87, 89.

[85] Islamic Culture (Guidance Cycle, Third Year), 94-96 [for Muslim students].

[86] Religion and Life (Secondary Education, Second Year), 57 [for Muslim students].

[87] Islamic Culture (Guidance Cycle, First Year), 16 [for Muslim students].

[88] Gifts from Heaven (Primary School, Grade 3), 40-51; (2004) Gifts from Heaven, Work Book: Islamic education (Primary School, Grade 3) [Hadiyehha-ye Aseman, Ketab-e Kar: Ta'lim va Tarbiyat-e Islami (Sevvom-e Dabestan) 1383] (Tehran: Ministry of Education, 2004), 34-37; (2004) Gifts from Heaven, Work Book: Islamic Education (Primary School, Grade 2) [Hadiyehha-ye Aseman, Ketab-e Kar: Ta'lim va Tarbiyat-e Islami (Dovvom-e Dabestan) 1383], 34. Tehran: Ministry of Education [all for Muslim students].

[89] Teaching Divine Religions (Secondary Education, First Year), 9 [for non-Muslim students].

[90] (2002) Teaching Divine Religions and Ethics: for religious minorities (Primary School, Grade 4) [Ta'limat-e Adyan-e Elahi va Akhlaq: Vizheh Aqaliyyatha-ye Mazhabi (Chaharom-e Dabestan) 1381], 26-27. Tehran: Ministry of Education [for non-Muslim students].

[91] (2002) Teaching Divine Religions and Ethics: for religious minorities (Secondary Education, Second Year) [Ta'limat-e Adyan-e Elahi va Akhlaq: Vizheh Aqaliyyatha-ye Mazhabi (Sal-e Dovvom, Amuzesh Motevasseteh) 1381], 75. Tehran: Ministry of Education [for non-Muslim students].

[92] Islamic Culture (Guidance Cycle, First Year), 32 [for Muslim students].

[93] Teaching Divine Religions (Guidance Cycle, Third Year), 48 [for non-Muslim students].

[94] (2004) Gifts from Heaven: Islamic education (Primary School, Grade 2) [Hadiyehha-ye Aseman: Ta'lim va Tarbiyat-e Islami (Dovvom-e Dabestan) 1383], 29. Tehran: Ministry of Education [for Muslim students].

[95] Gifts from Heaven (Primary School, Grade 4), 8-11 [for Muslim students].

[96] Religion and Life (Secondary Education, Second Year), 135 [for Muslim students].

[97] Ibid., 152.

[98] Islamic Insight (Secondary Education, Third Year), 32 [for Muslim students].

[99] Islamic Culture (Guidance Cycle, First Year), 66-70 [for Muslim students].

[100] *Religion and Life* (Secondary Education, Second Year), 137 [for Muslim students].

[101] *Islamic Culture* (Guidance Cycle, Second Year), 74 [for Muslim students].

[102] Ibid., 137.

[103] Ibid., 100.

[104] *Teaching Divine Religions* (Primary School, Grade 2), i [for non-Muslim students].

[105] *Teaching Divine Religions* (Guidance Cycle, First Year), 2-6 [for non-Muslim students].

[106] G. Mehran (2002) The Presentation of the 'Self' and the 'Other' in Postrevolutionary Iranian Textbooks, in N.R. Keddie & R. Matthee (Eds) *Iran and the Surrounding World: interactions in culture and cultural politics*, 232-253. Seattle: University of Washington Press.

[107] Ibid.

APPENDIX
Islamization of Public and Private Spheres

Great Islamic Civilization, Great Islamic Nation, Islamic Army, Islamic Banking, Islamic Beliefs, Islamic Clothing, Islamic Covering, Islamic Customs, Islamic Decrees, Islamic Dignity, Islamic Duty, Islamic Ethics, Islamic Faith, Islamic Feasts, Islamic Fighters, Islamic Glory, Islamic Grandeur, Islamic Honor, Islamic Insight, Islamic Justice, Islamic Land, Islamic Laws, Islamic Leader, Islamic Morality, Islamic Mottos, Islamic Nation, Islamic Observances, Islamic Order, Islamic Power, Islamic Prayers, Islamic Regulations, Islamic Revolution, Islamic Rites, Islamic Rule, Islamic Ruler, Islamic Society, Islamic Solidarity, Islamic Standards, Islamic State, Islamic Tenets, Islamic Territories, Islamic Thought, Islamic Unity, Islamic Values, Universal Islamic Rule (source: Religious Education Textbooks for Muslim and Non-Muslim Students, Islamic Republic of Iran, 2004-2005 Academic Year).

Aspects of Bilingualism in Iranian Kurdish Schoolchildren

IRAN MOHAMMADI-HEUBOECK

Introduction

Iran as a nation state is a relatively recent construction, dating back to the twentieth century, propagated by the Pahlavi dynasty (1925-79), and adapted after the Islamic Revolution of 1979. One of the distinguishing characteristics of the Iranian state is its multiethnic and multilingual composition. The biggest ethnic groups are Persians, Azeri and Kurds; other groups comprise Balouchis, Bakhtiyaris, Ghashghaais, Lors, Arabs, Turkamens, all speaking different mother tongues. This situation of high ethnic and linguistic diversification is paralleled by a strict administrative and political centralism, where the Persian language (Farsi) dominates local ethnic languages in formal settings. This is particularly true of the educational system. Despite article XV of the Constitution, which grants ethnic minorities teaching in their languages, almost all of the teaching in Iranian schools is delivered in Persian.

It has been noted that school is one of the major contexts where construction and unification of the nation takes place (Deloye, 1994; Legrand, 1988; Payet, 2000, p. 141). The experience of bilingualism in the new Kurdish generation and the role of language is thus to be considered a significant reflection of the process of the construction of individual identity. The contact of local and national languages at school, i.e. of Persian and Kurdish in our case, is at the core of the interaction between traits of ethnic and national identities.

For a number of reasons, school seems to be a social setting of crucial importance for the study of bilingualism in the Iranian Kurdish area. Historically, it has been one of the domains of conscious linguistic and cultural centralism by Iranian governments since the early twentieth century. School is certainly the one national institution which aims at assimilating the entire (young) population by incorporating them in a rigid system of power over a long period of time. At the same time, even though it is a sign of the centralist state, school cannot be completely rejected by local populations, as schooling is also perceived as a basis for their children's professional opportunities and prosperity in later life.

This particular role of the school as a location for indoctrination in national identity dates back to the 1920s and is linked to efforts towards modernisation of the country under the Pahlavi dynasty and the growing domination of a central state over the country to achieve a kind of national integrity. The creation of the modern school and an educational system, imposed as 'one of the major national institutions' (Paivandi, 1995, p. 1154), is one of the most important structural changes to have occurred during the period between 1920 and 1940. From the very beginning, Reza Shah (1925-41) thus perceived the field of education as 'a potential power in the country cohesion regarded as a Nation' (Menasheri, 1992, p. 94). Under his reign and afterwards in the Islamic Republic, debates took place over educational materials, content matters, and language policy. Schoolbooks in the whole country were published exclusively in Persian, and the entire content of teaching decreed by the national authorities propagated the one legitimate identity across the country (Castells, 1997, p. 18).

One side effect of this administrative and linguistic centralism imposed on an ethnically diverse country was that the official language, Persian, originally the language of the ethnic group of Persians, was put into close contact with a variety of regional languages, giving rise to politically motivated situations of bilingualism throughout the country. After the Islamic Revolution of 1979, the centralised structure in the educational system remains in place despite all the debates and negotiations and even the official recognition of the right of ethnic minorities to receive education in their own language.[1]

Since the creation of the modern centralised school, the claim for linguistic decentralisation of education, i.e. the right to deliver education in the Kurdish language, has become an important part of the political programme of Kurdish autonomists. The tension between autonomist claims and the uninterrupted centralist policy of Iranian governments resulted in two periods of crisis in recent history. For eleven months, educational autonomy of the Kurdish parts of Iran was attempted during the so-called Republic of Mahabad, established as the result of a civil war between Kurdish autonomists and the Iranian government in 1946, when for the first time education was delivered in Kurdish.

After the autonomists' defeat in 1946, the issue of autonomy in education stayed on the agenda and was raised again after the Islamic Revolution of 1979. The second attempt to deliver teaching in the Kurdish language was made by the Kurdish political parties, the DPIK [2] and the Komala [3], between 1980 and 1984, when the conflict once more reached a military dimension (depending on one's viewpoint, the parties speak of 'civil war' or 'armed resistance'). In the so-called 'liberated area' [4], both the DPIK and the Komala, united in their goals, but rivals as advocates of the cause of the Kurdish minority, opened primary and secondary schools where

Kurdish was the language of teaching and also published schoolbooks for the first two years of primary school in Kurdish.

Since the establishment of the centralised educational system, and in spite of an ongoing tradition of Kurdish protests against Iranian monoculturalism, the school has become an important agent in the process of socialisation of the Kurdish youth, where it takes on a particular role in the complex process of construction of the identity of Kurdish adolescents. This process is characterised by the interaction of three groups of actors – the state, present in the official institution of school; traditional Kurdish culture, represented to Kurdish adolescents by their parents; and the peer group of the young generation of Iranian Kurds. The interplay between school and family institutions illustrates the problematic relationship between minority and majority in a dualism of local and national identification.

This chapter aims to draw attention to some basic aspects of bilingualism in Iranian Kurdish schools and proposes a preliminary analysis of the complex system in which the Persian and Kurdish languages interact in the everyday experience of Iranian Kurdish adolescents.

The data on which the present chapter is based consists of 120 interviews with schoolchildren, their parents and teachers in the two Iranian Kurdish provinces of Kermanshahan and Sannandadj, conducted in the wider context of investigating the process of construction of Kurdish adolescent identity through a range of dimensions – linguistic, political, religious and various aspects of everyday culture (Mohammadi, 2004). It turns out that school plays a crucial role in shaping the attitude of Kurdish adolescents as well as that of their parents towards Kurdish language and culture – resulting in either the abandonment of their traditional ethnic culture, or its transmission in a form adapted to the reality of institutionalised hegemony of Persian culture. I will commence by discussing those forces that lead parents to abandon the transmission of the Kurdish language within the family, followed by the effects of this rupture on the experience and identity of Persian-speaking Kurdish adolescents. Another pattern of reaction to this forced bilingualism, to be discussed in a following section, consists of the emergence of Kurdish nationalist tendencies among Kurdish schoolchildren. I will then go on to briefly discuss the question of self-image and the feeling of belonging.

Continuity and Rupture in the Transmission of Kurdish Language and Culture

To the young generation, traditional Kurdish culture is in the first place represented by their Kurdish-speaking parents and family. However, the role of families as the site of transmission of traditional ethnic culture is nowadays rivalled by school, oriented by the reference culture of Persian. Whereas formerly, Kurdish culture and language were transmitted homogeneously from one generation to the next in the private sphere, two models arise nowadays: one of continuity, opposed to the other of discontinuity in the transmission of the ethnic culture. In the case of discontinuity, i.e. a rupture in the transmission of the Kurdish language, Kurdish is substituted with Persian as the language parents use when talking to their children. Persian thus is no longer perceived by the parents exclusively as the 'language of school' or 'language of Persians' but the language of 'our children', even if the command of Persian by many parents is rather poor and inadequate. Despite their attachment to Kurdish identity, these parents proceed to a 'self-elimination' (Bourdieu, 1982, p. 53) by substituting Persian for Kurdish at home. A new pattern of linguistic identity gradually emerges, as the transmission of Kurdish is on the decline and the young generation's linguistic identity shifts towards the official language.

This rupture in the transmission of the Kurdish language can be observed in three types of families: first, in young or middle-aged illiterate parents from either the lower or the middle class speaking Kurdish as their first language, but who use Persian or a mixture between Persian and Kurdish when speaking to their children. Second, in large families, Persian is often the language of only the youngest children whereas the other family members (parents and the elder children) still speak Kurdish as their first language. Thirdly, the substitution of Kurdish with Persian is practised by young parents who have themselves received education in Persian in the centralised educational system.

There are various considerations for the linguistic substitution of Kurdish as the language of the new generation. It should be pointed out, however, that this practice does not imply any negative attitude towards Kurdish culture and identity. In the first place, education in the Persian language is here perceived as giving the children better chances in a situation of stiff competition as it is faced in school. In this case, the desire for success at school motivates parents, especially mothers, to speak Persian with their children even before they start school. They thus proceed to 'anticipated socialisation' (Merton, 1965, p. 84) in Persian in order to maximise their possibilities to climb the social scale.

A mother of three children, thirty-nine years old, from the city of Kermanshah says:

> My husband is Kurdish, I speak to him in Kurdish, but I speak
> Persian with my children because it is for school, especially for the
> elementary level. I am concerned if they do not learn their lessons.

A mother of four children, also in Kermanshah, says:

> With my elder son we used to speak Kurdish, poor child, he was
> completely lost at his first year at elementary school. His teacher
> advised us to speak to him in Persian because he had not
> understood anything at school. Then we spoke to him in Persian,
> and we saw that his marks got better and better and that he
> understood his lessons.

Whether advised by teachers as the representatives of state authority or undertaken by the parents at their own will, based on considerations of utility, substituting Kurdish with Persian in the family has become more and more a common phenomenon, in particular since the Islamic Republic, as the incidence of schooling is higher than before the Revolution of 1979 for both boys and girls. The parents are more concerned about the professional future of their children, which is closely related to mastering the official language.

The cultural disapproval of Kurdish is another result of the modernisation of school, contributing significantly to the discontinuity of the transmission of Kurdish. The 'hierarchy of linguistic use' (Bourdieu, 1982, p. 34), attributing Persian the valued status of the language of school and social promotion, encourages parents (whether they be illiterate or have themselves received education) to neglect the transmission of Kurdish to their children to avoid cultural and social stigma attached to speakers of Kurdish.

For instance, a mother of three children, aged forty, says:

I am Kurdish, I speak with my children both in Kurdish and in Persian, but mostly in Persian. Outside, in the street and in our area, they make fun of Kurdish speakers, that's why I prefer Persian. It is also good for their school. I thought they could learn Kurdish later.

A secondary school teacher explains why she wants to speak to her newborn child in Persian:

If we can take myself as an example, as I have spoken Kurdish from the start, in certain situations when I was in a group of speakers of Persian, I could not make myself understood as I wanted. If I had learnt Persian from the beginning of my life, I would probably be more at ease to express my opinions and feelings.

Conflicts of Identity

Whether cultural or educational considerations cause parents to substitute Persian for Kurdish, the young generation's identity is shaped in a conflict-laden environment. The resulting dichotomous intergenerational opposition of the two languages, together with the dominance of Persian over Kurdish within the family, also entails a shift in the way in which these young Kurds perceive their relation to their ethnic group. They are simultaneously characterised by a detachment from this group and a differentiation within the complex question of ethnicity. Thus, they see themselves as distinct from both Persians and from Kurds: what separates them from Persians is the fact that their families' language is Kurdish. However, speaking Persian, they do not consider themselves as being Kurds either. Characteristically, other aspects of the Kurdish identity, such as the historical, cultural and religious, are totally obscured by the question of the language.

The experience of linguistic difference that separates these young Kurdish speakers of Persian from their parents directly leads to a depreciation of signs of Kurdish ethnic culture, now stereotypically associated with rural areas. The relation between speakers of Kurdish and Persian is conceived in terms of a logic of exclusion, as one between 'the installed and the excluded' (Elias, 1997, pp. 55-56), where the attributes 'urban', 'educated' and 'cultivated' are associated with speakers of Persian, whereas speakers of Kurdish are perceived as 'rural' and 'uneducated'.

This stereotypical stigmatisation of the Kurdish language can already be seen in schoolchildren's discourse; for instance, Mahasti, aged fourteen, says:

> Today, Kurdish is only spoken by the farmers, and for me who
> has never been to the countryside, there is no reason to speak it.

Taraneh, aged seventeen, says:

> I am very happy to speak Persian, because the Kurds do not have
> culture. I do not like the Kurdish language. It reminds me of the
> countryside, the village, it is disgusting. As I see that only farmers
> speak it, it does not have any value for me. I do not like it.

According to Teymour, aged sixteen:

> I speak Persian at home and at school. Persian is more important
> and more valuable. As the Kurds are not really cultured and they
> behave roughly. I don't like to speak that language, nor read or
> write it.

Cultural references are then expressed in more individualistic terms detached from any Kurdish collective identity. These young Kurds do not consider themselves as members of the Kurdish ethnic group any more, but as individuals. Individual benefits and self-image are at the focus of their attention.

The individualistic focus of youth culture contributes to widening the intergenerational gap between children and the older members of their family. The struggle for an identity defined in individualistic terms, therefore, is directed not only against the model of 'rural' (as it is perceived) Kurdish culture, but also against the parents, who belong or at least belonged to this culture. This contradiction between cultures within the one family is experienced as a crisis of identity on two levels, concerning the relations within the family on the one hand, and the adolescent's presentation of self in their surrounding social environment on the other.

In the private sphere, the adolescent cultural references are not defined any more by the family culture, but emerge as the result of personal preferences. These young Kurds seize every opportunity to distance themselves from their parents' cultural references and values by introducing elements of the Persian culture in their everyday lives, which bring them closer to the dominant national culture of speakers of Persian. A cultural gap separates them from their parents: they question their families' values and opinions, associated with the Kurdish language, considering the fact that they speak Persian as a sign of modernity and social prestige that separates them even more from their parents. The cultural gap and situations of conflict are expressed where adolescents are talking among themselves and criticising their parents' attitudes and opinions by mocking them in Kurdish. The disagreement with their parents is interpreted by these young Kurds as conflict between generations and associated directly with detachment from their ethnic community.

In public, even though these adolescents successfully present themselves as having assimilated the national identity by speaking Persian either in a local or a Tehranian accent and thus conceal their Kurdish origin, they suffer from a constant threat that this origin might be revealed to others. The feeling of discomfort and shame for their parents, or their family who master Persian only poorly, is common among them. These adolescents put much effort into concealing their parents' Kurdish identity in the social sphere, both in front of their peer group and at school. Fearing that they may 'lose the façade' (Lipiansky, 1990, p. 187) of being Persian, they refuse to let their parents, their mothers in particular, come to school in person.

Demand for Self-recognition in the Educational Centralised System

In contrast to the previous group of Persian-speaking Kurds who have made the Persian culture their frame of reference and detached themselves from Kurdish for either practical or aesthetic reasons, another group of Kurdish adolescents defend their ethnic identity, demanding recognition by the same centralised school.

It is important to note that, in the case of adolescents who stick to the Kurdish language, domination of Persian is not viewed exclusively in terms of refusal and contestation but in terms of coexistence between the ethnic and local identities. They approach school in two parallel ways: on one hand, they see it as a legitimate place for the creation of a national unity, including linguistic cohesion. However, protestation against the Persian-speaking culture arises when the pupils cannot find any traces of their local and ethnic identity in the centralised system.

A fifteen year-old boy from Kermanshah writes:

> There is nothing on the Kurds in our books at school. In Iran, we
> have many minorities, and the Kurds are one of them. It would be
> good if our books would speak about us, our language, culture
> and religion alongside the Shiites and the Persian speakers.

According to this young Kurd, the role of schoolbooks in reflecting the multiethnic reality of the people of Iran has two sides. On the one hand, by demanding that their ethnic minority with its particular history and cultural characteristics be mentioned in the schoolbooks, they express, in Lipiansky's (1990, p. 180) terms, a need for 'existence and valuation' on the local scale. On the other hand, schoolbooks are thought of as a means to achieve 'social visibility' (Moscovici, 1979, pp. 223-225) on a national level.

As for the linguistic aspect of the centralised educational system, the demand to be taught in the Kurdish language reflects the desire to be recognised as Kurds as a reaction to the perceived threat to the existence of their ethnic group.

> It is the wish of everybody in my class that the Kurds have some hours of classes in the Kurdish language. As the majority of us are Kurds, that would have positive effects. We like to speak Kurdish as it is our language. (Siyavash, seventeen year-old boy from Kermanshah)

> We are not demanding everything in Kurdish or all of our books to be written in our language. But we would like some units of teaching in that language. Nowadays, it is planned that two hours per week be taught in Kurdish at the faculty of Sannandadj. Do you realise how proud that makes us? (Parastou, a sixteen year-old girl at secondary school in the city of Sannandadj)

The need for identifying themselves by means of school and establishing a close relationship with their place of education is grounded in the fact that the Kurdish language, as one integral part of their identity, is systematically denigrated by the central power. The fear of a loss of the Kurdish language is growing more and more, as national educational policy aims to form everybody through the same language (Persian).

> All of our classes are in Farsi, the students do not see the necessity to learn Kurdish, while the government, in parallel, aims to devalue our language. Our young generation thinks that Kurdish is an accent, not knowing that Kurdish is an independent language which has its own proper writing system. They know Kurdish only as a means of oral communication. It is said that one day the Kurds will separate themselves from the rest of Iran. There is no place for linguistic minorities in the schoolbooks and in our educational system. I am being sectarian about condemning Persian, I even listen to Persian music. (Nashmine, seventeen year-old girl, from Sannandadj)

The claim for recognition of the Kurdish minority by education in general is supported by teachers concerned about the preservation of Kurdish ethnic identity. While their task is to transmit the political objectives of the centralised school, and accept the centralism of Persian at school to be judged as positive for the education of the young generation, they also defend the right to be taught in Kurdish within the centralised school:

> It is true that Persian is our official language and common to all Iranians; it must find its roots within every Iranian. But imperatively, we must think of other languages besides it. We must not let other languages disappear in Iran. (Teacher in Sannandadj)

The fear of the loss of the Kurdish language is only one aspect of the teachers' concern; a further aspect is that by demanding the right to have some Kurdish courses, teachers react to what they perceive as a feeling of shame and discomfort among Kurdish-speaking pupils, caused by the official institution's intolerance towards the linguistic minority.

> Besides Persian, there must be Kurdish. Kurdish children must be taught in Kurdish so that they do not think they are nothing, and that importance is given to the Persian language only. (Female teacher in Sannandadj)

> The pupils like us to speak to them in Kurdish. But we insist that they learn to speak Persian. If they are strong at it, it is better for them. If they are unable to speak Persian, tomorrow in their place of work they feel inferior to others. They will be timid and will not express themselves. Therefore, it is our duty to teach them Persian. But, at the same time, it is our wish that they should not forget their Kurdish mother tongue. (Teacher in the city of Sannandadj)

The demand for recognition of Kurdish culture in the centralised school suggests a lack of balance between local and national culture and identity. This feeling of imbalance leads Kurdish adolescents to question the centralised system, in which they risk being deprived of their local identity in a number of respects. At this point, their experience becomes politically relevant. Where Kurdish pupils do not contest the educational system, it is, among other things, because of the hope that the fifteenth article of the Constitution, granting linguistic minorities the right to be taught in their own language, will be fulfilled.

Bilingualism at School as a Political Issue

The feeling of belonging to the Iranian nation, either by denying the local identity or accepting the coexistence between the ethnic and official identities, is not the only reaction engendered by linguistic centralism at school. Another, more violent reaction consists in refusing the government's claim of linguistic and cultural hegemony, perceived as a political issue. With adolescents speaking Kurdish, we have a new group who view school as a political tool employed by the central state in the interest of domination of Persian culture at school. Within the fragment of school, they oppose their own political goals, the struggle for the 'Kurdish cause', to the ones of the central state. This way of politicising the institutional environment of school may be thought of as ethnic nationalism. We will see that three different patterns of behaviour and identity at school may be subsumed under this label.

The first group of pupils includes those who are most successful at school and have a positive approach towards Persian. One major aspect of their acceptance of Persian as the language of the state is that they see the Kurdish minority related to speakers of other minority languages and Persian as a means of inter-ethnic communication common to all Iranians as a lingua franca. Most importantly, however, they believe that only by succeeding in a system dominated by Persian will Kurds have the possibility to assist the Kurdish people. They hope to achieve, in the long term, an influential professional position, which will give them the power and the opportunity to participate in developing the Kurdish area. Being schooled in another language, and in particular being successful at it, may lead to problems in their everyday lives for these adolescents, whose parents mostly do not know how to read or write, and are still illiterate, like their parents, in their own language. As a consequence, they are developing a feeling of guilt, the fear of loss and the feeling of responsibility for their ethnic language.

Faroukh, a nineteen year-old student from the city of Sannandadj, says:

> We are forgetting the Kurdish language. We do not know how to read or write in our language. On the oral level, this language is losing its richness. Many Farsi words have entered into it, because we did not learn their equivalent in Kurdish. If some subjects at school were taught in our language, it would be better. In any way we are going to speak Kurdish forever and with our children as well.

Parastou, sixteen years old, from Sannandadj, says:

> If I have the possibility to choose between these two languages, I choose Kurdish. This is my mother tongue. I speak it with my friends. The only exception is when I speak to my teachers because it is obligatory to speak Persian with them. Our identity is Kurdish, our roots are Kurdish. It does not mean that I do not like Persian, but there should also be some subjects at school taught in the Kurdish language, for example, Kurdish literature or religious instruction.

Besides these successful students with a marked Kurdish identity, a second group of schoolchildren, unsuccessful and unable to cope with the difficulties they face at school, develop a political resistance against the ideology of the centralised school. In the first place, they view their lack of success as a personal failure. In many of our interviews, young boys and girls who have abandoned school started out by saying that they may be useless for the interview because they quit school and had no access to further education. They interpret their experience of school failure right away as a lack of motivation and effort, or of intelligence, because in the same situation other pupils from the same monolingual Kurdish area are successful at school. This often gives rise to a feeling of shame. However, as the interview goes on, they may come up with other reasons, political ones, such as their opposition to the central government, to account for their lack of success. Often, it is implied, or even said explicitly, that had they been allowed to study in their own language they might have done so with more success. They link their failure at school to the language of teaching, and this becomes the point of departure for ideological exploitation on the part of both the central government and the Kurdish resistance.

Finally, a third group of adolescents categorically oppose any presence of the state on a local scale. This third group perceive in the present centralism a reflection of historical attempts of the state – both of the Islamic Republic and Pahlavi dynasty – to dominate the Kurdish people. School as an institution is regarded as a political tool of the government to divert the new generation from their ethnic origin and thus constitute a threat to the Kurdish society. Speaking of Kurdish culture and society, they refuse all changes in Kurdish linguistic practice, whether they be imposed by the government or brought about by the new Kurdish generation's own attitudes and behaviour. Their criticism goes beyond the dominant role of Persian at school and spreads to other fields such as art or the local media. While in general it is largely believed that Kurdish language programmes on the local radio or television ease the political tension between the minority and the government, for this group of adolescents, all local programmes in the Kurdish language are seen as a strategic ploy used by the government, which plans a gradual deterioration of Kurdish by mixing Kurdish and Persian.

Whenever there seems to exist a chance to obtain some degree of autonomy or decentralisation, from the government, the political resistance of this group of actors is directed towards the Kurds who have contributed to any changes in the Kurdish society. This is because they see them as a force in the decline of Kurdish identity among the new generation.

Once more, the phenomenon of stigmatisation can be observed in the relations between Kurdish adolescents of these different groups: those who introduce Persian words into the Kurdish language or who speak Persian are stigmatised as 'collaborators' or 'traitors'. Such segregation within the Kurdish society is expressed in the words of Gelareh (eighteen years, from Sannandadj):

> There are Kurds who have been Kurds for several generations and
> who now speak Persian. They think by doing so they can gain
> prestige. I know a child of Kurdish parents who continues to

speak Persian only because she used to live in Teheran for some time. She has lived in Sannandadj for eight years now, and there is no reason for her to speak Persian. To punish such people, we do not address one word to them in Persian. We, the Kurds, will never speak Persian with other Kurds, even if they want it.

We can thus see that the linguistic choice has important implications concerning both peer-to-peer relationships and the projection of a legitimate frame of cultural reference for social actions. On the one hand, the Kurdish language is used as a tool for discriminating young Persian-speaking Kurds, legitimated by the idea of the Kurdish ethnic community (as practised by the third group discussed above) to display political and cultural resistance. On the other hand, Persian is employed by Kurdish adolescents as a tool for exercising social pressure on speakers of Kurdish, drawing its legitimisation from the frame of a national culture (linked to 'official' political power).

Conclusion

It has been shown in the preceding discussion how the Iranian school is a crucial factor in the process of construction of a linguistic identity for young Iranian Kurds, whereby the situation has been described as one of a conflict-laden contact between two cultures, represented by two languages, the local, ethnic culture of Kurdish and the national, dominating one, of Persian. Characteristic identity patterns have been illustrated emerging out of this conflict, and so we can now attempt, with a few concluding remarks, to provide a synthesis of these complex relations.

Firstly, a process of cultural detachment from the ethnic minority can be observed with young Kurds whose parents, in spite of their attachment to the ethnic identity, choose to discontinue the transmission of the traditional language by speaking Persian to their children. The adolescents from these families view this discontinuity as a sign of modernity and social prestige distinguishing themselves from their – 'traditional', 'outdated' – Kurdish parents. They disapprove of the Kurdish culture and community and try to conceal their ethnic origins both in their private and social lives. Thus, the Kurdish–Persian bilingualism implies an unequal relation between the local and the official language, diametrically opposing local and national identities.

In the second category, when the young Kurds' mother tongue remains Kurdish, bilingualism can lead to a feeling of discomfort, illustrated in the overwhelming feeling of shame for linguistic errors or a strong local accent when these Kurdish adolescents speak Persian. The adolescents in this second group stick to their local identity and despite the denial of a linguistic programme for the minorities at school, claim to be recognised equally in the same centralised school. Their demand to be granted the right to be taught in their own language in a centralised school demonstrates their need to identify themselves through their school, as well as the new generation's quest for a balanced relationship between their national and local identities.

Finally, the conflict-laden bilingualism caused by Persian dominance throughout school results in the growth of Kurdish self-awareness, reinforcing nationalist tendencies in young Kurds still educated in the continuity of their ethnic tradition and culture. We have distinguished three categories of pupils that defend their linguistic identity whereby their attitude towards the central government may be more or less tolerant or hostile, but who are united in considering the dominating language of school as a political tool directed against their minority.

Notes

[1] There have been two notable initiatives to decentralisation; the first under the project title 'Auto-gestion programme of the departments of the Islamic Republic', handed out to the Democratic Party of Iranian Kurdistan in December 1979, in which the central government announced the liberty to teach minority languages as the principal language from the primary school, equal to Persian. The second project dates from 1981 and concerns an internal document of the Ministry of Education which suggests modification of the structure of the training system proposing two types of programmes: one fixed and common on the national scale, the other variable and open to modification by the individual ethnic minorities. However, neither of these two projects has been followed up.

[2] The Komalaye zhiyaani kordestan, the 'Organisation for the renaissance of Kurdistan' was created in 1942 and renamed to its current name of Hezbz domocrate kordestan iran (Democratic Party of Iranian Kurdistan) in 1945. Cf. Eagleton (1991) and McDowall (2000).

[3] Saazemane enghelaabiye zahmatkeshane kordestane iran-Komala, 'Revolutionary Organisation of the Workers of Iranian Kurdistan', was founded in 1969. Cf. More (1984)

[4] During the two first years after the Revolution of 1979, the relation between the Iranian government and the Kurdish autonomists alternated between negotiations and violence. From 1980 to 1984, the Kurdish guerrilla (*peshmerghehs*) gained control over the triangle of Mahabad, Sardach and Bokan (the so-called 'liberated zone'). PDKI and Komala installed their general quarters, schools, radio stations and hospitals. They lost this area in spring 1984 after a new offensive by the Iranian army.

References

Bourdieu, P. (1982) *Ce que parler veut dire, l'économie des échanges linguistiques*. Paris: Fayard.

Castells, M. (1997) *The Power of Identity*. Oxford and Malden, MA: Blackwell.

Deloye, Y. (1994) *Ecole et citoyenneté, l'individualisme républicain de Jules Ferry à Vichy, controverse*. Paris: Presse de FNSP.

Eagleton, William, Jr (1991) *La Republique Kurde*. Brussels: Complexe.

Elias, N. (1997) *Logique de l' exclusion.* Paris: Fayard.

Legrand, L. (1988) *Les politiques de l'éducation.* Paris: PUF.

Lipiansky, E.M. (1990) *Identité subjective et interaction, Stratégies identitaires*, 173-212. Paris: PUF.

McDowall, D. (2000) *A Modern History of the Kurds.* London: I.B. Tauris.

Menasheri, D. (1992) *Education and the Making of Modern Iran.* New York: Cornell University Press.

Merton, R.K. (1965) *Eléments de théories et de méthode sociologique.* Paris: A. Colin.

Mohammadi, I. (2004) Le rôle de l'école dans la recomposition de l'identité des jeunes Kurdes dans la République Islamique d'Iran, PhD dissertation, Paris: Ecole des Hautes Etudes en Sciences Sociales (EHESS).

More, C. (1984) *Les Kurdes d'aujourd'hui, Mouvement national et Parties politiques.* Paris: L'Harmattan.

Moscovici, S. (1979) *Psychologie des minorités actives.* Paris: Quadriage, PUF.

Payet, J.P. (2000) L'ethnicité dans l'école française, de la censure républicaine à la reconnaissance democratique? *Pour Educations, Société*, No. 165, 109-151. Paris: L'Harmattan.

Paivandi, S. (1995) L'analyse démographique et d'analphabétisme en Iran, *Population*, 50, 1155-1184.

Israel's Education System: equality of opportunity – from nation building to neo-liberalism

YOSSI DAHAN & YOSSI YONAH

The value of equal opportunity has always been proclaimed by the founders of Israel and its prominent political leaders as the main ideal that should guide the articulation and implementation of public policies in the field of education. Their alleged commitment to this value echoes the egalitarian ethos of Labour Zionism, being the most dominant of Zionist movements both in pre-state Israel and in the first three decades following the inception of the state in 1948. Furthermore, this value was deemed essential to the realisation of the goal of cultivating a cohesive national community and solidarity among the members of the budding Jewish state. But how has this value fared in Israel's education system over the years? To what extent does it receive meaningful expression in Israel's educational policies?

Although it is rather difficult to provide clear and conclusive answers to these questions, we argue that the ideal of equal opportunities was never sufficiently implemented in the education system as to prevent the emergence of deep scholastic gaps among children, correlated with their respective national, ethnic, racial and gender-based divisions characterising Israeli society. Although we do emphasise the impact of exogenous factors in determining the capacity of the education system to secure equal opportunities to all children irrespective of family background, we do not perceive the emergence of these gaps to be merely the result of these factors. We argue that the very policies themselves were also largely responsible for undermining equal opportunities in the Israeli education system. That is, while on the one hand, these policies spoke the language of equal opportunities, on the other hand, they also spoke the language that combined ethno-nationalism and meritocracy and were often marked with prejudices and systematic discrimination against marginalised social and cultural groups.

Due to limited space, we do not intend to provide a comprehensive account of all major policies implemented in the Israeli education system. Rather, we focus on two educational reforms – actually the two most important ones – which the education system has faced to date. The first one is the Integration Reform, implemented in 1968 and the second, a more recent one (Ministry of Education, 2005), is presented in a voluminous and detailed document titled *The National Task Force on Education*. The latter reform is widely known in Israel as the 'Dovrat Reform', named after the businessman, Shlomo Dovrat, head of the 'Task Force'. This reform was endorsed by the Israeli government in that same year.

Despite their very different ideological and political nature, both reforms decree that educational policies are desirable only to the extent that they significantly contribute to the realisation of the value of equal opportunities. Generally understood, this value dictates that educational opportunities should be granted to all children irrespective of social background, including their nationality, ethnicity, race, gender, family milieu and economic status. This conception of equality of opportunity is often referred to as 'fair equality of opportunity'. Thus, for instance, according to John Rawls:

> Fair equality of opportunity is said to require not merely that
> public offices and social positions be open in the formal sense, but
> that all should have fair chance to attain them. To specify the idea
> of a fair chance we say: supposing that there is a distribution of
> native endowment, those who have the same level of talent and
> ability and the same willingness to use these gifts should have the
> same prospects of success regardless of their social class or origin,
> the class into which they are born and develop until the age of
> reason. (Rawls, 2001, pp. 43-44)

Our main argument then is that on the whole the policies implemented in the field of education have actually undermined 'fair equality of opportunity'. We also argue that the implementation of both reforms counteracts Israel's policy makers' aspiration to cultivate a society that enjoys a considerable degree of social cohesion and solidarity among its members.

The Israeli Education System 1948-1968:
main patterns of inequality

The Mandatory Education Act of 1949, passed in the parliament a year after the establishment of the state of Israel, and the State Education Act enacted in 1953, formally nationalised Israel's educational system, which prior to the establishment of the state was run mainly by the Jewish National Committee, the main Jewish governing body in the British mandatory era. According to the 1953 Act, the system was to be guided by a set of values that endeavour to combine national and universal values. Thus the Act states that the policies and practices in the field of education are to be guided by the following values: scientific achievement, the love of the nation, loyalty to the state and the people of Israel, agricultural work, pioneering training and the aspiration for a society based upon the values of liberty, equality, tolerance and love of mankind.[1]

Guided by these values, the Education Act is designed to provide equal opportunity to all children so that they can fully realise their potential. Ben Zion Dinur, Israel's Minister of Education during the years 1951-55, argued that:

should the state transfer the concern to future generations,
personal capacity, social happiness, and moral, intellectual and
technical level of each member of society to someone else, it
would abdicate its duty. (Dinur, 1958, pp. 26-28)

He then concluded:

that the aspiration for the intellectual and cultural equality of all
the children of Israel should guide the education system's actions
and that the system should not distinguish between pupils of
different ethnic origins and different sectors of society. (Dinur,
1958, pp. 26-28)

Despite these official declarations, Israel's education system in the years following the establishment of the state (1948) was characterised by geographical segregation and systematic discrimination against various social groups. This discrimination was manifested in the allocation of material resources, in the supply of high-quality teaching personnel, in drafting different school curricula, in differential expectations from children and more (Swirski, 1990, pp. 47-139).

Combining physical segregation and explicit and implicit forms of discrimination, these policies were not equally implemented against all groups; some groups faced more severe forms of discrimination than others. Thus, the severest forms of discrimination were manifested against Arab children. In the years following the establishment of the state, Israeli Arab citizens lived under military rule, since they were considered a potential security threat to the state of Israel. Hence, Arab children were confined to segregated schools and subject to blatant discrimination in the allocation of resources (Swirski, 1990; Mazawi, 1999; Saban, 2002).

Jewish children were supposed to be spared this harmful combination of geographical segregation and systematic discrimination, since they were all considered potential members of a future Jewish community, to be cultivated as a cohesive and homogeneous nation. Schools, it was commonly believed, constitute the main vehicle for bringing about this desirable outcome. But as a voluminous corpus of research indicates, this was not usually the case. The education system has generally resulted in reproducing existing patterns of geographical segregation and structural inequalities between Mizrahi and

Ashkenazi children, thus practically creating two educational sub-systems characterised by a disparity of material conditions and different school curricula (Swirski, 1990). Most of the Mizrahi children attended separate and impoverished schools, located in their secluded and deprived towns and neighbourhoods. Facing low expectations, many of them dropped out of schools or channelled to vocational high schools (Swirski, 1990, Yonah & Saporta, 2006).

Compared to the first two groups (Arab and Mizrahi children), the group comprising children of veteran Israelis (Ashkenazim), of mainly European origin, attended privileged schools that were located in affluent areas.[2] These schools provided high-quality education, preparing their children for institutes of higher education and consequently for prestigious and lucrative positions in the job market. Aside from this quasi sub-system serving these children, the Israeli education system created a segregated and privileged sub-system serving children of the Kibbutzim.

Finally, the Israeli education system has contributed significantly to the reproduction and reinforcement of gender-based biases in school, bolstering gender-based division of labour in Israeli society (Yonah & Saporta, 2006).

School segregation and discrimination in the allocation of material resources have greatly contributed to the emergence of wide scholastic gaps among children belonging to different social groups. The main gap in this regard, occupying the attention of policy makers in the field of education, was the one existing between Mizrahi and Ashkenazi children. This gap particularly attracted their attention since it was commonly believed that its continuous existence might undermine attempts to cultivate a cohesive Jewish community and a stable political order. Thus, for instance, in a conference held in 1958, attended by supervisors from the Department of Education, it was reported – with a pronounced sense of urgency and a deep concern – that 'a two year learning gap exists between a pupil from a new immigrant settlement and a pupil from the city; many of the new immigrant students cannot read'. The drop-out rate among Mizrahi students, the report continued alarmingly, was much higher than Ashkenazi students, and their rate of representation among high school and university students was very low (Swirski, 1990, p. 57).[3]

The Educational Reform and Social and Ethnic Integration

In the mid 1960s, amid growing dissatisfaction with pupils' poor achievements and the perceived need to modernise the educational system, politicians and decision makers at the Ministry of Education initiated a major educational reform. The reform restructured Israel's schools according to a model that was imported from other Western countries such as the United States and Sweden. Despite widely shared concerns about growing scholastic gaps between children of different ethnic origins, the main purpose of the reform was to create organisational and structural mechanisms in the service of a school tracking system aiming to distinguish, in early stages, between two groups of children: high achievers and low achievers. While the first group of children was to receive high-quality education, preparing them to enrol in institutions of higher education and consequently to acquire prestigious and lucrative positions in the job market, the second group was supposed to receive basic (mainly vocational) education, preparing them for low-skill positions in the job market. According to the reform, the distinction between the two groups of children would take place in junior high school.

The main principles guiding the Integration Reform were contained in a special report prepared by a parliamentary committee – the Rimalt Committee – which was approved by the Israeli parliament in May 1968. The reform sought to restructure the elementary and secondary school system by replacing the binary model (eight years followed by four years, 8:4) with a tripartite model (6:3:3), consisting of a six-year elementary school, three-year junior high school and three-year high school. The logic underlying this restructuring is obvious – introducing children into a more demanding curriculum at an earlier stage of their schooling.

Nevertheless, it was often overlooked in academic and public debates. Supporters and critics of the reform focused on the component of the reform that dealt with the integration between children of different ethnic and cultural backgrounds in junior high schools. This component has been so often discussed that the reform is very commonly referred to as the Integration Reform. Therefore, it is important to emphasise that at the early stages the educational integration of children of different ethnic and cultural backgrounds (i.e. Mizrahi and Ashkenazi children) was not part of the reform (Amir & Ballas, 1985, p. 73). The integration component of the reform was introduced only after Mizrahi parents exerted pressure to end school segregation and demanded quality education for their children in integrated schools. It is also important to note that the inclusion of the integration component in the reform was endorsed by Zalman Arran, the Minister of Education at the time, believing that its inclusion would promote public support in its favour. That is, he believed that the inclusion of this component in the reform might reduce objections to its more controversial and supposedly meritocratic components.

Those arguing in favour of the integration component of the reform presented several arguments to support their position, giving the impression that the main purpose of the reform was to secure equality of opportunity for all children 'regardless of their social class or origin'. Thus they argued first that educational integration is a necessary condition if the newly emerging Jewish state aspires to create a strong sense of cohesive national community based on common historical heritage (real or imagined). And indeed, the 'melting pot' project, otherwise known as 'the gathering of the exiles', which has been guiding social and educational policies in Israel since its inception, owed much to this nation-building logic. Ethnic segregation and educational

145

and economic inequalities, they argued, could encourage and accelerate tendencies toward social disintegration and ethnic rifts in Israeli society (Ben Ari et al, 1985, p. 17).[4] The idea of restructuring the educational system according to the principle 'separate, but equal' was considered practically impossible politically, and morally undesirable.

The value of equality of opportunity, then, was allegedly one of the main concerns, leading many to advocate ethnic integration in the education system. The equalisation of educational opportunities, they contended, cannot be attained in a school system separated along ethnic, social and economic lines. They claimed that education services provided exclusively to the poor would ultimately be poor services, since, among other things, schools in middle-class and rich neighbourhoods have the ability to extract more resources from the state and have the ability to utilise these public resources and their own private resources in a much more efficient way than schools in poor neighbourhoods. Schools in rich areas attract better teachers and their children possess a privileged cultural capital that is instrumental to school success. Social and ethnic integration, argued its supporters, would make children from middle-class and rich families function as role models for poor children, who lack these attributes and usually face low educational expectations (Ben Ari et al, 1985, 19-25). In conclusion, supporters of integration argued that adding the integration component to the reform was in line with two central and complementary goals of the Jewish state: creating a homogeneous and cohesive national community and promoting social equality through equal educational opportunities (see Kfir et al, 1993, pp. 3-4).

However, despite a common belief that school integration between children from different social and cultural backgrounds would provide equal opportunities, the scope of the desired integration was in practice severely limited. Thus, the reform did not aspire to change official policies regarding enrolment in elementary schools. At that stage children were still assigned to schools according to their area of residence. As mentioned before, the main thrust of the integration component of the reform came in the three-year junior high school. The reform imposed registration zones (cross-neighbourhood) on the school enrolment of junior high school students, with the aim of restructuring the school environment and guaranteeing the mixing of pupils from different ethnic groups and socio-economic classes. The policy officially denied parents the option of enrolling their children in schools outside their assigned registration zone, while prohibiting schools from denying admittance to children on the basis of any selective criteria. The reform also did not impose zone restrictions on students' registration to high schools.

Furthermore, the reform, which was supposed to be imposed, was only to be implemented in the two main streams of Israeli education – state education and state religious education. It has been applied neither to children who were enrolled in the state-independent, religious, ultra-orthodox stream nor to Arab children. The reasons for the reform's limited scope of application were different in each case. In the former case, the reason was that the state expediently complied with the demand of ultra-religious communities to exercise autonomy in educational affairs. In the latter, however, the reason was rather simple: since the Integration Reform was fully subordinated to national goals and interests, Arab children were deemed irrelevant in this regard. However, the exclusion of Arab children was rationalised by the argument stating that integrating between Jewish and Arab children would amount to forcing a Jewish identity on Arab children, whose community has a separate and distinct national identity (Adler, 1985, pp. 52-52). The Integration Reform was silent on the subject of Arab children, who could have benefited the most from educational integration, due to their poor social and economic conditions.[5]

It is important to note that the integration component of the reform was never universally enforced, even in the educational streams to which it was officially directed, i.e. state education and state religious education. The limited scope of application was due to fierce objection voiced by parents and social groups who were concerned that the Integration Reform would compromise the interests of their children (Gaziel, 1994). Thus, although integration was required by law, a mere 56% of the Jewish children attended integrated schools in the late 1970s, a period signalling the peak of the efforts to implement the Integration Reform (Israel, 1981). One of the most common methods of circumventing the Integration Reform was the rapid establishment of new communal settlements by affluent parents, mainly of Ashkenazi background. As Blanck argues, this development is actually analogous to the 'white flight' phenomenon existing in the USA, figuring the escape of white families from inner cities to the suburbs, thus shunning desegregated schools (Blanck, 2004).

Another method of avoiding the integration was used by the kibbutz movement. In clear contrast with its socialist ideology, the kibbutz movement vehemently objected to the enrolment of Mizrahi children in the same schools as their children, on the ground that such enrolment may undermine the unique culture and way of life of the kibbutz. This objection proved successful, and the kibbutz movement was exempted from the Integration Reform and was allowed to maintain its segregated educational system.

Furthermore, in many affluent districts, the reform was not implemented because parents were able to 'enlist the help of their municipalities' in their refusal to send their children to integrated schools (Stahl, 1991, p. 61). Moreover, in many municipalities in which integration was implemented, many schools still maintained social and ethnic segregation by channelling Mizrahi students into separate classes.

In a comprehensive study examining the implementation of the Integration Reform, Resh & Dar (1996) have discussed the elaborate mechanisms employed by schools to circumvent the goals of the integration part of the reform and thus to maintain 'segregation within integration'. As they put it, 'integration at the school level is counteracted at the classroom level, negatively affecting the achievement of the social and educational goals of the integration policy' (1996, p. 11). An extreme example of this is the city of Tel Aviv/Jaffa, where the State Comptroller, in her 1990-92 report, put the blame for sabotaging the Integration Reform on the city's Educational Central Authority (Israel, 1990-92).

Another challenge to the reform came from the establishment of 'cross-district schools'. From 1992, there were between thirty-five and forty elementary schools and junior high schools that had been given permission to operate outside the framework of the Integration Reform. These schools – existing in both state secular and state religious streams – are permitted to recruit children irrespective of the officially defined registration zones. About 2% of the country's children in these age groups are enrolled in such schools, which are organised according to unique pedagogical, ideological, and curricular characteristics (Shapira, 1988; Kashti, 1991).[6]

The ways and means exerted by parents and social groups to avoid the Integration Reform were not the sole reason for its failure to effect meaningful equality of opportunity among different social and ethnic groups. As the relevant literature testifies, there were other fundamental deficiencies accounting for its meagre results in this regard. First, although the public, parents and educational experts agreed that in order for social and ethnic integration to succeed it should start at an early stage, in the elementary school, the integration took place only in a later stage and was limited to three years in junior high school. One of the main reasons for the government's refusal to implement the integration at an early age was that implementing the integration then would have necessitated public bussing of children, requiring an increase in the Ministry of Education's budget. Thus, as a result of this late implementation, many of the children from largely different, homogeneous, ethnic and socio-economic neighbourhoods met each other for the first time only at junior high school, which according to some experts was much too late (see Sharan et al, 1985, p. 204). Moreover, after three years, assuming the best case scenario of three years of educational and social integration, pupils were once more segregated upon entering high school, usually ending up in separate schools, segregated along socio-economic and ethnic lines.

High schools in Israel are divided into two categories: academic and vocational. Academic high schools are very selective and have very strict policies of disallowing students with low grades to continue their studies in the school at the end of the year. Moreover, these schools channel students to different classes based on their achievements and their prospects of future success. The academic high schools enjoy a high status and most of their students pass the matriculation examinations and are admitted into universities. Most of the academic high schools reside in middle-class and rich neighbourhoods and the majority of their students are Ashkenazim. Vocational high schools, on the other hand, are considered appropriate for those students (mainly of Mizrahi origins) whose success rate in the matriculation examinations is much lower than that of students attending academic schools (Swirski & Schwartz, 2005). These students are believed to be incapable of meeting the high standards of academic high schools (Kashti & Yosephon, 1985, pp. 14-15).[7]

The core curriculum of the Integration Reform also failed to contribute to the realisation of its original declared intent – securing the ideal of equal educational opportunities. According to a public committee investigating the reform in the Israeli educational system, when changes were made in the core curriculum for junior high schools,

> except for a few cases, the change took into consideration mainly
> the needs of students belonging to high and middle achievement
> groups, and ignored the needs of low achieving and weak
> students. (Swirski, 1990, p. 151)

Thus, for instance, in accordance with the 'melting pot' ideology – functioning according to assimilatory rather than integrative logic – the core curriculum in junior high schools lacked any learning materials, either in history, literature or any other discipline, that were based on or inspired by Mizrahi cultural heritage and history. One reason for this neglect was, as critics of the Israeli education system note, that those drafting the school curriculum believed that the inclusion of elements from Mizrahi cultural heritage and history counteracts efforts to modernise and resocialise Mizrahim in the light of values and ideals borrowed from the self-image of Israel as a modern and European state. Mizrahi cultural heritage and history were, and still are, believed to reflect backwardness and cultural stagnation, as opposed to the Western, modern, and progressive values of the hegemonic Ashkenazi culture (see Kashti & Yosefon, 1985, pp. 10-11). The idea that including elements from Mizrahi cultural heritage and history might contribute to the enhancement of a positive self-image of Mizrahi children and strengthen social integration was alien to the world-view of the founders of the Israeli education system (Sharan et al, 1985, pp. 217-291). Unfortunately, this idea still does not enjoy wide support among policy makers in the field of education (Dahan & Yonah, 2005).

According to its critics, the Integration Reform was severely plagued by other problems as well. They characterise it as a rigid, state-centred bureaucratic policy that did not seriously take into consideration the intricate challenges involved in its implementation at the school and class levels. It did not offer appropriate solutions to problems faced by principals, teachers and students, and neglected to take seriously communities' and parents' reactions to its effects.[8] Due to all these different problems many junior high schools have become schools where students are channelled onto different tracks according to their scholastic achievements correlated with their ethnic affiliations. Thus, contrary to the original intention, junior high schools are practically turned into educational sites where the main selection processes of differentiating between 'successful' and 'unsuccessful' students take place, processes which by their very nature defy fair equality of opportunity and social integration.

The persistent objections to the Integration Reform and its flagrant violations, occurring alongside a substantial shift in the values and ideals dominating Israeli society, have gradually infiltrated official attitudes and values vis-à-vis the field of education (Gaziel, 1994; Yonah & Dahan, 1999). As early as the mid-1980s, a noticeable change was taking place in the Ministry of Education. What was at first merely tolerated, and later tacitly encouraged, emerged as official policy. In the early 1990s the Ministry of Education initiated studies with the aim of examining the potential of reorganising the educational system. The guiding principles of the quest for new directions were borrowed from a specific value system and terminology, which includes concepts such as decentralisation, accountability, school self-management, autonomy, empowerment and parental choice.

The Dovrat Reform:
formal demise of the integration

The publication of the Dovrat Report, *The National Task Force on Education*, in 2005 best epitomises this paradigm change. The report, drawing its inspiration from similar neo-liberal reports drafted and implemented in many other countries, upholds the principles of decentralisation and accountability and the introduction of quasi-market mechanisms as its guiding principles (Dahan & Yonah, 2005).[9] The authors of the report present it as a proposal for a comprehensive and radical reform of Israel's educational system. This is only partially true, since the report is in fact a summary of several policies and mini-reforms that have taken place during the last two decades. In this respect, the report does not amount to a complete revolution. However, it does introduce new structural changes that integrate the various policy changes that have taken place in Israel's educational system into a comprehensive and unified plan. As the authors of the report themselves state, 'the dire state of education in Israel requires a general reform; not piecemeal alterations' (Ministry of Education, 2005, p. 69).

As stated, the report's main thrust is oriented towards decentralisation and accountability. The orientation of the Dovrat Committee is clear from the very fact that its head (Shlomo Dovrat) and other major members of the committee are prominent figures of the Israeli business community. As one of them stated, 'never before were business people given such a great opportunity to influence public policy in matters not-economic'.[10] And indeed this unprecedented opportunity reverberates throughout the report. Its analysis and solutions are inspired by organisational principles and global business values.

Thus, the reform recommends transforming the educational system into a goal-oriented venture, guided by cost–benefit evaluative criteria. All policies and programmes introduced into the educational system are to be evaluated in terms of their financial costs versus their intended results. To allow for such a transformation, the reform recommends strict measuring principles and assessment of the performance of the various components of the system in light of the goals ascribed to it. The goals to be measured include not only student scholastic achievements but also the inculcation of values (i.e. civic and moral virtues) and their effectiveness in reducing the level of violence among schoolchildren. The authors of the report write that

> the proposed plan embraces this concept. Underlying it is the assumption that the achievements and results of the educational process can be measured and evaluated, and that the educational process can and should be directed and managed in such a way that it is aimed at achieving specific objectives. According to our perception, goals and objectives should be defined in advance in as much detail as possible at the level of the education system as a whole, at the local level, and at the level of every pre-school and school. For each objective, a way of measuring success should also be determined in advance.[11]

This vision of the educational system is guided by the belief that effective management of the system requires decentralisation and simplification of the existing mechanisms. That is, the report decrees that the education system as a whole will consist of only three administrative echelons as follows:

(a) the Ministry of Education is faithful to the report's neo-liberal spirit, as it limits the role of the state substantially and transfers some of its main responsibilities to the two other organisations. The Ministry of Education is supposed to bear overall responsibility for the education system, delineate policy, handle budgeting, set standards, and oversee compliance with the standards. As part of the decentralisation of the system, the report introduces a new body:

(b) the Regional Education Administration (REA), which is supposed to have an overall authority and responsibility over the education system in its region, including provision of services, management of professional personnel and providing measurement and evaluative services. At the bottom of the hierarchy we find:

(c) the educational institutions themselves, which will have maximum control over their own educational activity. One major change that is to take place in schools is the central role and authority that the report grants to the school's principal. Under the report's vision, schools will be self-managed. They will enjoy managerial, pedagogical and financial autonomy. The school principal bears a responsibility to meet its goals – to hire and fire school personnel, to run a balanced budget, and to initiate fund-raising schemes from non-public resources, for example, leasing school facilities to generate extra revenues.

The neo-liberal spirit of the report is also expressed by introducing quasi-market mechanisms such as competition and choice into the educational system. These include the recommendation to deregulate assigned registration zones and the establishment of a controlled choice programme. According to the report's recommendations, parents will be allowed to choose between several schools in certain geographical areas. The diminishing role of the state and the introduction of competition to the educational sphere are also expressed by allowing non-governmental organisations to run schools. The report authorises the REA to certify such organisations to run schools which are under its jurisdiction. These schools are supposed to be quite similar to 'Charter Schools' in the United States.

However, the Dovrat Report does not officially renege on the value of equality of educational opportunity. On the contrary, it heralds this value and declares that the recommendations it proposes were articulated in its light. In addition to economic measures, the Report declares:

> education is one of the central tools to eliminate hardships, to
> reduce social gaps and to facilitate a well-ordered society, one
> characterised by solidarity. A high level of education for all is a
> means to equal opportunities, enabling the breaking of the circle
> of poverty and the opening of possibilities and social mobility, so
> that the achievements of all individuals will neither depend on the
> economic standing of their parents, nor on their national and
> ethnic origin nor on their gender or place of dwelling. (p. 42)

Thus, one of the main reasons for the acutely needed educational revolution is due to what the committee calls the deep crisis that Israel's educational system is experiencing. The crisis is exhibited, among other things, by large academic gaps between pupils; the committee points out that Israel is among the world's leaders in academic gaps on the basis of socio-economic background, national background (between Jews and Arabs), origin (Ashkenazim and Mizrahim), time in the country (immigrant and veteran Israelis), and place of residence (rich towns and neighbourhoods versus poor towns and neighbourhoods). According to the committee, these gaps are blatantly evident in academic achievements, drop-out rates, and success rate in the matriculation examinations.

In order to reduce these different forms of inequality the committee recommends several new and more direct equality enhancing policies, among them the introduction of differential criteria for the allocation of public resources. According to these criteria, schools belonging to the lower strata will receive up to 60% more than the basic level of public resources allocated to regular schools. It also recommends compulsory early childhood education, beginning at the age of three. This change, according to the committee, will bring about the 'turning of the pyramid', and set different priorities for the Ministry of Education, which would be required to invest more money in early education than in adult education. That is, the committee recommends investing more resources in early age education and less in later stages of education, as it is currently the case. The committee also recommends that, instead of six days, pupils will study for only five days, with a long school day, from 8 a.m. to 4 p.m., and the improvement and upgrading of the physical infrastructure of schools, aiming mainly to reduce classroom overcrowding.

However, these equality-enhancing recommendations of the report, which require additional budgeting, contradict the report's main working assumption, which states that 'the recommendations it suggests will not encumber the state with unreasonable burden'. It further states that it intends to 'offer a long term model allowing quality education, taking into account, however, the limitations of national resources' (Dovrat Report: Ministry of Education, 2005). The report uses the 2003 Ministry of Education Budget as its benchmark, which was the lowest budget since 1996. The committee ignores the painful fact that in the two years prior to the report's publication, the Ministry of Education budget has undergone fourteen successive cuts. According to an estimate of the 'Centre for Local Government', the additional budget required to implement early childhood education, the long day school and improvements in schools' infrastructures is approximately 1.5 billion dollars.[12]

The conclusion is that these recommendations essentially do not have any practical budgetary implications and are merely declarative, paying homage to the value of equal opportunity. That is to say, as far as the report goes, these recommendations belong in the realm of the remotely desirable – not of the feasible. But even when we consider the recommendations to introduce differential criteria for the public allocation of resources, intending to compensate for socio-economic gaps, doubts remain as to its effectiveness. That is, it is highly questionable whether it can compensate for other recommendations that allow and legitimise privatisation and commercialisation policies, which increase educational inequalities in an already unequal society. As studies conducted elsewhere in the world indicate, the introduction of quasi-market mechanisms to the field of education tends to undermine equal opportunities, not to enhance them (Whitty, 1997, 2002).

The declarative commitment of the committee to equality of opportunity is also greatly undermined by some of the other specific recommendations. The report recommends that schools institute three learning standards: a core programme which would be required of each pupil, an additional standard which will be more demanding than the core, and over and above these two standards, an excellence standard for bright pupils. Such a policy amounts to groupings which would inevitably infringe upon the principle of equality of opportunity, since the practical implication of implementing this policy is that most children from underprivileged social and economic backgrounds, mainly Arab and Mizrahi pupils, would populate the lower standard classes. The likelihood that this would inevitably happen receives support from studies examining programmes of this kind that have already been implemented elsewhere in the world (Hallinan, 2004; Glass, 2005).

Socio-economic Reality:
equality in unequal circumstances?

The Dovrat Committee completely disregards the causal relationship between social and economic inequalities and equality of educational opportunity. Social and economic inequalities have been exacerbated in recent years in Israel due to different factors, among which are the introduction of neo-liberal economic policies, which are expressed in the deregulation of the labour market, and the dramatic weakening of labour unions and cuts in various services of the welfare state. In 2004 the gross household income for the wealthiest 10% of households occupied by a wage earner was over US $8000, more than 12 times higher than the income of households (US $665) belonging to the poorest 10%. The gap between these two groups indicates an increase of 5.2% compared to 2003. The increase of the gap is mainly due to income increase of the top 10% (Adva, 2005, p. 10). The net income of households belonging to the top 10% in 2004 was $5313, which is 8.6 times higher than the net income of households belonging to the lowest 10% (US $614).[13] These figures are echoed in the sharp increase in the number of people living below the poverty line. Compared with West European countries and North America, Israel currently witnesses the highest poverty rates among families (20.5%), individuals (24.1%) and children (34.1%). It is important to note that the figure concerning the poverty rate among children reveals a sharp increase compared to the year 1997. In that year the poverty rate among children was 22.9%, indicating an increase of over 50% of children living below the poverty line within an interval of nine years (Adva, 2006). Furthermore, current data in this regard indicate a sharp increase during the period extending between the years 1977 and 1990. The percentage of people living below the poverty line during these years was, respectively, 3.3 in 1977, 4.8 in 1978, 5.6 in 1979 and 7.3 in 1980. One of the main reasons for this increase has been the steady rise in the rate of unemployment, which is nearly double that of 1980. The rate of unemployment that year was 5.4%, while in 1990 the rate was 9.8%; it currently stands at 8.7%, totalling 239,000 unemployed (Israel Central Bureau of Statistics [ICBS], 2006).

These social and economic inequalities also manifest themselves in the educational realm. The Israeli government expenditure on education is 82.6% of the total national expenditure on education. This figure is not below the average of the government expenditure on education of Organisation for Economic Cooperation and Development (OECD) countries; however, it indicates a significant retreat in comparison to previous years (Adva, 2002). Between the years 1975 and 2000 households' share in national expenditures on education increased considerably. Private expenditures on education within these years, which include private school tuition, private lessons and parents' payments, rose by 360%, while public expenditures rose by a mere 120%.

These figures, we should note, do not reflect equal distribution of private expenditures among households. Wealthy households spend larger amounts of money on education than poor households (Adva, 2002, pp. 4-5). Thus, in 1980 families belonging to the top 10% of households paid 2.3 times more for educational services than families belonging to the 51-60% range and 7.3 times more than families belonging to the 11-20% from the bottom. In the year 2000, families belonging to the highest 10% of households paid 2.7 times more for educational services than families belonging to the 51-60% range and 10 times more than families belonging to the 11-20% from the bottom (Adva, 2002). These findings, however, are clearly manifested in the spread of the phenomenon known in Israel as grey education, a phenomenon that Inbar (1989) aptly describes as 'a back door process of privatisation'. This phenomenon clearly attests to the dominance of economic factors in spurring the demand for 'more choice and variety in education'. Grey education is a privately sponsored additional curriculum (PAC) operated within the school framework. This phenomenon has emerged in response to sharp cuts in school teaching hours in the 1980s and is currently very pervasive. A study designed to examine the extent of PAC showed that 73% of schools operating such programmes were located in affluent neighbourhoods and only 10% in poor neighbourhoods (Bar-Siman-Tove & Langman, 1988, p. 9). Furthermore, a more recent study shows that the spread of 'grey education' has taken place mainly in affluent areas (Cohen & Cohen, 1996).

The relationship between financial means and equal opportunities in education has always been a major concern for educational policy makers in Israel. The philosophy guiding educational policy in the past was for the state to assume an almost exclusive role in financing the educational system, in order to curb parents' desires to be directly involved in the administrative affairs of the school and its curriculum. It was feared that this involvement might compromise the principle of equality of educational opportunities (Hen, 1987, p. 11). It is widely agreed that those in charge of public education have displayed too much zeal in sheltering the school from parental involvement. Nonetheless, their concern that by requiring parents to share in the financial burden, class interest might compromise the principle of equal opportunities in education, does indeed seem not unwarranted. And indeed, it would be accurate to state that what is referred to as 'the social movement in Israel calling for more choice and variety in education' (Goldring, 1991, p. 413) is more about what money can buy, and less about autonomy or enlightened processes owing to the alleged democratic nature of the Israeli political system and culture.

155

As claimed, the background socio-economic conditions are a prerequisite for realising equal opportunities in education. Surveying economic and social trends in Israeli society, it becomes virtually impossible for the education system to secure a meaningful measure of equal opportunities.

The Dovrat Report, however, does not easily follow in the footsteps of the reports and reforms preceding it, i.e. those heralding the decline of the Integration Reform. As previously noted, the Integration Reform of the mid 1960s was the main means employed by the state in the service of Israel's nation-building project. Thus, many experts on Israeli society tended to believe that the various attacks against the Integration Reform indicated a major shift in Israel's self-perception (Shapira, 1988). It is no longer a society consumed by existential anxieties and fears and by the desire to consolidate its existence in hostile surroundings, but a self-confident society manoeuvring comfortably in 'the brave new world' – a world dominated by neo-liberal economics. However, the newly emerging alliance between the national discourse and neo-liberal ideology questions this interpretation. It is an alliance, we should remember, seen worldwide (Whitty, 1997, 2002). Thus, like many other societies around the world, Israeli society also gives rise to these dialectical and elusive processes. That is, while the state, undergoing neo-liberal reforms, has become weaker due to a radical decrease in subsidising public services, it simultaneously has tightened its grip on certain social services by dictating external goals and criteria for evaluating the products of these services. As to the field of education, the products are children who firstly command skills enabling them to function effectively in the global economy, and secondly, who display the virtues rendering them all loyal and committed citizens of the nation state. These inconsistent goals become patently evident in the Dovrat Reform. Thus, while economic and social background conditions have become more unequal, and while the education system has undergone processes of privatisation, commercialisation and quasi-marketisation, the state grip on the values and belief systems of Israeli pupils has become tighter. That is to say, while these processes have been taking place, the state became more zealous in its desire to dictate a core curriculum which emphasises ethno-nationalistic values, attempting thus to counter the disintegrating effects of the increasing social and economic inequalities. [14]

Conclusions

As stated before, throughout the existence of the state the principle of educational equality of opportunity has been considered one of the main constitutive building blocks of Israel's state ideology. We claimed, however, that despite the alleged commitment of the state to this principle, the public policies carried out over the years in its name have tended to undermine it. To substantiate this claim, we examined two of the major educational reforms in Israel's history: the Integration Reform of 1968 and the Dovrat Reform of 2005. These reforms, we demonstrated, contravened the principle of educational equality despite the fact that they stem from very different ideologies.

The Integration Reform, neglecting Israeli Arab pupils, included educational policies intended to bridge the educational gap between different Jewish ethnic groups. But these policies were accompanied by other policies that have undermined the declared purpose of the reform. The latter policies include grouping according to achievement levels within each class, 'segregation within the integration' – namely, separating pupils from different ethnic groups into different classes within the same school, and the division of high schools into two main categories – prestigious academic high schools, populated mainly by Ashkenazi children, and low-prestige vocational schools, attended mainly by Mizrahi students. The implementation of these policies has greatly contributed to the emergence of protracted and persistent scholastic gaps between pupils from the two respective Jewish groups.[15]

While the Integration Reform was conceived as state controlled and part and parcel of the Zionist nation-building project, the Dovrat Reform draws its raison d'être allegedly from a different world-view: a neo-liberal philosophy that urges the unfolding of the state. Thus, the latter reform has emerged against a social, economic and ideological background assuming the gradual dismantling of the welfare state, a sharp reduction in the allocation of public resources to social services and speedy privatisation and commercialisation of these services. The Dovrat Reform actually demonstrates the intrusion of neo-liberal philosophy into the field of education. Its main thrust is to introduce quasi-market mechanisms such as consumer choice, competition among schools, along with organisational and managerial principles, which would dramatically transform the school power structure and redefine the roles, rights and duties of principals, teachers, students and parents.

However, despite its immersion in neo-liberal philosophy, one of the Dovrat Reform's main declared purposes is to bridge the dire educational gap between different groups in Israeli society. Accordingly, this reform includes important equality enhancement recommendations, such as free early age education and major investments in school infrastructure. But, as we demonstrated, the Report apparently vacillates in this regard. On some occasions it deems these recommendations necessary conditions for equal opportunities in education, yet on others it views them as ancillary and not an integral part of the Reform. This apparent vacillation, we argue, is not sincere, since the Report is faithful after all to the neo-liberal philosophy guiding its articulation, a philosophy that adheres to the policy of fiscal austerity and downplays the significance of budget increases as a necessary means to improve the education system. Furthermore, it is the same philosophy that upholds the introduction of market mechanisms into the field of education and recommends its semi-privatisation. We argued, then, that implementing this philosophy would most probably infringe upon the principle of equality of opportunity, and increase educational inequalities among different national and ethnic groups. The evidence accumulated in other societies in the world where such philosophy has been adopted provides support for our apprehension (Robertson & Dale, 2002; Whitty, 2002; Bonal, 2003).

Now, although the two major reforms we examined in this article differ from each other substantially, they still share an important common feature. The curricula and pedagogies aim at cultivating a very strong collective Jewish identity. Neither of these reforms adopts, as part of its curriculum, multicultural perspectives that leave enough room for the expression of other national identities, or includes the history and literature of Mizrahi pupils in any significant way. Thus, dialectically, while the economic, social, and educational gaps increase, and the equality of educational opportunity is undermined, leading to social alienation and disintegration, a strong nationalistic curriculum has been developed in order to counteract these disintegrating processes by forming in Israel's future citizens a robust national Jewish identity and a strong sense of community.

Notes

[1] In the year 2000 the act was changed so as to 'adjust it to contemporary educational reality'. Most changes, however, concerned the purpose of the state-secular stream and indicate a growing recognition of the multicultural nature of Israeli society. For instance, the act decrees that one of the purposes of education is to grant the children the possibility 'to know the language, culture, history, heritage and the unique tradition of the Arab population and other populations existing in Israel and to recognize the equal rights of all Israeli citizens' (article 2.11).

[2] Israel's Central Bureau of Statistics distinguishes between two categories of Israeli Jews, those who were born or whose father was born in Europe or America, who nowadays are referred to also as 'Ashkenazim', and Jews who were born, or their father was born in Asia or Africa, most of them from Islamic countries, and nowadays referred to as 'Mizrahim'. In this article we will use the terms 'Ashkenazim' and 'Mizrahim' to refer to these two categories of Israeli Jews.

[3] According to the data from Israel's Central Bureau of Statistics the total number of people living in Israel at the end of 2005 was 6,999,700, 76% of them Jewish, 19.7% Arabs and 4.3% defined as 'others', a category that consists mostly of non-Arab Christians. Out of the total Jewish population 39% are Ashkenazim, i.e. they or their father were born in Europe or America, and 27.4% of the total Jewish population are Mizrahim, i.e. they or their father were born in Asia or Africa. The rest are defined as native Israelis, i.e. they or their father were born in Israel.

[4] Ben Ari et al, write, 'Integration in the educational system is a preliminary necessary condition for building national social solidarity. It seems that ethnic integration in the educational system is a social imperative for Israel, in which all Jewish ethnic groups see themselves as an integral part of the Jewish nation and the Jewish people' (1985, p. 28).

[5] The reform in terms of creating new junior high schools among Israeli Arabs was very limited. In 1980 there were only twenty-five junior high schools serving Arab children (Swirski, 1990, pp. 157-158).

[6] As stated in a report prepared by the research and information centre of the Israeli Parliament, there are up-to-date figures concerning the extent of this phenomenon. However, it is commonly believed that it has grown drastically in the last decade (Knesset [The Parliament], 2003, p. 7).

[7] Kashti & Yosephon cite the Ministry of Education Peled Committee Report from 1976 that states, 'Vocational schools should be the answer for the education and socialization of students from the poor classes who need special treatment, this is their main and only alternative' (p. 15).

[8] The deficiencies in the implementation process included also the lack of special and unique teaching methods in the heterogoneous classes, appropriate learning materials, educational experimentations in order to find solutions to problems which might arise from such a drastic educational change, social activities geared to improving ethnic relationships and a pluralistic and multicultural core curriculum that includes learning materials from the different ethnic cultures (see Sharan et al, 1985, pp. 210-219)

[9] One of the educational reforms that some of the recommendations of the Dovrat Report is inspired by is the No Child Left Behind Act signed by US President George Bush in 2002.

[10] *Haaretz*, 30 May 2004.

[11] The Dovrat Report, Main Points of the Plan (English Translation), p. 9. http://cms.education.gov.il/NR/rdonlyres/EEE94632-B3D0-4D68-99DC-DE52F78FB0FC/960

[12] Yuli Hurmchenko, 'The Local Government Center against the Dovrat Report: most recommendations already exist but have not been yet allocated the necessary budgets,' *Haaretz*, 18 May 2004.

[13] Israel Central Bureau of Statistics, Press release, 3 August 2005.

[14] We have explored this dialectical process in our paper (Dahan & Yonah, 2005).

[15] See Dahan et al (2002).

References

Adler, H. (1985) Integration in Schools and the Developments in Israel's Education System, in Y. Amir, S. Sharan & R. Ben Ari, (Eds) *School Desegregation*. Tel Aviv: Am Oved Publishing [in Hebrew].

Adva (2002) *The Growth in Households' Expenditures on Education 1986/7-2001*. Tel Aviv: Adva Center.

Adva (2005) *Annual Report*. Tel Aviv: Adva Center.

Adva (2006) *The War on the Budget: 2006's budget and the war on poverty*. Tel Aviv: Adva Center.

Amir, B. & Ballas, N. (1985) The Development of the Ministry of Education's Social Integration Policy, in Y. Amir, S. Sharan & R. Ben Ari (Eds) *School Desegregation*. Tel Aviv: Am Oved Publishing [in Hebrew].

Bar-Siman-Tove, R. & Langerman, S. (1988) *Parent-Sponsored Additional Curriculum in Elementary Schools*. Jerusalem: Henrieta Szold Institute [in Hebrew].

Ben Ari, R., Sharan, S. & Amir, Y. (1985) Ethnic Integration in Education, What For? in Y. Amir, S. Sharan & R. Ben Ari (Eds) *School Desegregation*. Tel Aviv: Am Oved Publishing [in Hebrew].

Blanck, Y. (2004) Decentralized Statism: local government, segregation and inequality in public education, *Legal Studies*, 282, 347-417.

Bonal, Xavier (2003) Managing Education Legitimation Crisis in Neoliberal Contexts: some semiperipheral evidence.

http://www.keele.ac.uk/depts/ed/events/conf-pdf/cPaperBonal.pdf

Cohen, E. & Cohen, E. (1996) *The Gray Education in Israel: privately-sponsored additional curriculum (PAC) in the 90's*. Jerusalem: Institute of the Study of Educational Systems [in Hebrew].

Dahan, Y. & Yonah, Y. (2005) The Dovrat Report: on the neo-liberal revolution in education, *Theory and Criticism*, 27, 11-38 [in Hebrew].

Dahan, M., Mironichev, N., Dvir, E. & Shai, S. (2002) *Educational Gaps in Israel: have they narrowed? On the Factors Determining Eligibility for Matriculation Certificates*. Jerusalem: Van Leer Institute.

Dinur, B. (1958) *Values and Paths*. Tel Aviv: Urim [in Hebrew].

Gaziel, H.H. (1994) Implementing Reforms in a Centralized Education System: the case of Israeli education, *Oxford Review of Education*, 20(2), 237-252.

Glass, Jene (2005) *Grouping Students for Instruction*. Tempe: Arizona State University, Education Policy Studies Laboratory.

Goldring, E.B. (1991) Parents' Motives for Choosing a Privatized Public School System: an Israeli example, *Educational Policy*, 5(4), 412-426.

Hallinan, Maureen (2004) The Detracking Movement, *Education Next*, Fall, 73-76.

Hen, M. (1987) Education in Israel: between equality and excellence. Symposium, Skira Hodshit [in Hebrew].

Inbar, D. (1989), A 'Back Door' Process of Privatization: the case of Israel, in W.L. Boyd & J.G. Cibula (Eds) *Private Schools and Public Policy: international perspectives*, 268-284 (London: Falmer Press).

Israel (1981) *Report to the Knesset Education Commission of the 1968 Education Reform*. Jerusalem: Knesset Publication [in Hebrew].

Israel (1990-92) State Comptroller Reports. Jerusalem Government Publications [in Hebrew].

Israel Central Bureau of Statistics (ICBS) (2006) 19 March.

Kashti, I. (1991) *Cross-District Educational Framework*. Public Committee Report. Jerusalem: Ministry of Education [in Hebrew].

Kashti, Y. & Yosifon, M. (1985) *Education as Bargaining*. Tel Aviv: Hakibbutz Hameuchad [in Hebrew].

Kfir, D., Resh, N., Adler, H. & Safran, K. (1993) *School Integration: policy and implementation*. Jerusalem: The NCJW Research Institute for Innovation in Education, The Hebrew University of Jerusalem [in Hebrew].

Knesset Information and Research Center (2003) *Allocation of Resources in Education and Magnet Schools*. Jerusalem: The Knesset.

Mazawi, A. (1999) Concentrated Disadvantage and Access to Educational Credentials in Arab and Jewish Localities in Israel, *British Educational Research Journal*, 25(3), 355-370.

Ministry of Education (2005) *The National Task Force on Education: the National Education Plan* (The Dovrat Reform). Jerusalem: Ministry of Education.

Rawls, J. (2001) *Justice as Fairness – a restatement*. Cambridge, MA: Harvard University Press.

Resh, N. & Dar, I. (1996) Segregation within Integration in Israeli Junior High Schools, *Israel Social Science Research*, 11(1), 1-22.

Robertson, Susan & Robert Dale (2002) Local State of Emergency: the contradiction of neo-liberal government in New Zealand, *British Journal f Sociology of Education*, 23(3), 463-482.

Saban, I. (2002) The Collective Rights of the Arab-Palestinian Minority: what there is and what there is not and the sphere of the taboo, *Legal Studies*, 26(1), 241-319 [in Hebrew].

Shapira, R. (1988) *Socio-Educational Specialty: special schools, background, development and problems – a proposal*. Tel-Aviv: Tel-Aviv University, School of Education [in Hebrew].

Sharan, S., Amir, Y. & Ben Ari, R. (1985) Ethnic Integration in Schools: future challenges, in Y. Amir, S. Sharan & R. Ben Ari (Eds) *School Desegregation*. Tel Aviv: Am Oved Publishing [in Hebrew].

Stahl A. (1991) Education Reform in Israel: the implementation of integration in intermediate school, *Curriculum and Teaching*, 6(1), 59-66.

Swirski, S. (1990) *Education in Israel: schooling for inequality*. Tel Aviv. Brerot Publishing [in Hebrew].

Swirski, S. & Schwartz, I. (2005) Matriculation Exams Success Rate 2003-2004. Tel Aviv: Adva Center.

Whitty, G. (1997) Creating Quasi-Markets in Education, in M.W. Apple (Ed.) *Review of Research in Education*, 22, 3-47.

Whitty G. (2002) *Making Sense of Education Policy*. London: Sage.

Yonah, Y. & Dahan, Y. (1999) The Education System in a Transition Phase: from collectivism to civil individualism – parental choice as a case study, in Elad Peled (Ed.) *Fifty Years of Israeli Education*, 163-179. Jerusalem: The Ministry of Defense Press.

Yonah, Y. & Saporta, I. (2006) The Wavering Luck of Girls: gender and pre-vocational education in Israel, *Journal of Middle East Women's Studies*, 2(3), 71-101.

The Moment of Education: the politics of education among the Negev Bedouin, Israel

RICHARD RATCLIFFE

Introduction

In recent years, the Negev Bedouin have come to show a new political interest in education. Over the last 10-15 years, the provision of Bedouin education in the Negev has become a political issue. For a brief period state provision of education became one of the key sites of Bedouin political activism and a vehicle for a range of other political struggles among the Negev Bedouin community. This moment of education can be interpreted as shedding light on a number of politicised debates on Negev Bedouin 'modernisation' and their positioning vis-à-vis various political projects in Israel/Palestine. This chapter will argue that Negev Bedouin educational politics was significant both for the way it facilitated new modes and forms of politics within the community, and also for the way in which it was sufficiently pliable to become a channel for many older agendas. It will also argue that educational campaigning was politically significant for what it did not speak about, and for the limits of education's political role. In all this, the case of the Negev Bedouin highlights the fundamental ambiguity of education's political role in state–society relations.

This chapter attempts to look at what happened within this educational activism, and why. This activism is relevant to an established body of literature on education and the contestation of power, a body that is characterised by two mutually opposed trends, looking either at formal education's liberatory potential (Paulston, 1980; Petherbridge-Hernandez, 1990; Millar, 1991; Freire, [1970] 1996; Dyer & Choksi, 1998; Champagne & Abu Saad, 2005), or its inherent coercive dimension (Illich, 1973; Foucault, 1976; Karabel & Halsey, 1977). More locally, this contestation of formal education provision is significant due to its implications for conventional wisdom about the Negev Bedouin. There is a large body of academic knowledge charting the distant relationship between the Bedouin and education, highlighting the gap between Bedouin parents and the school

(Abu Saad et al, 1998); the school as a culturally alien environment (Abu Saad & Hendrix, 1995); high Bedouin drop-out rates and low achievement rates (Abu Saad, 1991, 1997). The rising profile of education among the Negev Bedouin is also significant as a potential indicator on specific debates on Bedouin development, where an increasing engagement with education is often a key component of the modernisation of nomads (Meir, 1997); on Bedouin integration into the state, where the processes of social change lead them to want the same norms as everyone else; and on increasing Bedouin nationalism, since education is often central to nationalist movements and seen as a sign of a nationalist or even Islamist awakening. The rise of a concern about education is significant for all these different debates on the Negev Bedouin, but it allows for ambiguous and even contradictory interpretations. This is part of its interest.

Negev Bedouin and Education

The Negev Bedouin constitute approximately 140,000 (Palestinian) Arab citizens in Israel. They live in the metropolitan Beer Sheva area, in the north-east of the Negev desert. Historically, the Negev Bedouin have been administratively, and to a certain extent socially, segregated from the rest of the Arab population in Israel. Until recently, the Negev Bedouin were a peripheral and rather romanticised minority within both Israeli and Palestinian political landscapes. They have been subject to a process of state-planned sedentarisation, which has involved a mixture of in situ urbanisation and geographic concentration. This process has been narrated through a discourse of modernisation and development. At present, the process as planned is incomplete since half the Negev Bedouin live in state-planned localities, and half outside, in what have come to be known as the 'unrecognised villages'.

In recent years, however, the Negev Bedouin have come to take on a new centrality in Israeli politics. Over the past decade, rising contestation of the state's sedentarisation plan has made the Negev Bedouin central both to the new post-Oslo Nationalism [1] of the 'Palestinian national minority in Israel', where the Negev has become 'Al-Naqab', an iconic symbol of Israeli state discrimination; and also to neo-Zionism, where in place of the old romanticism they have come to symbolise the internal Arab threat, in terms of demography, land, security, and perhaps even the existential impossibility for social integration.

Negev Bedouin education is provided by the Israeli state. At present, education is free from ages 5 to 18, and compulsory from ages 5 to 16, and in some areas from 3 to 16. Over the past century Bedouin schools have experienced a process of expansion, and extension to more and more areas. This is narrated as one of linear growth, even if provision has been denied and schools have been closed as well as opened for political reasons (Abu Saad, 2001; Abu Rabia, 2001). Bedouin formal education provision is largely universal today. The Bedouin education system is segregated from other Israeli communities either by language, geography or administrative structure. Its curriculum is standard for Arabic medium schools, and is highly controlled (Mar'I, 1978; Copty, 1990; Al-Haj, 1995). The educational outcome is characterised by low achievements. As of the late 1990s, there was a matriculation rate from high school of only 6%, a drop-out rate of over 60% of students, and only 2 in 1000 Negev Bedouin students went on to further education (Abu Saad, 1997). The Bedouin school system also employs many non-Bedouin teaching staff, historically acting as the employer of last resort for Arab graduates within the segregated Israeli labour market. Within this school system, decision-making and managerial appointments are highly controlled by the state, with the security services involved in all appointments (Human Rights Watch [HRW], 2001)

> Facilities and equipment are insufficient and in some cases, altogether lacking. This is especially true for the schools in spontaneous tribal settlements which the government considers temporary. Currently there are eleven temporary and eighteen permanent Bedouin primary schools in the Negev. These temporary schools in unplanned settlements are poorly equipped, have low budgets, inadequate facilities, poor buildings and furnishings, and few teaching materials. They often suffer from a complete lack of facilities and materials such as audiovisual, computers, laboratory and sports equipment etc. They are mostly housed in tin, wooden or concrete buildings with insufficient classroom and office space. In general, they are not supplied with running water and electricity, although some are found next to water pipes or electric lines. As a rule, these schools are not expanded and are poorly maintained. In contrast to temporary schools, permanent schools are located in government planned settlements or on the sites of future developments, and are better equipped. Most of them are housed in modern buildings, and have electricity and running water. But even they do not have sufficient laboratories, libraries or other teaching materials.'(Katz Committee Report, 1998)[2]

The Moment of Education:
educational contestation 1994-2005

Since the mid 1990s, there has been much discussion among community groups, political parties, and among the national and even international media on education provision for the Negev Bedouin. This led to what might be called 'the moment of education', where education became both the most prominent political issue in the community, and a vehicle for a wide array of other politics, including struggles over land, development and demography. Though a number of institutional factors are relevant to this increased interest in education, such as, in particular, the establishment of the Shatil Beer Sheva office [3], which coordinated efforts which led to the establishment of the Katz Committee, whose findings are encapsulated in the quotation above, a campaign explicitly to lobby for improved Bedouin education in the wake of these findings was initiated through the funding of an American Jewish philanthropist, Bob Arnow.[4] Though there was opposition to the campaign from other community groups, particularly with regard to control over funding, from its first meeting in October 1999, the campaign gradually came to form a unanimous demand from community representatives and to become increasingly institutionalised.

The campaign was oriented around two main interests: to improve the material provision of education, and to raise the importance of education within the Bedouin community. As part of the campaign, Bedouin groups began preparing briefing papers on the state of Bedouin education. They held a series of demonstrations on the situation of Bedouin education, and even school strikes were organised. A number of specialist lobbies on different aspects of Bedouin education were organised, with a pre-school lobby, a special education lobby, and a union of parents' committees. A local Arabic language newspaper was published on the development of Bedouin education. Significant efforts were devoted to lobbying the Knesset, particularly its Children's Committee, which led to a regular special hearing for Bedouin education. Other bodies were enrolled to the cause: as a result of this dynamism, national organisations, such as the Follow Up Committee on Arab Education, and non-governmental organizations (NGOs) such as the Arab parliamentiary lobbying group, Mosawa, and Adalah: the legal Centre for Arab Minority Rights all started to lobby on behalf of Bedouin educational rights. The campaign reached out even more widely, with speaking tours to New York, and it even involved Human Rights Watch in a report on Arab education (HRW, 2001). Political parties also took up the issue of Bedouin education as part of their programme, and eventually a whole structure of lobbying was organized, with the aim of improving the Bedouin school system.

The main issues on which the campaign focused were material. Though it was to become a general critique of structural discrimination, in its initial stages, the campaign focused on the most tangible issues of education provision. Its first activity was to challenge the building quality of Bedouin schools, and in particular their asbestos roofs. There was pressure over the number of schools serving the community, and then on the general quality of conditions in the temporary schools of the unrecognised villages. Most prominently, this pressure identified their lack of electricity and water, though it remained a rolling critique of a number of issues.

There was also a sustained attempt to establish a new high school for the unrecognised villages, which ultimately failed. The campaign highlighted the economic absurdity of the Ministry's transportation policy that bussed children up to 70 km each way daily rather than open a high school nearer to their homes. A similar approach was taken in lobbying for kindergartens to be established for the Bedouin community and especially for the unrecognised villages, which made use of a new pre-school law which called for compulsory free kindergartens for all children aged three and over. There had been no state-funded kindergartens in the unrecognised villages prior to 2000, although lobbying successfully secured the promise of thirty-nine kindergartens from the Ministry of Education. The campaign also focused on special education, and especially educational provision for deaf children, since there had been none for the Bedouin previously.

Among this discourse of a lack of schools and problems of transportation, there was a particular focus on the issues of Bedouin children dropping out of school, and on girls' education. These two concerns were often conflated, since there were many families who did not send their girls to school after eighth grade, and some who did not send them beyond sixth grade. The campaign also highlighted the achievement levels of the Bedouin education system, focusing on the low pass rates, matriculation rates, and numbers going to further education. It consistently made the link between the poor material situation and the low achievements in Bedouin schools.

As the campaign progressed, its material focus became more diversified. It went on to discuss the quality of teachers and lack of Bedouin teachers in Bedouin schools, emphasising the prevalence of teachers who were unqualified and outsiders. Moreover, as more fundamental successes were achieved, the material focus shifted towards discrimination in general auxiliary services, highlighted through services such as educational psychologists or afternoon enrichment programmes provided for Jews and not Arabs. In this critique, there was little that addressed the curriculum.

Nonetheless, perhaps the most memorable cause of the campaign was the one that was not actually material. The high point of the campaign was an attempt to replace the head of the Bedouin Education Authority, Moshe Shohat, in the wake of his racist comments about Bedouin activists. His comments to the effect that the educational activists' complaints of a lack of running water in their schools should be disregarded as they were 'blood-thirsty Bedouins [*sic*] who commit polygamy, have 30 children and continue to expand their illegal settlements taking over state land ... In their culture, they take care of their needs outdoors. They don't even know how to flush a toilet' [5], were to take on an almost iconic status, even beyond his eventual removal from office.

New Knowledge

As part of the campaign, there was a whole new body of knowledge produced on Bedouin education, with statistics on achievement levels, years of education, *bagrut* pass rates, drop-out rates, literacy rates, the number of Bedouin teachers, the proportion unqualified. All the schools and pupils in the unrecognised villages were surveyed, so as to be able to prove numerically the lack of facilities. Much of this statistical material had to be gathered independently, as the authorities were uncooperative. Much of this information on Negev Bedouin education was produced in English, or simultaneously in English and Hebrew for an external audience, such as for foreign media or international fora, such as the United Nations human rights system (Levinson, 1999; 2004; Maan, 2005), or was even produced by external bodies such as Human Rights Watch (HRW, 2001).

The overriding aim of this knowledge was to prove that the low status of Bedouin education was not caused by 'cultural' reasons, but rather by unequal material conditions and discrimination. In order to do so, the form that this knowledge took was very significant. It made great use of statistics, with budgets, and pass rates and numbers of classrooms. It put the idea of Bedouin education into numbers, and had a credibility with the outside world because it did so. Similarly, it made use of resonant quotations, which represented discrimination and the racism underpinning it, and representative visual images. Visually, the schools in the unrecognised villages came to embody discrimination, and especially the school in Wadi Naam, which was the most overcrowded school in Israel, and was situated next to a foul-smelling chemical plant that even the nearby military camp had been relocated from.[6] The narrative of this new knowledge was quite simple: There is discrimination; here are some manifestations of it. Paradoxically, this notion of discrimination was to take on an increasingly amaterial quality. The discourse had almost an autonomous quality, as though there was discrimination which had material examples, but was anterior to them.

Court Cases

As a key component of the campaign, a number of cases went to the High Court to improve different aspects of Bedouin education. Court activism became an increasing part of the campaign strategy. Initially, this activism was led by Jewish groups, though a nascent Arab human rights infrastructure soon came to focus on Bedouin issues. Moreover, non-legal Arab NGOs came to be increasingly involved in a number of court cases, and legal strategies came to dominate the activists' work, to the extent that court cases came to be the hallmark of a new activism.

As a whole the human rights groups organised a series of court challenges to state policies that were strikingly effective. There was a petition to provide electricity for the temporary schools built in the unrecognised villages. There was a petition for three more schools to be built in the unrecognised villages. There was a case for more schools to be provided for the Azazmeh, the most remote of the Bedouin tribes, which resulted in the school at Wadi Naam being divided into two, and a new school being established at Bir Haddaj. There was a petition for pre-schools to be provided in the recognised locality of Segev Shalom. There was a case for more educational psychologists in Bedouin schools. Not all school cases were won: there was the petition for a high school for the unrecognised villages, which was lost. The most celebrated case was the Shohat, the court case to remove the head of the Bedouin Education Authority for racist statements mentioned above. This was partially successful, in that he was removed for corruption rather than racism, though for the activists it felt like a success of their strategy.

Impact

As a whole, the lobbying to improve education had a significant impact on Bedouin education provision. It had an impact that went far beyond the previous achievements of the political parties and personal petitions. In its wake, the Government established a series of committees, including the Katz Committee and the Melitz Committee, to discuss Bedouin education. These investigatory committees led to an increased investment: NIS 50 million extra was promised to be spent on Bedouin education over the coming five years, and there was an increased focus on Bedouin education in a new five-year plan for Arab education. Education in Bedouin localities, recognised and unrecognised, was awarded National Priority Status A by the Government. Specifically, their main recommendation was to improve facilities in the temporary schools. Concrete action was taken on a number of the other issues raised: the Minister of Education made it a priority that pre-schools be established in the unrecognised villages. There was a new effort to recruit and train more Bedouin teachers. There was an increased focus on Bedouin pass rates in matriculation examinations, and a real increase in the pressure on schools to improve their achievements. There was also a focus on the issue of girls dropping out of school, and simultaneously on the numbers of girls in university.

In particular, extra efforts were made by Ben Gurion University, the regional university in the Negev, to improve especially Bedouin girls' educational achievements. A scholarship programme was established, which grew in the space of ten years from funding two girls from unrecognised villages to every Bedouin girl at university, whose numbers increased from an annual intake of 10 to over 150. Similarly, a Centre for Bedouin Studies and Development was set up, as a channel for research on the Bedouin and also to provide extra programmes for Bedouin students. To support this work, a whole infrastructure of university NGOs was set up around this to further Bedouin education, such as the Association for the Promotion of Bedouin Women's Education, and a Study Guidance Centre. This push resulted in a number of firsts, with the first Bedouin girl studying medicine, the first starting a PhD programme.

Politically, the court case to remove Shohat marked the most open attack on a whole structure of governance, though it was always couched as a personal challenge, of a man inappropriately employed, rather than an inappropriate system. Throughout the lobbying efforts, the campaign experienced considerable manoeuvring by different arms of the authorities however, such that while one arm gave a permit, another prevented it, and an instability to their gains, since the courts never actually ruled in favour of the Bedouin, but would merely pressure the authorities into making extra-judicial concessions. At the height of the campaign, however, Bedouin activists did observe quite optimistically the sense of achievement and development in their community. Similarly, Jewish activists felt they had contributed to democracy in Israel. As times changed, and the authorities became less willing to concede gains, this sense of achievement began to feel increasingly hollow, and many of the key Bedouin activists moved on to other concerns.

Nonetheless, for Bedouin politics, the education campaign was significant in three ways: firstly, it marked a new political discourse, citizenship, and a new mode of politics, which I term 'technopolitics'; secondly, it was sufficiently pliable to allow the articulation of many older forms of politics; and thirdly, it also highlighted some of the political boundaries facing the Negev Bedouin.

New Politics

The campaign marked a new politics in the Negev. This was both a new discourse for politics, and a new mode of politics.

New Discourse: citizenship and discrimination

The education campaign also marked a new political discourse among the Bedouin of Arab 'citizenship'. Citizenship was taken up as a distinctive slogan and political aspiration by the Arab leadership in the wake of the Oslo process. The slogan of the 'State for all its citizens' underpinned a campaign for the de-Zionisation of the state, for a new Israel in the wake of the new peace agreements that would include the Arabs as a constituent part of the nation rather than as a potential 'Fifth Column'. Education was the vehicle for repackaging Bedouin concerns around these ideas of discrimination and citizenship rights.

Thus the Bedouin lobbied for education, no longer on the grounds that they had special needs as Bedouin, but because they were citizens, and had rights. The new citizenship discourse had a new sense of entitlement, and it gave the Bedouin a different way of relating to the Government. The new discourse was very effective at challenging the special treatment of the Bedouin and the structural discrimination focused at them. It presented this discrimination as an active process, *'siyasat al-tajhil'*, rather than passive neglect. There was a whole infrastructure built up consistently identifying 'gaps' and 'lacks'. The logic of the discrimination discourse was, however, adopted gradually, and the focus on education, and particularly on issues such as special education and kindergartens, was the softest way to discuss discrimination, appealing to an image of the government's patrician benevolence.

The education campaign also facilitated the growth of the Bedouin at the centre of the citizenship discourse nationally, as the symbol of Palestinian Arab citizens suffering from discrimination. While Bedouin schools did not represent discrimination, as the unrecognised villages came to, Bedouin schools most effectively articulated to the external world the discrimination that Bedouin villages came to represent. Thus, Bedouin education became a way to talk about discrimination for the whole Arab minority.

New Mode of Politics: technopolitics

The educational campaign not only marked a new discourse for politics in the Negev, it also became a key site for introducing a new mode of politics which I have termed 'technopolitics'. Technopolitics is the contestation of issues in a manner that styles itself as a neutral dispute of a technical issue. It develops in a context where governance operates in a manner that styles itself as the neutral implementation of technical regulations, for instance, conceiving a process of forcible eviction and house demolition as the due process of planning regulations, or upholding the rule of law. Within technopolitics, since power is asserted as a technical issue, it is also contested as a technical argument. A territorial conflict is reconfigured as a discussion over the most appropriate form of planning, a movement for cultural autonomy is reconfigured as an argument over the safety aspects of including Arabic on road signs. Technopolitics is thus simultaneously both a mode of politics, and also the way in which this politics is euphemised. In practical terms, technopolitics involves the use of the courts, of lobbying and campaigning, the use of demonstrations and speaking tours. It operates to challenge administrative decisions, planning policies and so on, specifically within the terms of their own moral universe.

Technopolitics is distinctive in its indirect relationship to power, in that it neither constitutes a direct claim to power, nor an invocation of power politics. Rather, it has an integrationist logic. It operates through a complex mechanics of persuasion. Its campaign methods are far more related to the articulation of a narrative. Thus, while it uses courts, or lobbying, or campaigning, and even holds demonstrations, these are often done for coverage rather than as a demonstration of power.

This engagement with technopolitics was new for the Bedouin. To a national and international audience, the campaign marketed the technical idea that something needed to be done about Bedouin education. Technopolitics reconfigured the idea of Bedouin education as a technical problem that needed to be addressed through such issues as planning, zoning and budgets. It used the discourses of rights and of professionalism to challenge a number of governmental practices, and to coalesce a number of forces behind them. Technopolitics was able to deconstruct much of the ontology that had built up about tradition and modernity. With time, the community became increasingly skilled in their operation of technopolitics, and their capacity to highlight increasingly specific complaints, rather than an easily dismissed, if not inaccurate, general rhetoric.

It was also aimed at a local audience and devoted many resources to the regular production of an Arabic language newspaper reviewing the situation of Bedouin education. Compared to earlier competitive strategies of patronage, this mode of politics was particularly good at uniting the community. The campaign highlighted this by providing an issue around which everyone could mobilise.

Education's Pliability

The education campaign was also significant for what was old about it. The call for Bedouin education was pliable and ambiguous, and meant different things for different people. This ambiguity allowed for the euphemised articulation of older struggles and politics, as education came to coalesce around a number of different discourses and agendas.

Development

Ironically, at one level, the educational discourse was a vehicle for the continuation of the state's policies of development and sedentarization. In its focus on a material citizenship, education lobbying was strikingly normative. It called for educational development, to have the same provision as the Jews for Bedouin daughters, or for the youngest Bedouin children. In this, the education campaign replicated the kind of territorial modernity that is so prominent in Israel (Sa'di, 1997), both vis-à-vis the Jews (wanting to be modern like them) and within Bedouin society (wanting the Bedouin of the unrecognised villages to be modern like the Bedouin of the towns).[7] People were not confronting this discursive regime, but making some space for themselves within it.

In the brief post-Oslo period, the citizenship discourse was focused on inclusion in national development. Bedouin educational development was translated into a series of normative demands, of wanting the same as other Israeli communities, and notions such as closing the 'gap'. At the structural level, this approach had an integrationist logic, where the expansion of education was for the authorities closely related to the idea that the Bedouin needed to be included in Israeli society and economy, and where an equality discourse among activists was predicated on demanding sedentarised norms.

Consequently, the education campaign focused a significant proportion of its efforts on a local audience, and on convincing them that they needed to develop, that education specifically is the way for them to develop, and that accordingly, they needed to invest in education. Thus they needed to send their daughters to school; thus parents needed to get involved in their children's education again.

Land

Simultaneously, the education campaign was also an articulation of Bedouin land politics. More specifically, it was about the instrumental use of public services in the battle to resettle the Bedouin, or for them to be able to stay on their land. It was this land dispute that gave the educational lobbying such a material focus. One of the key justifications for the relocation of the Bedouin had always been the need to provide them with modern public services. This was backed up materially by a lower grade provision of services outside the state-declared 'modern' areas. The argument was premised on their special characteristics as nomads, which meant that they were too scattered and remote, and even transient, to be able to provide them with an education. This approach was even written into the school curriculum, which emphasised the wretched life of those Bedouin outside the planned towns.

Bedouin tribes who were looking to get their tenure acknowledged had no chance when lobbying directly for land rights. However, within the wider 'recognition' paradigm, they were able to lobby for education provision on their lands. Education was especially useful because there were a number of enshrined legal rights that the Bedouin could claim. They adopted a strategy of creeping consolidation of tenure, lobbying for the extension of public services and the de facto recognition of the community by the state authorities.

The education campaign should be seen in terms of subverting this paradigm, for de-linking service provision from the land struggle, turning it into an autonomous 'right' or an aspect of 'citizenship'. Whereas previously people had been faced with a binary choice, either to learn or to stay on their land, now, within the new rubric, they were able to stay on their land and get their rights. The new discourse undercut the whole positive justification of the resettlement policy. Campaigners were able to highlight how far more remote new Jewish farmers were getting all the services that the Bedouin were deemed too remote to be provided with, to point out how needlessly far Bedouin schools were from Bedouin localities, the educational impact of the travelling involved, and the overcrowded nature and deliberately poor environmental quality of existing Bedouin schools. The approach of the campaign was effective in disproving the romantic idea that there were all these tiny remote village schools that the Ministry was struggling to run for the Bedouin, much like it did on the neighbouring kibbutzes. Rather, it observed that the Azazmeh school, notionally the most remote school in the country, also happened to be the biggest elementary school in Israel, with over 1300 pupils bussed in daily from as far away as 70km to a site on the outskirts of a toxic chemical dump.

Education was particularly useful in this land battle because it was on the surface so depoliticised. Paradoxically, this strategy deliberately packaged itself as claims for education 'rights' without reference to the land dispute. The focus was on special education, kindergartens and schools, the most innocuous forms of provision. It called simply for what the state claimed it wanted to provide. Like Scott's 'infrapolitics' (Scott, 1990), it used the terminology and moral universe of the state's own discourse. The effectiveness of the discourse lay in the fact that it pointedly denied that it was about land. Rather, it asserted consistently that the land dispute and service provision should be de-linked: While negotiations over land are continuing, Bedouin children should not be punished. The outcome was the extension of public services, and ultimately subsequent recognition for a number of villages.

Gender and Demography

Throughout the educational campaign, there was a specific interest in women's education. In part this was a function of development, and a notion of modernisation and modern culture which implies certain roles for women and their equal participation on a socio-economic level. Thus, a focus on women's education is a keen concern of developmentalists generally, and Bedouin women's low levels of education are often a symbol for Bedouin backwardness. In part, however, this concern was a function of Israeli notions of security, though obviously addressed in a euphemised form. The idea of the (Arab) demographic threat, and the need to maintain a demographic balance between Arabs and Jews, has always held within Israel, though it took on a new prominence with the arrival of the new Palestinian citizenship discourse. A concern for women's education was an articulation of this concern, due to the established correlation in development between lower fertility rates and higher levels of female education (Sen, 1999). Indeed, the National Demographic Council identified Bedouin women as a key concern for its work. Their demographic concern was a key impetus behind the focus on Bedouin women's education and especially further education to delay their fertility and lower Bedouin birth rates. Thus, the focus on Bedouin education was for many of the institutions involved a focus on Bedouin women's education and there was a great rhetorical focus on girls' schooling. For example, the drop-out problem was presented as though it was just a female issue.

Segmentary Politics

At the same time, the education campaign also turned out to be an articulation of the segmentary mode of politics traditionally observed by anthropologists of the Bedouin (Dresch, 1986; Caton, 1987; Shryock, 1997; Parizot, 2001), a politics of a shifting balance of opposition between tribes and kin-groups agonistically testing each other's power. The modes of competition within this politics were evident in two ways. Firstly, the logics of segmentary organising and alliance building underpinned the new activism. While there was the idea of a new coalition, and a discourse that for the first time they were all working together rather than for narrow partisan interests, the old modes of segmentary mobilisation were predominant in terms of who came, and how the different lobbying groups were organised.

Secondly, the new technopolitics came to be a vehicle for segmentary politics, such that segmentary battles often seemed to underpin the demands of the education campaign. Within segmentary politics, there is not really a political focus on educational output, or on the educational project itself, but rather in a localised sense on the politics of occupation, of getting one's own tribe in control, and of one's family, tribe, community acquiring more of the public service 'cake'. The education campaign tended to focus on arguments that fitted within the logic of these segmentary demands. Thus, for instance, the broad slogans of the campaign argued for more local teachers, and for the replacement of the northern teachers on the grounds that the children could not understand their accents. Similarly, the demand for new schools gave a lot of scope for inter-tribe competition over the siting of these schools. This had the effect of families boycotting schools awarded to the wrong family, and increased trouble between the pupils from different families, until each got their own school. Moreover, control of schools, and the education department became a prominent part of local elections.

This segmentary politics could often seem to give the discrimination discourse quite a parochial quality, and to sustain the narrative and self-perception of the Bedouin as having special problems. Thus, while the citizenship discourse implied a different relationship to the Government, it still took a while before it stopped being effectively a call for special treatment.

Limits of Education

There were limits to education's pliability with regard to all issues. The education campaign was conspicuous in its silence on addressing three issues: the politics of culture; structures of surveillance and control within the education system; and the internal complicity with the networks of patronage that had developed within it.

Cultural Politics

One might have expected a cultural focus to the education campaign, as the citizenship movement it articulated was also the site for a new identity politics, of the Palestinian national minority in Israel, of putting Arabic into the public sphere and asserting 'recognition' for Arab culture.[8] Thus, one might have expected this cultural focus to have been a core strategy for the educational activism, since it was a motivation for a number of the groups involved. This is aside from the fact that cultural politics is a key part of the use of education by most nationalist movements.

Beyond this trend, there were further reasons why one might have expected a cultural concern from the Bedouin when education became such a political issue. Nomads are notoriously wary about the state intruding on their ways, and held to be keenly aware of the reconfiguring effects that education has on culture (Kratli, 2001). Moreover, the destruction of the pastoral way of life under state sedentarisation has provoked a cultural disorientation and profound sense of moral loss. Similarly, the modern planned urban settlements are critiqued heavily for being unsuitable for their culture. Combined with a growing discourse of a clash of civilisations, there is a sense among the Negev Bedouin that their culture is actively under threat. Accordingly, there has been an increasing concern for their *adat wa taqalid* (customs and traditions) over the past two decades, and a growth in mosque building, religious observance and a newly standardised Islamic dress. This trend in particular is much politicised in the Israeli media, and supports in turn a developmentalist discourse that there is a need to modernise Bedouin culture further to prevent extremism.

Yet it is striking how little of these concerns entered the political debates on education during the educational campaign. Within the campaign, formal education was not identified as part of the alien modern world. Though it is seen as modern, and though historically perceptions may have been different (Abu Saad, 1991), the school is now broadly seen as a Bedouin environment: it is in a Bedouin town, it has Bedouin students and Bedouin teachers; the Bedouin occupy it. Cultural activism in so far as it occurs in schools is almost entirely folkloric celebrations of Bedouin heritage.

Moreover, any references to culture within the educational campaign tended to replicate one of two kinds of politics that were the opposite of nationalism. They either furthered a politics of special claims. Cultural needs were used in a pre-citizenship sense to justify an entitlement to special treatment, and most usually quite pragmatically, either to obtain more funding, or more employment for relatives or neighbours. Similarly, educational initiatives to lobby for the right to their culture did not challenge the cultural transformation of modernisation, but if anything facilitated it, since they used culture primarily for egalitarian demands within a certain form. In doing so, they subordinated this culture not to an orthodoxy, but an orthopraxy of the contemporary secular order. This can be seen most clearly in Bedouin MK Talab Al-Sane's campaign to draft a new law getting the education system to acknowledge the same number of feast days for both Muslim and Jewish students, which implicitly constructed Bedouin culture as a series of homologous diacritics framed by the majority's sense of its own culture, while experiencing this culture within that framing as something authentic. Like so much contemporary orthopraxy, it is experienced as a kind of resistance that is simultaneously a kind of cooptation. It did not attempt to safeguard culture in the terms discussed by political agendas elsewhere in the community.

Internal and External Control

The second area where the educational discourse was conspicuously silent was in the control of the education system, specifically the control of its higher echelons, of curriculum design, and of the involvement of the security services. Generally a close control of the Bedouin education system is maintained by the Jewish authorities, and Bedouin head teachers are very wary of political activities, since they are held to account for their political involvement. The Bedouin education system is closely monitored by the security services and all appointments are vetted by them. Appointments of unqualified candidates are often made for political reasons.

The educational campaign made no challenge to this system of control, except for an effort to personally remove the head of the Bedouin Education Authority, and references to an abstract need for greater professionalism. In meetings it barely even discussed it. This is somewhat surprising, as one would expect the new citizenship discourse to have addressed these control mechanisms, since they are the clearest violation of educational rights. Discourse notwithstanding, in terms of power relations they are also one of the clearest points at which to contest state control.

While on a national level there was some discussion of the control and administration of Arab education throughout the 1990s, nothing of this was mentioned by the Bedouin campaign activists, even if the structures of control were made visible by the Shohat case. Control over curriculum design remained unchallenged, and was not mentioned as an issue, since the campaign derogated its position to that of the national body, the Follow Up Committee on Arab Education. Most pointedly, however, the educational lobbying was silent on the interference of the General Security Services in the Arab education system, policing teacher and head appointments, and monitoring the 'political' activities in school and of those involved with the Bedouin education system. The security concerns highlight the fact that the cohesion and unity of the campaign was precarious. The Negev Bedouin are a structurally divided community, and there was a need to avoid internal disputes. Even though broadly education was an easy point of commonality, the campaign's initial strategy was to avoid anything that was internally controversial and that was perceived to be too confrontational.

At the same time, the campaign averted controversy by not challenging any of the community's material interests, and only working to further them. Thus the campaign was largely silent on the internal dimensions of the patronage system that had built up around the segregated system of Bedouin governance, and indeed was sustained in part by the security services interventions. The criticism was personal to Shohat, rather than a more systemic critique of the Bedouin Education Authority's divisive policy of patronage networks. There was little concrete discussion of the internal aspects of the corruption in educational appointments, beyond the affirmation of the need for 'professional' teachers and heads. There was a criticism of the old sheikhs involved in the Bedouin Education Authority, but for their lack of qualification as educators rather than their structural position within the state's system of patronage. Moreover, the campaign avoided any discussion of more parochial issues that might have proved internally divisive, such as in which tribes the new schools or kindergartens should be sited. This silence was a marker of the campaigners' limited weight within the community, despite their external prominence. It also gave the discourses of communitarian and national unity, deployed extensively by the Bedouin and external activists, a somewhat complex quality.

Conclusion: after the moment

This limited pliability has become more evident over recent years, as history has moved on. With the end of the Oslo period and outbreak of the second Intifada, there has been the end of the moment of inclusive citizenship, a return to older forms of power politics, a trend towards separation between Arabs and Jews, and a series of measures and statements delegitimising Arab citizenship (Sultany, 2003; Cook, 2006). This changed climate has had a profound effect on the efficacy of attempts to lobby for improved Bedouin education provision, and educational technopolitics suddenly became far less effective. Moreover, education has been far less able to euphemise other struggles, or be a channel through which all agendas were passed. There has been a breakdown of the old consensus among the different agendas working for education, which has created an increasing sense of ambiguity in their partnerships. Accordingly, over the last five years, the campaign has become intermittent, and struggled to hold a coherence. Active educational lobbying has gradually lost its political orientation and only been sustained as a material track for educational NGOs and individual academics and activists.

Even allowing for these setbacks, the education campaign has had a number of lingering consequences. Though it is beyond the scope of this article to do more than mention them in passing, at the political level, the past decade of educational campaigning has marked the passing of a segregated mode of governance for the Bedouin, and the extension of modern modes of governance as elected local authorities were established among them. It has also been relevant to the growth of moral orders that support this mode of governance; to three 'modern' political discourses surrounding the Bedouin; to notions of Bedouin 'modernisation', in that it led to a shift in aspirations away from an autonomous 'freedom' and towards a normative 'equality', and the growth of a new class of Bedouin activists working for 'social change' and 'development'; to notions of Bedouin 'democratisation', in that it led to a sincerely held assertion of Bedouin rights and citizenship, and their integration into mainstream Israeli and Palestinian structures of representation; and even to notions of a Bedouin nationalist awakening, in that for all its cultural silence, material focus and integrationist logic, the education campaign marked the increasing structural engagement of the Bedouin with Palestinian nationalist activism, concerns and iconography.

The way the campaign was fought, the structures it developed, and the subjectivities it engendered all highlighted the development of a new mode of international governance and structure of power that is increasingly significant in the Negev, as well as in Israel/Palestine and beyond. The contestation of education highlighted processes that have led to the creation of a new Bedouin civil society and advocacy industry, and the indigenous subjectivities to embody it; and to the 'NGOisation' of politics through the medium of advocacy and the construction of all political struggles as predominantly technical issues marketed by a narrative that is simultaneously a problem and solution, where any given political incident is relegated to become an iconic manifestation of this narrative. It produced new ideas about the Bedouin and 'the Bedouin's struggle', sustained both by outsiders and increasingly the Bedouin themselves. It marked the internationalisation of Bedouin politics, and the reconfiguring of the Bedouin as locals for an international audience, and the rise in power of international institutions and fora at the expense of the national. In Israel/Palestine, with the focus on competing national projects, this transformation is often overlooked.

At the educational level, it changed the way people talked about Bedouin education, both within the Bedouin community, and also about the Bedouin community. The idea of Bedouin education became in itself an icon, representing discrimination, and something that was doubly reified and deployed in the interest of a variety of other political agendas and battles, with an amorphous, and even ambiguous pliability.

The fecundity of its deployment, and the ambiguity, where it simultaneously promoted contradictory and notionally mutually exclusive agendas, highlights an interesting point for educational theory. Educational literature discussing education's role in politics tends to take one of two approaches. Either it considers education's role in a disciplinary sense, moulding and shaping society (Illich, 1973; Foucault, 1976), or, it is reviewed in an oppositional sense, looking at the ways education can be used to contest power relations (Freire, [1970] 1996). Yet the political role of education among the Negev Bedouin is neither oppressive nor libratory. It is both, and crucially it is both always and at the same time. It is this ambiguity which makes education such an interesting lens for looking at the interaction of competing political agendas. Yet it is also this ambiguity which underlines the fact that Cartesian notions of either/or resistance or subordination are not necessarily the most fruitful frame of analysis.

Notes

[1] The 1993 Oslo Agreement between Israel and the Palestinian Liberation Organization (PLO) and the creation of the Palestinian National Authority in the West Bank and Gaza Strip had a significant impact on Palestinian nationalism among all Palestinian communities. Among its consequences within Israel were the legalization of flying the Palestinian flag and other expressions of Palestinian nationalism as the PLO was no longer declared a terror organization. Simultaneously it also led to the reorientation of these nationalist expressions towards an articulation as a discrete community, the Palestinian national minority in Israel, with a political struggle distinct from Palestinians elsewhere, and with a new strategy of civic activism focused around collective demands and civil rights challenging structural discrimination within the Israeli state. The situation of the Negev Bedouin was central to this activism, and new nationalist idiom.

[2] Katz, Y. et al (1998) *Report of the Investigatory Committee on the Bedouin Educational System in the Negev*. Yaakov Katz was the Head of the Bedouin Development Authority and Chair of the Pedagogic Secretariat at the time of this report. Previously he had been the appointed Mayor of Laqiyya.

[3] The Shatil Beer Sheva office was opened in 1994, and was to become a significant factor in the development of Negev Bedouin civil society in the post-Oslo era, acting as a focal point for attracting and orienting Jewish American and international funding for social development projects in the Negev, and also hosting the education campaign.

[4] The campaign began due to a joint initiative from Ismail Abu Saad, a Bedouin professor of education, Bob Arnow, and Shatil, the capacity building centre for Israeli civil society founded by the New Israel Fund. It was initially given a grant of $300,000 by Bob Arnow, a New York real estate developer and the former Chair of the Board of Governors of Ben Gurion University of the Negev. Upon retirement from this Chair, he has devoted his energies to the cause of Bedouin education. The funding was channelled through Shatil (Jerusalem office), on the condition that it was only spent on educational advocacy.

[5] Moshe Shohat, Head of Bedouin Education Authority, July 2001. The comments were to lead to his eventual removal from office in 2003. See: Berman (2001).

[6] Hence, the 2001 HRW report observes:

Several days later we visited a school bordering an unrecognised Bedouin community outside Beer Sheva. An electrical plant was visible nearby and electric wires ran overhead; however, neither the community nor the school was connected to a central power supply. Two years ago, following the Israeli High Court's 1998 ruling that the state was obligated to provide electricity to all government schools in unrecognised villages, the Ministry of Education provided the school with a generator. When we visited, the generator was operating but was noisy and disruptive inside the classrooms. According to a representative of the parents' committee, it is weak and often shuts down. Like all Bedouin schools in the Negev that we visited, the building had no central heating or air conditioning. The principal described the extreme desert temperatures – both heat and cold – and showed us a small space heater and a small fan mounted on the wall. 'That's it,' he told us. Most of the buildings at this school were concrete block, although two were new prefabricated buildings. To one side of the school were eight toilets, housed in a separate concrete structure. These served all fifty-two teachers and 1,330 children, except for the kindergarteners who had a single toilet in their classroom. Next to the toilets and about twelve feet from a classroom was an open, foul-smelling garbage pile, taller than a kindergarten child. We were told that the school is supposed to burn the pile every few days, but it had not done so recently because the fumes blow into the school and the nearby houses. There are cyanide and bromine factories in a nearby industrial zone, and a first grade teacher complained to us that a bad smell, which she attributed to the factories, often fills her classroom. (HRW, 2001, *Second Class*, p. 86)

[7] Throughout its history Israel has considered itself a modern project, building a modern state, which has involved both building a new nation and a new landscape. Among other things, this has involved constructing the Negev Bedouin as a 'traditional' society, in need of an eschatological modernisation, of joining the melting pot of the modern world.

[8] The new politics of the citizenship moment was also the site for a new politics of culture and a new nationalism that seemed to galvanise the Arab minority in the post-Oslo period, and to give them a far greater national and especially international visibility. In a variety of forms this movement focused on asserting a collective presence in Israel, such as the attempt to put Arabic on road signs and other parts of the public sphere, to put the unrecognised villages on the map, or to assert recognition for Bedouin culture.

References

Abu Rabia, A. (2001) *Bedouin Century: education and development among the Negev tribes in the twentieth century*. Oxford: Berg.

Abu Saad, I. (1991) Towards an Understanding of Minority Education in Israel: the case of the Bedouin Arabs of the Negev, *Comparative Education*, 27(2), 235-242.

Abu Saad, I. (1997) The Education of Israel's Negev Beduin: background and prospects, *Israel Studies*, 2(2), 21-39.

Abu Saad, I. (2001) Education as a Tool for Control vs. Development among Indigenous Peoples: the case of Bedouin Arabs in Israel, *HAGAR International Social Science Review*, 2(2), 241-260.

Abu Saad, I. & Hendrix, V. (1995) Organisational Climate and Teachers' Job Satisfaction in a Multicultural Milieu: the case of the Bedouin Arab schools in Israel, *International Journal of Educational Development*, 15(2), 141-153.

Abu Saad, I., Abu Saad, K. Lewando-Hundt, G. et al (1998) Bedouin Arab Mothers' Aspirations for their Children's Education in the Context of Radical Social Change, *International Journal of Educational Development*, 18(4), 347-359.

Al-Haj, M. (1995) *Education, Empowerment and Control: the case of the Arabs in Israel.* Albany: SUNY Press.

Caton, S. (1987) Power, Persuasion and Language: a critique of the segmentary model in the Middle East, *International Journal of Middle East Studies*, 19, 77-102.

Champagne, D. & Abu Saad, I. (Eds) (2005*) Indigenous and Minority Education: international perspectives on empowerment.* Beer Sheva: BGU, Negev Center for Regional Development.

Cook, J. (2006) *Blood and Religion: the unmasking of the Jewish and democratic state.* London: Pluto Press.

Copty, M. (1990) Knowledge and Power in Education: the making of the Israeli Arab educational system, PhD thesis, University of Texas, Austin.

Dresch, P. (1986) The Significance of the Course Events Take in Segmentary Systems, *American Ethnologist*, 13(2), 309-324.

Dyer, C. & Choksi, A. (1998) Education is Like Wearing Glasses: Nomads' views of literacy and empowerment, *International Journal of Educational Development*, 18(5), 405-413.

Foucault, M. (1976) *Discipline and Punish.* London: Penguin.

Freire, P. ([1970] 1996) *Pedagogy of the Oppressed.* London: Penguin.

Illich, I. (1973) *Deschooling Society.* London: Penguin.

Karabel, J. & Halsey, A. (Eds) (1977) *Power and Ideology in Education.* New York: Oxford University Press.

Katz, Y., Abu Saad, I., Abu Ajaj, M., et al (1998) *Report of the Investigatory Committee on the Bedouin Educational System in the Negev.* Jerusalem: Ministry of Education.

Kratli, S. (2001) *Education Provision to Nomadic Pastoralists: a literature review.* IDS Working Paper 126, Institute of Development Studies, University of Sussex.

Mar'i, S. (1978) *Arab Education in Israel.* New York: Syracuse University Press.

Meir, A. (1997) *As Nomadism Ends: the Israeli Bedouin of the Negev.* Boulder: Westview Press.

Millar, C., Raynham S. & Schaffer, A. (Eds) (1991) *Breaking the Formal Frame: readings in South African education in the eighties.* Cape Town: Oxford University Press.

Parizot, C. (2001) Le Mois de la Bienvenue: Reappropriations des Mecanismes Electoraux et Reajustements de Rapports de Pouvoir Chez les Bedouins du Neguev, Israel. PhD thesis, Ecole des Hautes Etudes en Sciences Sociales.

Paulston, R. (1980) Education as Anti-Structure: non-formal education in social and ethnic movements, *Comparative Education*, 16(1), 55-66.

Petherbridge-Hernandez, P. (1990) Reconceptualising Liberating Non-formal Education: a Catalan case study, *Compare*, 20(1), 41-51.

Sa'di, A. (1997) Modernisation as an Explanatory Discourse of Zionist-Palestinian Relations, *British Journal of Middle Eastern Studies*, 24(1), 25-48.

Scott, J. (1990) *Domination and the Arts of Resistance: hidden transcripts.* New Haven: Yale University Press.

Sen, A. (1999) *Development as Freedom.* Oxford: Oxford University Press.

Shryock, A. (1997) *Nationalism and the Genealogical Imagination: oral history and textual authority in tribal Jordan*. Berkeley: University of California.

NGO Publications & Newspaper Articles

Berman, R. (2001) Israeli Official Slurs Bedouins, *The Jewish Week*, 19 July.

Human Rights Watch (HRW) (2001) *Second Class: discrimination against Palestinian Arab children in Israel's schools*. New York: HRW.

Levinson, E. (Ed.) (1999) *Statistical Yearbook of the Negev Bedouin*. Beer Sheva: Center for Bedouin Studies and Development.

Levinson, E. (Ed.) (2004) *Statistical Yearbook of the Negev Bedouin*. Beer Sheva: Center for Bedouin Studies and Developmen.

Maan (2005) *The Arab Woman in the Negev: realities and challenges*, Beer Sheva: Maan, Forum for Bedouin Women's Organisations.

Sultany, Nimer (2003) *Citizens without Citizenship*. Haifa: Mada.

The Struggle for Palestinian National Education Past and Present

BILAL FOUAD BARAKAT

The struggle over Palestinian education offers interesting insights at several levels. On the one hand, it brings into sharp focus issues raised by the role of education in anti-colonial and modernisation projects throughout the world. On the other hand, its historical development places it in a highly exceptional position, the reality of which must be acknowledged even if a 'cult of uniqueness' is to be rejected as unhelpful.

There is no pretension at comprehensiveness in this discussion. Indeed, some omissions – such as the controversy surrounding textbooks – are immediately obvious. A recurrent theme is the notion of 'education as liberation'. While the dilemmas and paradoxes this raises are not resolved here, it is worth highlighting the problem, which is all too often glossed over. A central aim is to demonstrate that it would be wrong to believe that the conflict over Palestine merely disrupted the development of education, and that an otherwise 'typical' development trajectory was adapted to the obstacles the conflict presented. It can be seen that on the contrary, the history of the conflict over the land and its integrity provided not only a unique context for educational development, but fundamentally shaped the very aims, expectations and attitudes towards education and schooling.

A note should be made on the order of presentation. Palestinian education is extraordinarily fragmented in space and time (see Figure 1). Maintaining a strictly linear chronology would no doubt serve more to obscure the structure than to avoid confusion. Accordingly, the reader is asked to excuse the necessary discontinuities in presentation.

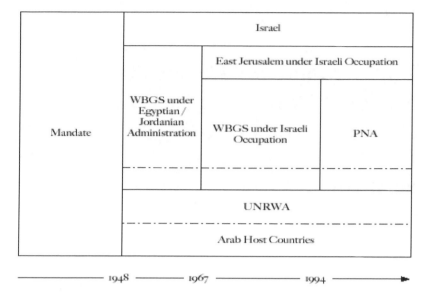

Figure 1. Palestinian education under foreign control:
from the Ottomans to the first intifada.

Commencing in 1846, a series of Ottoman education laws provided the framework for public schooling in Palestine. It was modelled largely on the French system, even to the extent of using straight translations of French textbooks into Turkish. Initially, the uptake of educational opportunities was heavily class-dependent. The rural elites began to supply their sons with formal education and migrate from their villages into urban areas, as positions in the bureaucracy became increasingly important to maintaining their influence (Kimmerling & Migdal, 2003). In 1913, primary education became compulsory and universal by law. In reality this was never fully achieved (Mazawi, 1994). This can partly be explained by a lack of relevance. The curriculum adopted in 1908 was not only French in origin, but uniform throughout the Ottoman Empire. Even the Arabic language itself was taught through Turkish. A switch to Arabic was decided upon in 1913, but not implemented due to the onset of the First World War (Al-Haj, 1995).

At the same time, private schools were more responsive than public schools to the needs of their constituencies. In the nineteenth century, the Ottomans had granted concessions to various European powers to establish missionary schools in Palestine. The number of such private schools – Christian, but nonetheless open to all denominations – had increased greatly by the end of the century (Tibawi, 1961).

This was also time of private Jewish schools, often with support from Jewish communities in Europe, in response to the perceived threat of attempts at conversion in Christian missionary schools. Partly because proselytising among Muslims was illegal, but no doubt also due to their under-representation in urban centres, the number of private Muslim schools, while significant and increasing, never reached the level of the other religious communities. Private schools also provided the only opportunity for education beyond the primary level. Only during the First World War was the first public secondary school established to rally Arab support. One result of the large number and variety of foreign schools was that teachers were from the beginning viewed as agents of social and political control (Mazawi, 1994).

Britain's influence in Palestine goes back at least to the defence of Acre against Napoleon (Tibawi, 1961). But it was her role as governing power between the end of the First World War and her withdrawal in 1948 that became her lasting legacy to Palestine in many areas, including education. The British Mandate government changed the medium of instruction in public schools to Arabic and almost immediately embarked on a programme of expansion of public education. Like two further school expansion programmes that followed at critical junctures to shore up Arab support, it rapidly ran out of steam. By the end of the British Mandate still fewer than one in three Arab children of school age were enrolled and only a third of Arab villages had schools. The necessary funding for greater expansion was never made available. As a matter of British policy, under the Mandate, Palestine was expected to be self-financing, and consequently investment of British resources was not forthcoming. A reluctant exception was made only for security expenses. As a result, 'towards the end of the Mandate, government expenditure on police and prisons was five times the budget for education' (Shepherd, 1999, p. 127). That more money could have been made available given the political will was explicitly recognised at the time by the British Royal Commission of 1937. Indeed, the limited expansion of public schooling was a deliberate policy. The Director of the Mandate government's education department in the early 1920s stressed 'the danger of giving too literary a bias to village education ... tempting the village boy to the town where he may become unemployed and unemployable' (Shepherd, 1999, p.155). Likewise, access to secondary education remained extremely limited due to the conviction on the part of some officials that only a small proportion of children had the 'natural' capacity for it.

For the British, the point of Arab education was mainly to supply minor bureaucrats and primary school teachers. Because private Christian schools were already providing sufficient government staff, there was no incentive to invest in public education (Elboim-Dror, 2000). But

> if the aim of government education in Palestine was to enable the
> Arabs to acquire better agricultural and technical, rather than
> 'literary' skills, this was precisely what the Education Department
> failed to encourage. [Systematic agricultural instruction took
> place] in fewer than half the village schools, many of which were

personally financed by the fourth High Commissioner, Arthur
Wauchope (a keen gardener). (Shepherd, 1999, p. 162)

As a result, technical education was neglected even more, because 'arts and
crafts' enthusiasts in the administration favoured traditional handicrafts and
objected to industrialisation, a bias not shared by the local population. This
was an unfortunate colonial legacy. Arab higher education was all but non-
existent. While the two Jewish universities were theoretically open to Arabs,
instruction was in Hebrew. Even by the mid 1940s, the only Arab post-
secondary institutions were a school of law operating as a night school and
two teacher training colleges with negligible enrolment (Abu-Lughod, 2000).
The elites had nevertheless become keenly aware of the value of further
education and 'upper-class families were increasingly sending their sons to
universities in Cairo, Beirut, and sometimes Europe' (Kimmerling & Migdal,
2003, p. 57). So while Arab popular demand for schooling was high, it was
not met, and every year large numbers of prospective students hoping to
enrol in village schools were turned away. Despite the demand, many villages
were not provided with a school at all, and the situation was much worse for
girls than for boys. In a drive to supplement government provision, private
contributions by the Arab population towards education in kind and in cash
were substantial, and eventually exceeded the amount of public funding
(Tibawi, 1956).

Arab dissatisfaction with the public schools was directed not only at
insufficient capacity, but also at a curriculum perceived as deliberately failing
to support Arab nationalism. This stood in obvious contrast to Jewish
education, which was fully integrated into the Zionist nationalist project.
Nonetheless, despite the lack of nationalist content in the official Arab
curriculum, village schooling – incomplete as it was – did help the spread of
revolutionary zeal to the countryside, by physically bringing educated young
men – often nationalists – into the villages as teachers (Kimmerling &
Migdal, 2003). Consequently, during the Arab revolt of 1936-39, teachers
and students played a revolutionary role that led to suppression and the
occupation of many schools. In a move anticipating later Israeli practice, the
British Mandate government abused its control of access to education, so
that while 'bad' villages were subject to collective punishment, 'good' villages
were rewarded with the establishment of schools (Shepherd, 1999).

In the build-up to, and the aftermath of, the British withdrawal in 1948,
war between the Zionists and the Arabs resulted in the displacement of
hundreds of thousands of Palestinians to parts of the country not under
Zionist control, and even beyond, to the neighbouring countries of Lebanon,
Syria and Jordan. A United Nations Relief and Works Agency (UNRWA)
was established to provide humanitarian support to these refugees. UNRWA
educational support focused almost exclusively on the primary level. The
curriculum used was that of the respective host country. Owing to the young
age structure of the Palestinian refugees, education made, and still makes up
a significant part of UNRWA's activities. While the Agency has been credited

with major educational achievements, such as the rapid universalisation of primary education (see also an early romanticising account ['merry banging'] of its vocational schooling [Faherty, 1959, p. 47]), UNRWA's role as an educational leader is declining, even if it remains a major (and in some countries the only) provider of schooling to Palestinian refugees. Its precarious budget, dependent on donations, coupled with strong demographic pressures, has resulted in a situation where previous achievements are threatened by lack of new capacity to meet the demand. UNRWA was unable, for instance, to follow suit when compulsory schooling was extended from 9 to 10 years in the West Bank, for Jordan and Egypt had taken control of the West Bank and the Gaza Strip respectively and implemented their own education systems. Just like the refugees outside Palestine, students in these territories – refugees and non-refugees alike – were thus exposed to a foreign curriculum that lacked specifically Palestinian content, even if it covered the conflict over Palestine as such (Abu-Lughod, 1973).

On the other hand, instruction in the curriculum of the host countries and participation in their secondary school examinations and certification facilitated access to universities in these countries. Indeed, in many Arab countries this access was granted to Palestinian refugees on the same basis as to nationals. Apart from the propaganda value of providing this privilege, Palestinian graduates were desperately needed by the modernising economies of these Arab states. In some Gulf states, for example, modern schooling had not been in existence long enough to provide sufficient native high-level manpower. To a large extent, Palestinians were able to fill this gap and as a result, during the 1950s and into the early 1970s, they made up a large part, or even the majority, of the teaching force and other professions, in Kuwait especially and the Gulf States in general (Badran, 1980; Mazawi, 1994).

In 1967, Israel seized control of the West Bank and Gaza Strip, which became known as the Occupied Territories (OT). Under military occupation, the 'Israeli Defence Forces (IDF) controlled all governmental, legislative, appointive, and administrative activities of government schools' (Van Dyke & Randall, 2002, p. 19). This authority was severely abused. Investment in buildings, teacher training and other essentials was almost entirely absent, despite the rapid growth of the school-age population and the collection of funds for public services from the local population. The clear aim of reducing the schooling process to its functional minimum was evident in that teachers in public schools were actively prevented from attending in-service training offered by local universities (Khaldi & Wahbeh, 2000) and also that 'extracurricular activities were banned, as well as social and cultural clubs' (Velloso, 2002, p. 149). Indeed, under occupation:

> Palestinian teachers and students were subjected to a plethora of
> human rights violations at the hands of the occupiers. These
> included arbitrary detention, torture and ill-treatment under
> interrogation, deportation, army raids on schools (which resulted

in the killing of many schoolchildren), intrusion of soldiers onto
school premises, and harassment of students and teachers.
(Velloso, 2002, p. 149)

De jure, the Jordanian and Egyptian curricula remained in place. They were,
however, heavily censored, mediation attempts by UNESCO
notwithstanding (Schiff, 1989; Brown, 2002). Censorship was not only
widespread, but applied by default: any book not specifically approved for
purchase or import was considered illegal (Sullivan, 1994). The use of
outdated but approved textbooks in place of censored current ones resulted
in the teaching of obsolete information (Van Dyke, 1996).

Shortly after the occupation of Jerusalem, Israel claimed sovereignty
over the 'united city', unilaterally annexing its Palestinian quarters.
Ostentatiously Jordanian legislation, including the education law, was
replaced by Israeli laws. However, this attempt to actually implement the
Israeli school system in Arab Jerusalem failed. Students and teachers refused
to return to school at the beginning of the academic year (Masarweh &
Salhout, 2002). This boycott of municipal schools that introduced the Israeli
curriculum continued, as parents registered their children with private and
Islamic trust schools instead. Secondary students in particular refused to sit
for the Jewish *bagrout* school-leaving examination, which would not have
granted them access to Arab universities. As a result of popular pressure, the
Jordanian curriculum (subject to the same restrictions as elsewhere on the
West Bank) was resumed in phases, beginning with the secondary cycle in
1973, to allow students to sit for the Jordanian *tawjihi* examination, and
finishing with the primary cycle in 1980 (Ministry of Education, 2000;
Masarweh & Salhout, 2002). This failure put an end to any ambitions to
replace the curriculum throughout the West Bank (Heeps, 1993, p. 78).
Even after reverting to the Jordanian curriculum, however, the teaching of
Hebrew and Israeli civics remained compulsory (El Nammary, 2001).

After 1967, the difficulties Palestinians encountered when wanting to
study abroad or return to the OT from their studies accentuated the need for
Palestinian universities at home (Baramki, 1987; Abu Lughod, 2000).
Moreover, by the early 1970s, 'the capacity of Arab universities to absorb
them [Palestinian students] with the same degree of willingness as they have
exhibited in the past' was open to question (Abu-Lughod, 1973). The
establishment of Palestinian universities in the OT was tolerated, though not
supported, by the occupying power. Sullivan (1994) suggests that during the
1970s, some Israelis might have believed access to Palestinian universities
would offer youth an alternative to Palestine Liberation Organisation (PLO)
membership and they also wished to discourage study in the Soviet Union.
Most important, however, was the ability to monitor ideological and political
trends, for 'Palestinian universities were rife with informers' (Sullivan, 1994,
p. 171).

The extent of this 'toleration' should not be overestimated. The
universities suffered from much of the same kinds of oppression as schools,

including deportation and censorship. In addition, they suffered from administrative harassment, such as the denial of value-added tax (VAT) exemptions, or permits for expansion, the construction of buildings or the introduction of new courses being delayed for many years. Military order 854 of July 1980 sought to place Palestinian universities under direct Israeli administration, based on the misapplication of a Jordanian law for the regulation of schools rather than higher education (Assaf, 1997). This order would have given the Israeli authorities the power to licence institutions annually, set curricula, select textbooks, admit students, prohibit political activities of staff and to approve and dismiss instructors (Roberts et al, 1984; Sullivan, 1994). It was not implemented after international and Israeli academic protests and local pressure, but never officially rescinded.

Apart from providing individual students with access to higher learning, the Palestinian universities also aimed 'to prepare responsible generations ready to take part in changing the history of the Palestinian people' (Shahin, 2000, p. 95). In an effort to serve the community as a whole rather than merely create a new indigenous elite, community work as a graduation requirement was introduced in Birzeit University in 1971, and since 2001, all undergraduates in the OT are required to perform 120 hours' community service in volunteering (UNDP PAPP, 2000). Other outreach programmes were added over time: literacy and adult education in 1976, community health services in 1980, and environmental health and public safety in 1982 (Baramki, 1987). The universities also served as important sites for gender interaction, since most schooling was single sex. Though the impact has been slow and patchy,

> positive interaction between females and males in classes, on campus, and through other university activities has contributed considerably to the acceptability of the Palestinian female in the 'educational place'. (Abu-Lughod, 2000, p. 91)

Despite being technically private, their uniquely independent position meant that:

> Palestinian universities have been obliged to assume some aspects of a national authority ... members of their administrations and many of their teachers have for years been recognized by Palestinians as among their most important representatives in negotiations with Israeli officials and foreign dignitaries. (Sullivan, 1994, p. 188)

This is echoed by Kimmerling & Migdal:

> in very important ways, the meetings, discussions, and political activity of the 1970s had had a cumulative effect, resulting by the 1980s in a much more tightly woven society. Probably no structures played a more important role in this regard than the new universities. (2003, p. 289)

191

Given that a substantial share of Palestinians lived in the diaspora without access to these 'national' universities, it is natural to consider the potential role of distance learning. Indeed, the idea of a Palestinian distance university emerged early on, and the final implementation of this idea in the form of the Al-Quds Open University is well described by Mazawi (1999).

During the popular uprising in the Occupied Territory at the end of the 1980s, known as the first intifada, repression in the education sector intensified and culminated in the blanket closure of schools and universities for months or even years at a time. In addition, at least 10% of the schools were utilised as military camps and detention centres during the intifada (Alzaroo & Hunt, 2003, p. 170). The experience of children at this time differed from that in politically violent crises elsewhere because of their own important role in it (Barber, 1997). The effect this had on their attitudes towards authority was continuously hotly debated. The complex relationship between revolt and conformist behaviour is highlighted by Usher (1991), who quotes a child as saying: 'Everyday when I come home from school, I wash my hands and have lunch. I wash my plate and do my homework. Then I go out and throw stones' (p. 3).

By contrast, Yair & Khatab (1995) took a much more negative view of student 'empowerment' and noted that some students were impelled by their newly gained self-confidence towards violence and threats against teachers, extortion of higher grades and looting. Initially, periods of closure were compensated for through remedial measures within the formal framework, such as longer classes, more teaching days per week or shorter holidays (Baramki, 1987). When closures persisted, 'neighbourhood schools' appeared, which were held in private homes and other places out of sight of army patrols. These initiatives were not entirely spontaneous and ad hoc, but planned, with attempts to produce guidelines and a handbook for alternative schooling (Mahshi & Bush, 1989). Even though the official curriculum was taught, there was a lack of confidence that work in alternative schools would count towards promotion. This made the erratic reopening of regular schools by the Israeli authorities an effective tactic aimed at undermining these efforts.

The educational effects of the intifada experience were mixed. Some anticipated a profound positive transformation. An example of a somewhat romantic account is provided by Fasheh (1990):

> Talking about education among Palestinians in the future
> necessarily means talking about more than just opening schools
> and going back to the syllabi and tests. It will not be easy, for
> example, under the old system to control a child who has
> discovered his power and his dignity. It is not going to be easy to
> teach history to a child who feels that he or she has been making
> history. (p. 29)

Others, however, anticipated the intifada to have a lasting damaging effect on education. At the tertiary level in particular it was noted that quality could not be provided off-campus during closures (Baramki, 1987) and that alternative arrangements such as distance learning materials represented 'a weaker education that lacked the intellectual support of libraries and laboratories, the synergy that comes from personal and group encounters' (Abu-Lughod, 2000, p. 88). A balanced assessment is provided by Mahshi & Bush (1989, p. 274), who in an early verdict on its effects concluded that the intifada resulted in 'a loss of literacy and numeracy skills, but a growth in self-reliance and self-esteem'.

The official Israeli reason for the closure of schools and universities was that they were centres of political activism and youth violence. Of course, 'fear of "unrest" or student demonstrations on campus cannot justify barring academic staff from tending their laboratories and equipment. It cannot be a reason for stopping librarians from maintaining the university libraries' (World University Service [WUS], 1991). The fact that closures were applied even to primary schools and kindergartens further called the ostentatious security rationale into question. Palestinians perceived a deliberate policy of holding their children hostage to ignorance.

> Desperate to deprive the movement of its youthful energy and leadership, the Israelis have used their control over education as a way of pressuring the Palestinian population ... the authorities are well aware of Palestinian reliance on education as a solution to their many problems, and that they have exploited this vulnerability by closing schools ... as a collective punishment. (Mahshi & Bush, 1989, p. 273)

This was no mere speculation. The Israeli authorities were quite explicit that education as such was to be criminalised. In April 1988:

> all government schoolteachers in the Ramallah area were called to a meeting by the Civil Administration and reminded that any attempts to provide education to students would be considered illegal and grounds for immediate dismissal. (Mahshi & Bush, 1989, p. 275)

The following month, cultural and educational activities – even of neutral subjects – organised by popular committees were likewise outlawed. In August, a military order set a punishment for involvement in popular committees of up to 10 years in prison, whatever their purpose. This prohibition was by no means theoretical. Fasheh (1990) documents the example of a Professor of Botany who was jailed for six months for community gardening. The *Jerusalem Post* of 25 November 1988 reported an incident where soldiers raided private homes to interrupt informal lessons by parents (Gabarino et al, 1991, p. 114). Both providing and seeking education was criminalised: 'If we find anyone teaching, or any students carrying books we will take appropriate measures against them', stated Major Micha, Deputy Head of the Civil Administration, 24 April 1989 (quoted in WUS, 1991, p. 15).

It was not lost on outside observers that statements such as the one above were unconditional and failed to mention genuine security concerns. The Israeli decision to finally reopen schools and universities was brought about by pressure applied by the European Parliament, which in January 1990 recommended sanctions and the suspension of scientific cooperation and bilateral cultural accords with Israel (WUS, 1991).

With the withering of the intifada, the signing of the Oslo accords shortly afterwards, and the entry of the Palestinian National Authority, the context of Palestinian education in the Occupied Territories changed radically, and it is to this new phase that the discussion will now turn.

Developments since Oslo, Current
Realities and Future Perspectives

The Oslo accords formally transferred control of the education system in the OT to the newly formed Palestinian National Authority (PNA or PA). Because the transfer of authority occurred only two days before the commencement of the school year 1994/95, no overhaul was attempted in that year, except for reverting to the uncensored versions of existing textbooks and the outlawing of corporal punishment.

UNRWA's schools were not able to follow suit with all changes, in particular the increase in compulsory schooling from 9 to 10 years and new minimum requirements for the recruitment of teachers (Ramsden & Senker, 1993). However, this did not necessarily lead to lower quality (Lempinen & Repo, 2002). The education sector was an extraordinarily important arena for the PNA to demonstrate its credibility and establish a successful relationship with the local population, a very large proportion of which was directly affected by schools as students, parents or teachers. In addition to explicit policy, the PNA also affected the education sector indirectly, by virtue of emerging as the single largest employer and stimulating demand for educated Palestinian labour at various levels of skills (Al-Qudsi, 2000).

Despite the incorporation of the existing Council for Higher Education into the Ministry of Education, the universities remained reluctant to cede the high level of independence they had acquired in the absence of a state, a unique situation that set them apart from other Arab universities (Mazawi, 2004). The PNA's focus on primary and secondary education, over which it exerted greater control, should be interpreted in this context.

PNA management of education was seen as reasonably successful by the general population, especially as compared to other public services (Bocco et al, 2003), and also deemed to be one of the least corrupt (Palestinian Legislative Council [PLC], 1997). Historically, Palestinian popular concern had been mainly about the expansion of schooling; under foreign control qualitative changes were nearly impossible to achieve. However, in the new situation, and once near universal enrolment in primary school had been achieved, the content of education began to receive more attention. This relatively successful development of the education sector contributed to the fact that enthusiasm for education remained high despite offering few economic returns (Angrist, 1995). The fact that higher levels of education did not necessarily lead to qualified employment, especially among females, also explains the notable absence of a significant impact on fertility.

One of the greatest advantages that Palestinian control of the education sector brought was the opportunity to develop a native curriculum. Progressive Palestinian educators had been looking forward to implementing their ideas for some time, and had been spurred on by the experiences with alternative education during the first intifada (Mahshi & Bush, 1989). A curriculum committee was set up that received much praise for the quality of the internal Palestinian curriculum debate it generated, its secular and politically independent approach and highly progressive and reform-oriented approach (Brown, 2001; Moughrabi, 2004a). However, after the submission of its report, civil servants directed by the Deputy Minister took over the task of producing the actual curriculum and textbooks, which ignored the radical recommendations for reform (Al-Ramahi & Davies, 2002).

The emergence of a native Palestinian education system invites the comparison of educational opportunities in the OT with those open to Palestinians within Israel, who attend Israeli Arab schools. Discrimination within Israeli education takes many forms, both overt and subtle. Different levels of funding of Arab and Jewish schools reflect the inequitable provision of funds and public services to these communities generally. A related concern is the inferior level of qualifications of teachers in the Arab schools, and the resulting attainment gap. The pass rate for the Jewish *bagrout* (matriculation examination) is far below the national standard in the Arab schools in Israel. As a result, Arab students are extremely under-represented in higher education, both as students and faculty. Moreover, they have at times been barred from many technological and scientific subjects, including meteorology. As a result, the benefits of higher education are low even for those who manage to obtain it against the odds. Because of a lack of alternatives, nearly all Arab graduates become teachers (80% in the late 1980s as compared to 15% among the Jewish graduates) (Mazawi, 1994). The overall effect is that the educational opportunities for Palestinians are better in the deprived Palestinian education system than within the highly developed and affluent Israeli state (see, for example, Mari, 1978, 1984 and 1985; Al-Haj, 1995; and Human Rights Watch [HRW], 2001). This is true in terms of access, while in terms of quality the conclusion is less clear. Even when disadvantaged as compared to Jewish schools, Israeli Arab schools are likely to compare favourably with Palestinian schools as far as equipment and facilities are concerned. On the other hand, true quality is precluded by the fact that the curricular content reflects the 'internal colonialism' (Zureik,

1979) that characterises the relationship between the two communities. Nonetheless, de-Palestinisation has ultimately failed, due to powerful informal forces of political socialisation (Mari, 1985). This has become increasingly evident over the years, especially in the show of solidarity with Palestinians in the OT in the face of Israeli military suppression of the second intifada which began in 2000.

Most serious are, of course, human casualties. Both students and teachers have been killed on their way to or from school or in some cases even inside their classrooms during lessons. Many more have been seriously injured. Direct Israeli military action has also caused considerable damage to the physical infrastructure; in some cases schools and universities have been directly shelled (Al-Qazzaz, 2001). But school buildings are also affected by indirect measures such as the withholding of funds or by preventing necessary repairs to be carried out (see UNICEF, 2003).

Furthermore road blocks and checkpoints that can appear at any time, including overnight, can reduce mobility to the point that the normal operation of the affected schools becomes impossible, as students and teachers suddenly find themselves unable to reach them on time or at all. The impact is even more severe in cases where access to schools is affected by the building of the separation barrier. In response to these obstacles, some teachers have been reassigned to schools closer to their homes, but such remedial measures can do little to compensate for a massive injustice. The effects of travel restrictions and closures on education are not limited to making school attendance more difficult. By choking the economy, they contribute to disastrously high levels of unemployment and poverty. These in turn have their effects on children. Children are more likely to drop out of school to undertake work (see UNICEF [2003] for a detailed discussion of child labour) or to get married early. Among those that remain, a not insignificant proportion suffers from a range of levels of malnutrition (Abdeen, 2002) that affect their physical and cognitive development and by implication their learning ability.

Not only is an insufficient number of Palestinian teachers trained specifically to deal with such issues. Many of the present generation of teachers were still students during the first intifada and their own education was severely disrupted so that they are ill prepared to teach. While early in the second intifada teachers reported being particularly gentle towards their students – who they knew were already suffering outside school – classrooms have since become tense and sometimes violent as teachers themselves have had to cope with years of worries over finances and their own families' health and safety (Arafat, 2003). Tensions are exacerbated by excessively large classes and overcrowded classrooms that leave little space for progressive teaching techniques.

Together these challenges threaten to undo previous achievements in the education sector. There is evidence that attainment is stagnating or even declining, as conflict-induced problems of quality multiply. Speaking of higher education, Moughrabi (2004b) points out that responses to the financial crisis have included, *inter alia*, an increased reliance on unqualified instructors, a relaxation of admission requirements, declining library holdings and other factors that 'eventually will lead to a precipitous decline in quality, something that Palestinians can ill afford and may take many years to remedy' (p. 10).

While there have been notable achievements 'under fire', such as the phased roll-out of new textbooks, educational development in line with the ambitious Five Year Plan has largely had to give way to emergency measures merely to keep the system in operation. But it is a testimony to the resolve of Palestinian educationalists that the slightest opportunity accompanying a period of calm has been used to work towards their ideal image of Palestinian education in peacetime, however modest the advances possible (see Van Dyke & Randall [2002] for articulations of this ideal). Successful schooling has a major impact on family and child well-being in terms of health, nutrition and treatment of children (Shibly & Tibi, 1996). Its disruption is therefore a major impediment to social development and positive attitudes. The deterioration of Palestinian education is also worrying because of its importance for future national development in a country that lacks any natural resources and space for large-scale agriculture or industrial development (UNESCO, 1994).

In this crucial development dimension, the comparative advantage Palestinians once enjoyed as compared to their neighbours is disappearing. Other Arab countries are catching up rapidly over the last twenty years, and some have overtaken already. All the while, in addition to the constraints that conflict imposes, rapid demographic growth among Palestinians (Goujon, 1997; see Palestinian Central Bureau of Statistics [PCBS], 2004) makes it difficult merely to maintain quantitative indicators at their current levels. Overcoming the biggest challenge, namely improving the quality of learning outcomes, seems to move further and further out of reach.

The deteriorating situation leaves little room for hope. But even assuming a positive development, major challenges will remain. Among them will be the challenge to overcome structural features of the education system that may no longer be appropriate in post-conflict scenarios. The 'mushrooming' of Palestinian universities, for instance, reflects their development under occupation, where their large number provided some measure of protection against closures of individual institutions and restrictions on movement. But ultimately it might be necessary to consolidate the higher education sector or at least increase cooperation to avoid the duplication of departments and resources, for instance, by establishing a joint library service (Pring, 1997; Abu-Lughod, 2000).

197

Education as Liberation: individual
interest and the collective struggle

In attempting to assess the contribution of education and schooling to the liberation of Palestinians, we need to ask 'Whose liberation, and from what?' For the individual refugee seeking to escape life in the camps, educational success was defined in terms of employability. This implied a focus on technical, scientific or professional subjects that did little to mobilize a spirit of Palestinian nationalism. On the contrary, educational patterns 'adapted to the Middle East labour market rather than to the needs of the Palestinian people'. As a result, Palestinians became 'agents of development and change everywhere', but contributed rather less 'to their own countries and communities' (Zahlan & Zahlan, 1977, p. 106).

Abu-Lughod (1973) raised concern about the potential effect of the kind of education Palestinians were receiving on their ability to wage revolutionary struggle, though Sayigh pointed out (1979) that the revolution was facilitated by educational progress by changing the intergenerational dynamic, because 'patriarchal authority was ... reduced by the greater earning power of the new educated generation' (p. 179). Nonetheless she too bemoaned the 'pride taken in a high rate of university graduates, irrespective of where they work or whether they contribute anything to the national struggle' (Sayigh, 1985). The dilemma is captured well by Nakhleh & Zureik:

> By and large, the consciousness which formal Western-style
> university education incubates is not a consciousness of collective
> liberation; it is a 'liberation' at the individual level, from job
> uncertainty, poverty, low prestige and some form of dependence.
> Such consciousness, if pursued – and it is in most cases, hence the
> contradiction – jettisons the individual in a direction of 'economic
> liberation' which contradicts the needed collective liberation ...
> especially, since the struggle may become economically
> debilitating ... and personally uncomfortable or fatal.
> (1980, pp. 195f.)

Host country curricula did not provide exposure to salient songs, poetry and literature or to Palestinian historiography. However, during periods of limited supervision, many teachers at UNRWA schools (who were largely recruited from among their own refugee graduates) found ways of introducing these topics to their students. Brief episodes of Palestinian-controlled schooling in Kuwait (Aruri & Farsoun, 1980) and southern Lebanon (Abu Habib, 1996) provided opportunities to formally include such nationalistic elements in the curriculum.

If national liberation was neglected in favour of individual escape from misery, national liberation in turn overshadowed other important liberation struggles, such as that of women (see, for instance, Abdo's [1991] discussion of this in the context of the first intifada).

Little has changed in this regard, as 'educational policies and practices remain still heavily entrenched in a collectivist and nationalist frame of reference, with less space devoted to issues of social diversity and equity' (Mazawi, 2000, p. 375). Even UNRWA, which has received much credit for first universalising schooling among the refugees, could not escape this tension. Critics such as Weighill (1995) conclude that UNRWA education was geared towards the top end and assisted individuals rather than the community. Accordingly, the effect of the rapid expansion of schooling as an equaliser should not be overestimated.

> Educational inequalities in Palestine contributed crucially to
> differential life-chances in the dispersion. Palestinians with
> diplomas were able to find jobs easily in the newly developing
> Arab countries. Palestinians without education, capital or modern
> skills – in other words the mass of the peasant/worker/bedouin
> population – were those who filled the camps. (Sayigh, 1979, p. 6)

Badran (1980) likewise affirms 'the immense discrepancy' in the living standards of the bourgeoisie and the 'destitute working class' among the refugees. The fact that those members of the bourgeoisie who had been Mandate officials received compensation payments from the British after 1948, alone undermines the notion that the refugees constituted a de-classed community. Accordingly, the drive for (higher) education was initially an initiative of the bourgeoisie as a means of staying ahead. Having experience in the modern sector, they devoted 'all their resources to making an economic recovery and to ensuring that their children obtained a university education' (p. 52).

Even so, Badran credits the middle classes with having been no less nationalistic, even if they were less revolutionary: 'Most groups of this bourgeoisie held fast to their Palestinian identity, and their university-educated children played an important role in the rise of the Arab nationalist movement' (p. 53). In fact, in some ways, the educated felt the humiliation of defeat more keenly:

> Because they were educated, they felt profoundly the bitterness of
> defeat, the extent of Arab backwardness and the grave impairment
> of national honour. For them the idea of Palestinian liberation and
> return represented an Arab revival and the rejection of the
> backwardness and colonialist domination that were holding back
> social and economic growth in the Arab homeland. (p. 54)

Nevertheless, 'the growth of their economic interests made them less revolutionary and more diplomatic, and less capable of understanding the real situation and the aspirations of the destitute masses' (p. 54). Sayigh's critique that the 'mystique around education ... has blinded national thinkers to defects in the way education works' was that education had failed to liberate the mass of refugees. Its role had been misconceived as a tool rather than an arena for the struggle, and its achievements had been exaggerated.

Graham-Brown (1984) observed that

> the symbolism which education has acquired for Palestinians, as
> an escape from poverty, a source of hope for the future, and a
> means of combatting the technologically sophisticated Israeli state,
> can obscure or oversimplify the role it has played in Palestinian
> society. (p. 12)

She notes that this 'ideological importance is attached to it by the Palestinian intelligentsia and the nationalist movement', while for most ordinary Palestinians, education 'is still locked in the patterns created by, and tending to recreate, the existing social structures' (p. 12). In the fascinating statement of a young camp woman, the inseparable connection between national liberation and class concerns becomes obvious: 'We can't be an uneducated people when we liberate Palestine, otherwise we shall just be exploited as cheap labour by the Israelis who remain behind, and we won't be able to develop our country' (Bendt & Downing, 1982, p. 68; quoted in Graham-Brown, 1984).

Unlike institutions of higher learning abroad, universities in the West Bank managed to reconcile at least individual and national liberation. Higher education did provide 'an avenue of social mobility for sons and daughters of peasants, refugees, and the urban middle and lower classes' with 'far-reaching social and political consequences for Palestinian society' (Taraki, 1999, p. 18). At the same time, there is no doubt that the Palestinian universities were part of the national project:

> by virtue of the fact that they were being supported by public,
> national funds ... As such, their administrations were expected
> (and often compelled) to allow full freedom of political activity
> and to align their institutions with the national movement.
> (Taraki, 1999, p. 18)

This national role did not, however, prevent them from providing bona fide academic instruction. Not only did they facilitate personal liberation by offering a route into professional careers, they also allowed a few individuals to combine the attainment of an improved social status with a position at the forefront of the national struggle. The activist student elite came mostly from modest family backgrounds, but as leaders of the student movement they acquired unprecedented influence in a highly politicised environment that valued activism and commitment to the national struggle. After having been imprisoned, they often 'gained leadership positions within various political organizations' (Taraki, 1999, p. 18). Mazawi & Yogev (1999) have shown how anti-occupation credentials, such as prison terms or resistance activism, could in fact act as a substitute for educational credentials for some members of this emerging elite. Nevertheless, in most contexts the inherent tension between individual liberation, national liberation and social transformation remained.

Just as serious was and is the failure to use educational resources to address internal Palestinian issues. Abu-Lughod (2000, p. 85) notes that 'thus far, the system has not produced adequately trained people to undertake the serious study of Palestinian society itself so that concrete society-based research can become the basis for national policies'. And Moughrabi (1997, p. 9) notes that 'those who run the universities have degrees from some of the best universities in the world' but are seemingly 'unable to create a viable and modern institution'.

The idea of education as key to the recovery of the homeland is deceptively compelling. But sovereignty is not handed out according to merit. High levels of education per se are not a liberation strategy; they must be actively leveraged for effect. Maintaining cultural awareness, while important for maintaining the struggle, could clearly not have been a means to bring about victory in itself. Nor could the aim realistically have been to achieve a technological military advantage. Smartness in international diplomacy, media mobilisation and direct negotiations was the only realistic channel for transforming a highly educated population into an asset for success.

During negotiations in the Oslo era, a human wealth of highly qualified Palestinian legal and technical experts was available, but not deployed to best effect. On the contrary, it was the Israeli negotiators who 'outsmarted' their Palestinian counterparts (Said, 2000). There has also in the past been a deplorable lack of national Palestinian expertise or a research centre on Israeli or USA society (Said, 2000, p. 119-124), a gap that the recently established Palestinian Forum for Israeli Studies (MADAR) has only in the last few years begun to close. Without a differentiated understanding of their dynamics, opportunities for positive leverage are bound to be missed.

While education must be judged to have failed as a weapon, it has nonetheless been a vital *defensive* strategy. The Israeli assault on Palestinian nationalism has from the beginning been not only physical, but also symbolic. Examples include the destruction and looting of the PLO research centre in Lebanon, theft and destruction of data and files during the re-occupation of the West Bank in spring 2002, the historical denial of Palestinian identity, the 'rebranding' of Palestinian cultural heritage as Israeli, the suffocation of Palestinian civil society, its structures and cultural institutions. This pattern has been apparent for some time under successive Israeli governments across political divisions. It has been termed 'sociocide', 'ethnocide' (McBride, 1983), 'politicide' (Kimmerling, 2003). While these are not synonymous and their authors introduce them for different kinds of arguments, their similarity is clear. They describe different dimensions of a policy by which Palestinians are to be reduced to a mere physical existence. Any expression, much less assertion, of their identity as political, historical, intellectual or cultural beings is sought to be minimised if not eliminated.

'Although the war is limited in its military features, it is often total in its political and cultural dimensions' (Gabarino et al, 1991, p. 115).

The apologists' defence that Israel does not threaten the physical *survival* of the Palestinians is therefore not only debatable but irrelevant. What is at stake is survival *as humans*: as thinking, dreaming, artistic, playful beings. Evidently the only defence against a denial of your humanity is to assert it. This is where a focus on education – for all its flaws – has served Palestinians well. It allowed the intelligentsia to provide 'the shared aesthetic and intellectual material for a concrete expression of Palestinism – a cultural glue helping to keep the society together' (Kimmerling & Migdal, 2003, p. 57).

Even the most shallow formal schooling offered an opportunity to socialise Palestinian children into a literate society and to encourage aspirations in some that transcend immediate material concerns. So 'from the moral perspective, large numbers of well-educated individuals within Palestinian society provide some immunity against attempts to dissolve the Palestinian national identity and shred the Palestinian socio-cultural fabric' (Development Studies Programme [DSP], 2005, p. 46).

Summary

The historical development of Palestinian education is closely tied to the specific history of their national project. For much of the twentieth century, the education of Palestinians was not so much disturbed by, but shaped and defined by the conflict over the land. Its discourse was likewise framed in nationalist terms, but remained vague when it came to concrete mechanisms through which education could contribute to the struggle. There is a need to demystify the educational narrative in order to face the real existing challenges. At the same time, we need to be clear about the true beneficiaries of educational development, and carefully distinguish individual and collective benefits.

While education has failed as a tool to forge the realisation of Palestinian ambitions, it has helped prevent their elimination as political, intellectual and cultural beings. Arguably, the emergence of a Palestinian-controlled education system has led to education and schooling being viewed in their own terms, with increased attention to questions of pedagogy and the transformation of society. While these aims are still expected to contribute to the liberation struggle by increasing the resilience of Palestinians, the educational ideal is now conceptualised in relation to peacetime, and the conflict treated as a disruption. Just as the process of decolonisation has only been partial, the transition from unrealistic expectations of the benefits of education for national development to disillusionment, that has characterised other emerging nations, has likewise been only partial.

References

Abdeen, Z., Greenough, G., Shahin, M. & Tayback, M. (2002) *Nutritional Assessment of the West Bank and Gaza Strip*. CARE International. http://www.reliefweb.int/library/documents/2003/care-opt-02jan.pdf

Abdo, N. (1991) Women of the Intifada: gender, class and national liberation, *Race & Class*, 32(4), 19-34.

Abu-Habib, L. (1996) Education and the Palestinian refugees of Lebanon: a lost generation? *Refugee Participation Network*, 21. http://www.reliefweb.int/library/RSC_Oxford/data/RPN/rpn21full.htm

Abu-Lughod, I. (1973) Educating a Community in Exile – the Palestinian experience, *Journal of Palestine Studies*, 2(3), 94-111.

Abu-Lughod, I. (2000) Palestinian Higher Education: national identity, liberation and globalization, *Boundary 2*, 27(1), 75-95.

Al-Haj, M. (1995) *Education, Empowerment, and Control – the case of the Arabs in Israel*. Albany: State University of New York Press.

Al-Qazzaz, H.R. (2001) Right to Higher Education. Right to Education Reports Series 1. Ramallah, Occupied Palestinian Territories: Democracy and Workers' Rights Center.

Al-Qudsi, S.S. (2000) Profiles of Refugee and Non-refugee Palestinians from the West Bank and Gaza, *International Migration*, 38(4), 79-107.

Al-Ramahi, N. & Davies, B. (2002) Changing Primary Education in Palestine: pulling in several directions at once, *International Studies in Sociology of Education*, 12(1), 59-76.

Alzaroo, S. & Hunt, G.L. (2003) Education in the Context of Conflict and Instability – The Palestinian Case, *Social Policy & Administration*, 37(2), 165-180.

Angrist, J.D (1995) The Economic Returns to Schooling in the West Bank and Gaza Strip, *American Economic Review*, 85(5), 1065-1087.

Arafat, C. (2003) A Psychosocial Assessment of the Palestinian Child. Research report, National Plan of Action for Palestinian Children/Save the Children. http://www.forcedmigration.org/psychosocial/papers/WiderPapers/psychosocial%20assessment%20pal%20children.pdf

Aruri, N.H. & Farsoun, S. (1980) Palestinian Communities and Arab Host Countries, in K. Nakhleh & E. Zureik (Eds) *The Sociology of the Palestinians*. London: Croom Helm.

Assaf, S. (1997) Educational Disruption and Recovery in Palestine, in T.Sobhi (Ed.) *Final Report and Case Studies of the Workshop on Educational Destruction and Reconstruction in Disrupted Societies*. Geneva: International Bureau of Education.

Badran, N.A. (1980) The Means of Survival – education and the Palestinian Community, 1948-1967, *Journal of Palestine Studies*, 9(4), 44-74.

Baramki, G. (1987) Building Palestinian Universities under Occupation, *Journal of Palestine Studies*, 17(1), 12-20.

Barber, B.K. (1997) Palestinian Children and Adolescents during and after the Intifada, *Palestine–Israel Journal*, 4(1), 23-33.

Bendt, I. & Downing, J. (1982) *We Shall Return: women of Palestine*. London: Zed.

Bocco, R., Brunner, M., Daneels, I., Husseini, J., Lapeyre, F. & Rabah, J. (2003) Palestinian Public Perceptions on their Living Conditions. Geneva: IUED (Graduate Institute of Development Studies, University of Geneva).

Brown, N.J. (2001) *Democracy, History, and the Contest over the Palestinian curriculum.*

Brown, N.J. (2002) The International Controversy Regarding Palestinian Textbooks. Lecture delivered at the Georg-Eckert Institute for International Textbook Research, 9 December 2002. http://www.geocities.com/nathanbrown1/

Development Studies Programme (DSP) (2005) *Palestine Human Development Report 2004.* Ramallah, Occupied Palestinian Territories: DSP/Birzeit University.

El Nammary, T.H. (2001) *The Status and Needs of Palestinian Education in Jerusalem.* Jerusalem: Arab Thought Forum.

Elboim-Dror, R (2000) British Educational Policies in Palestine, *Middle Eastern Studies*, 36(2), 28-47.

Faherty, R. (1959) *In Human Terms: the 1959 story of the UNRWA-UNESCO Arab refugee schools.* Paris: UNESCO.

Fasheh, M. (1990) Community Education: to reclaim and transform what has been made invisible, *Harvard Educational Review*, 60(1), 19-35.

Gabarino, J., Kostelny, K. & Dubrow, N. (1991) *No Place to be a Child: growing up in a war zone.* Lexington: D.C. Heath.

Goujon, A. (1997) Population and Education Prospects in the Western Mediterranean Region (Jordan, Lebanon, Syria, the West Bank and the Gaza Strip). Interim Report IR-97-046. Laxenburg, Austria: International Institute for Applied Systems Analysis (IIASA).

Graham-Brown, S. (1984) *Education, Repression and Liberation. Palestinians.* London: World University Service (UK).

Heeps, B. (1993) Trade Union Organisation and Professional Development, in S. Ramsden & C. Senker (Eds) *Learning the Hard Way – Palestinian education in the West Bank, Gaza Strip and Israel.* London: World University Service (UK).

Human Rights Watch (HRW) (2001) *Second Class: discrimination against Palestinian Arab children in Israel's schools.* New York: HRW.

Khaldi, M. & Wahbeh, N. (2000) Teacher Education in Palestine: understanding teachers' realities and development through action research. Presented at Selmun Seminar Conference, 'Teacher Education in the Mediterranean Region', at Selmun Palace, Malta.

Kimmerling, Baruch (2003) *Politicide: Ariel Sharon's wars against the Palestinians.* London: Verso.

Kimmerling, B. & Migdal, J.S. (2003) *The Palestinian People – a history.* Cambridge, MA: Harvard University Press.
Lempinen, J. & Repo, J. (2002) Palestine (West Bank and Gaza) Country Report – Education and Training Sector. Helsinki: Ministry for Foreign Affairs of Finland/Further Education Program.

Mahshi, K. & Bush, K. (1989) The Palestinian Uprising and Education for the Future, *Harvard Educational Review*, 59(4), 470-483.

Mari, Sami Khalil (1978) *Arab Education in Israel.* Syracuse: Syracuse University Press.

Mari, S.K. (1984) *Education, Culture and Identity amongst Palestinians in Israel.* London: International Organisation for the Elimination of All Forms of Racial Discrimination.

Mari, S.K. (1985) The Future of Palestinian Arab Education in Israel, *Journal of Palestine Studies*, 14(2), 52-73.

Masarweh, I. & Salhout, J. (2002) The Suffering of Children under Occupation. Documentary study. Jerusalem: Jerusalem Center for Social & Economic Rights.

Mazawi, A.E. (1994) Teachers' Role Patterns and the Mediation of Sociopolitical Change: the case of the Palestinian, *British Journal of Sociology of Education*, 15(4), 497-514.

Mazawi, A.E. (1999) Crossing the Distance: the Open University in the Arab States, *International Higher Education*, 18, 20-21.

Mazawi, A.E. (2000) The Reconstruction of Palestinian Education: between history, policy politics and policy making, *Journal of Education Policy*, 15(3), 371-375.

Mazawi, A.E. (2004) Wars, Geopolitics, and University Governance in the Arab States, *International Higher Education*, 36, 7-9.

Mazawi, A.E. & Yogev, A (1999) Elite Formation under Occupation: the internal stratification of Palestinian elites in the West Bank and Gaza Strip, *British Journal of Sociology*, 50(3), 397-418.

McBride, S. (1983) *Israel in Lebanon: report of the International Commission to Enquire into Reported Violations of International Law by Israel during Its Invasion of the Lebanon.* London: Ithaca.

Ministry of Education (MoE) (2000) *Five Year Education Development Plan.* Ramallah, Occupied Palestinian Territories: MoE.

Moughrabi, F. (1997) A Year of Discovery, *Journal of Palestine Studies*, 26(2), 5-15.

Moughrabi, F. (2004a) Educating for Citizenship in the New Palestine, in James A, Banks (Ed.) *Diversity and Citizenship Education: global perspectives.* San Francisco: Jossey-Bass.

Moughrabi, F. (2004b) Palestinian Universities under Siege, *International Higher Education*, 36, 9-10.

Nakhleh, Khalil & Zureik, Elia (Eds) *The Sociology of the Palestinians.* London: Croom Helm.

Palestinian Central Bureau of Statistics (PCBS) (2004) *Demographic and Health Survey.* Ramallah, Occupied Palestinian Territories: PCBS.

Palestininian Legislative Council (PLC) (1997) Special Committee Report (The Corruption Report). http://www.jmcc.org/politics/pna/plc/plccorup.htm

Pring, R. (1997) Higher Education in Palestine. Draft Report for the Qattan Foundation (unpublished).

Ramsden, S. & Senker, C. (1993) Vocational Education: technical and teacher training, in: S. Ramsden & C. Senker (Eds) *Learning the Hard Way – Palestinian education in the West Bank, Gaza Strip and Israel.* London: World University Service.

Roberts, A., Joergensen, B. & Newman, F. (1984) *Academic Freedom under Israeli Military Occupation.* Report of WUS/ICJ mission of enquiry into higher education

in the West Bank and Gaza. London: World University Service
(UK)/International Commission of Jurists.

Said, E.W. (2000) *The End of the Peace Process: Oslo and after.* London: Granta.

Sayigh, R. (1979) *Palestinians – from peasants to revolutionaries.* London: Zed Books.

Sayigh, R. (1985) Palestinian Education: escape route or strait-jacket? *Journal of Palestine Studies,* 14(3), 127-134.

Schiff, B.N. (1989) Between Occupier and Occupied: UNRWA in the West Bank and the Gaza Strip, *Journal of Palestine Studies,* 18(3), 60-75.

Shahin, V.A. (2000) Al-Quds University and Social Development in Palestine, in Guy Neave (Ed.) *The Universities' Responsibility to Society: international perspectives,* 95-101. Amsterdam: Pergamon.

Shepherd, N. (1999) *Ploughing Sand: British rule in Palestine.* London: John Murray.

Shibly, N. & Tibi, R. (1996) Empowering Parents to Change the Future: an analysis of changes in parental attitudes in East Jerusalem. Working Papers in Early Childhood Development 19. The Hague: Bernard van Leer Foundation.

Sullivan, A (1994) Palestinian Universities in the West Bank and Gaza Strip, *Muslim World,* 84, 168-188.

Taraki, L. (1999) Higher Education, Resistance, and State building in Palestine, *International Higher Education,* 18, 18-19.

Tibawi, Abdul Latif (1956) *Arab Education in Mandatory Palestine : a study of three decades of British administration.* London: Luzac.

Tibawi, A.L. (1961) *British Interests in Palestine 1800-1901.* Oxford: Oxford University Press.

UNESCO (1994) Higher Education in the West Bank and Gaza Strip. Report CS-94/WS-16. Paris: UNESCO.

UNICEF/DSP (Birzeit University Development Studies Programme) (2003) The Children of Palestine in the Labour Market. Ramallah, Occupied Palestinian Territories: UNICEF/DSP.

United Nations Programme of Assistance to the Palestinian People (UNDP PAPP) (2000) Focus Newsletter, Issue 6.3. Jerusalem: UNDP PAPP.

Usher, Graham (1991) Children of Palestine, *Race & Class,* 32(4), 1-18.

Van Dyke, B.G. (1996) Consensual Educational Perspectives in Post-Accord Palestine. Paper presented at the 1996 NRMERA Annual Research Conference.

Van Dyke, Blair G. & Randall, Vance E. (2002) Educational Reform in Post-Accord Palestine: a synthesis of Palestinian perspectives, *Educational Studies,* 28(1), 17-32.

Velloso, A. (2002) Palestinian Education: a national curriculum against all odds, *International Journal of Educational Development,* 22(2), 145-154.

Weighill, L. (1995) The Future of Assistance to Palestinian Refugees, *Asian Affairs,* 26(3), 259-269.

World University Service UK (WUS) (1991) *Palestinians and Higher Education: the doors of learning closed.* London: WUS.

Yair, G. & Khatab, N. (1995) Changing of the Guards: teacher–student interaction in the intifada, *Sociology of Education,* 68(2), 99-115.

Zahlan, A. & Zahlan, R. (1977) The Palestinian Future: education and manpower, *Journal of Palestine Studies*, 6(4), 103-112.

Zureik, E.T. (1979) *The Palestinians in Israel: a study in internal colonialism.* London: Routledge & Kegan Paul.

Formal Schooling in Morocco: the hopes and challenges of the current educational reform

ABDELKADER EZZAKI

In Morocco, education is currently viewed as a highly problematic area that needs large-scale reform. Despite the improvements made recently on rates of primary school enrolment and adult literacy, the sector remains faced with serious overall performance challenges. According to the 2003 United Nations Development Programme (UNDP) Human Development Report (UNDP, 2003), Morocco spends more than 25% of the total government annual budgets on education (about 5.5% of GDP), yet it ranks among the low-performing countries on human development indicators (rank of 126, with an education index of .50, compared to Egypt with a rank of 120 and an index of .63, Algeria with a rank of 107 and an index of .69 and Tunisia with a rank of 91 and an index of .73) [this is one of the three indices on which the human development index is built. It is based on adult literacy rate and the combined primary, secondary and tertiary gross enrolment ratio]). Equally serious in this sector are the problems of educational quality, such as the low practical usefulness of the learning, overloaded curricula, emphasis on rote learning and teacher-oriented instruction, the students' unsatisfactory communication skills, relatively low achievement results, and high rates of absenteeism among teachers and students.

In order to address the problems of the whole sector, a Special Commission of Education and Training ('Commission Spéciale d'Education et de Formation', or COSEF) was set up in the mid 1990s. A charter was drawn up and officially adopted in 1999. This charter (COSEF, 1999), which was the object and outcome of a national consensus, is currently the basis for all the reform initiatives taken by the different educational authorities in the country.

The charter, a document which consists of general guidelines rather than specific regulations, deals with the full range of educational areas, namely: (a) the fundamental principles; (b) the generalisation of education and its anchoring in the school's economic environment; (c) the reorganisation of the pedagogical system (the structure and objectives of each cycle); (d) the improvement of educational and training quality; (e) the human resources, (f) governance; and (g) partnership and funding.

In this chapter, we will review and discuss selected aspects of the educational reform in Morocco, with a focus on the generalisation of education and the main constituents of educational quality, namely, the curricula: the methods of teaching and evaluation, language education, and information and communication technology (hereafter ICT). In doing this, we will proceed from the terms of the reforms to a discussion of their implementation.

The Ambition to Achieve the
Universalisation of Education Schooling

As would be expected, the generalisation of schooling is presented in the charter as one of the primary goals of the reform, with specific targets to be achieved. For example, commencing in 2002, all six-year-old children are expected to be enrolled in primary school. As early as 2004, enrolment in the first year of pre-school was to be universal. In the subsequent cycles, out of the total number of children enrolled in first grade, 90% were expected to complete primary school by 2005, 80% to complete middle school in 2008, and 60% to complete secondary education (including vocational training) in 2011, with 40% completing the Baccalaureate.

Examination of the recent reports indicates that schooling rates have improved significantly. For example, according to the most recent evaluations (Ministère de l'Education Nationale et de la Jeunesse [MENJ], 2004; COSEF, 2005), the student population has increased from 1999 to 2004 by 11% in the system as a whole and by 17% in rural areas. The rates for primary schooling as a whole have increased from 66%, with an annual growth rate of 3.7%, compared with 2.2% in the previous decade. First-grade enrolment over the same period has increased from 66% in 1999 to 91% in 2004 (a significant gain). This is a considerable improvement, especially in that it concerns the underprivileged population. For rural children (males and females), the first-grade enrolment rates in the same period have increased from 58% to 85%. The rates for the specific population of females in rural areas have jumped from 25% to 82%.

Despite these improvements, the general picture is still largely unsatisfactory, given the pressing challenges and the fact that the reform is already in its sixth year – already beyond half the period declared as 'the decade of education'. The implementation targets set by the reform are far from being met and are not likely to be met in the near future. According to the most recent statistics (UNDP, 2003; COSEF, 2005; World Bank, 2005), the educational scene continues to show alarming indicators. For example:

- the illiteracy rate is over 40%, one of the highest in the Arab world;
- a large number of school-aged children are still out of school: about 2.5 million children, mostly females in rural areas;

- there is decreasing or poor internal efficiency, since the grade repetition rate has increased from 13.2% in 1997-98 to 13.7% in 2003-04 at the primary level and from 17.1% in 1996-97 to about 20% in 2003-04 at the high school level. With regard to the drop-out rate, about 25% of children leave school before Seventh grade and only about 10% reach eleventh grade. These rates undermine the efforts made in the area of first-grade enrolment;
- the pre-schooling system is weak, with enrolment declining from 55% in 1999-2000 to 50% in 2003-04. The poor performance of this component of the system severely compromises the chances of quality improvement, since many children will continue to join primary schooling with serious language and other educational deficits, especially those from disadvantaged families.

Redesigning Curricula and Pedagogy

The Main Provisions of the Reform

In the charter, several reform guidelines address familiar curriculum and teaching methodology problems in the Moroccan school system. These problems include the limited usefulness of the learning content; the dominance of rote learning; and content-oriented instruction rather than conceptual and problem solving.

The Emphasis on Useful Learning

One of the prominent issues in the charter is that of the relevance of learning content. Thus, a whole section (Section 7) articulates a general reform objective stated as 'Revising and adapting the programs, teaching methods and textbooks and teaching aids'. Speaking directly to this issue, this section calls for associating all theoretical content with practical learning activities and for instituting collaboration between institutions of general education and technical or vocational schools, thus maximising opportunities for practical learning and manual skill development. Students are called upon to open up to vocational training as early as the middle school.

The reform also calls for the creation of large-scale collaborative ventures between the school system and the outside world of economic and cultural activity (including local businesses, industry, agriculture, culture and sport) with the purpose of making full use of the available resources and ensuring practical or locally relevant skill learning for students.

One way put forward for strengthening the practical usefulness of school learning is the setting up of networks among different institutions at the provincial and local level. With this strategy, the system can maximise the deployment of the same resources in different institutions and enable each institution to do what it does best. For example, each middle or high school is to be linked to a local vocational or technical institution in such a way as to allow the former to focus on theoretical pre-vocational learning and the latter on practical vocational skills.

The Shift to Competency-Based Curriculum Design

With regard to actual curriculum design, the reform seeks to implement the competency-based approach in material development on the basis of the 'profile' or skills to be developed at the end of each cycle of study (primary, preparatory or secondary). This approach is to be supported by a system of a common core programme in the first year of secondary education, prior to branching out into more specialised fields of concentration in the two subsequent years, coupled with links or options to transfer among different fields of study, for example, across the branches of secondary education, and between formal schooling and vocational training. Accompanying these provisions is a flexible and locally adaptable organisation of the coursework, using – as much as possible – the semester-based and modular curriculum structure, instead of the traditional year-based and discipline-oriented organisation. The aim is to give students some choice in their courses and enable them to capitalise on their achievements across the different semesters, thus allowing them to move through their course of study at their own pace.

Adapting the Curriculum to the Students' Regional and Local Reality

This provision consists of dividing the curriculum into three components, one for each of the country's geographic constituents:

1. common core of 70% of school time deliverable to all students of the same level in the whole country;
2. a portion of 15% of school time devoted to the study of content about the region, and managed by the regional authority (AREF);
3. a portion of 15% of school time allocated to activities to be determined by the school and its community. These activities should include – but not be limited to – remedial instruction.

Privatising and Instituting the Plurality of References

Contrary to the traditional system characterised by the Ministry's monopoly over textbook authorship, the reform opens production of all educational materials to the private sector, on the basis of competition among the bidders. In doing this, the reform seeks to mobilise all capable educational authors and thus attain the highest level of quality in the instructional material. In addition, it calls for the plurality of contributors, thus giving provincial and eventually local educational authorities the possibility of making their own choices of instructional materials.

Naturally, this involvement of the private sector is subjected to certain quality control measures. These include the issuing of official 'Terms of Reference' to be used by all authors, the evaluation of the projects submitted by official teams of specialists (referees), and the overseeing of the entire programme of curriculum development and material production by a national curriculum committee whose task is not only to plan, supervise and validate the recommendations of the evaluators, but also to protect and promote the overall quality of the curriculum and ensure its continuous innovation.

The Quality of Teaching Methods and Evaluation

Regarding teaching methods, the charter highlights the need to implement a learner-centred pedagogy that aims at enabling children to achieve maximum development, with a focus on the use of active learning methods, cooperative learning, exposure to the economic and sociocultural activities in the school's environment, and the creation of a lively school environment. In the area of evaluation, the charter institutes, in Section 5: (a) the integration of continuous assessment in all cycles; (b) the distribution of evaluation responsibilities across the four educational authorities (local, provincial, regional and national); (c) the involvement of outside professionals in the practical examinations of the technological and vocational branches of study; (d) the combination of regional and national examinations in the high school final examination (Baccalaureate); and (e) the spreading of these examinations across the last two years of high school.

The 'Balance Sheet' of the Curricular and Pedagogical Reform

The achievements and difficulties of the reform in the curricular and pedagogical areas may be summarised as follows.

1. The upgrading of educational content. This includes the integration of new areas of study into the curriculum, such as human rights education, environmental education, citizenship, technology and computing. The downside of these improvements is the continuous overloading of the curriculum and the increasing demands on students' time and energy, not to mention the inevitable rise in the cost of school materials for parents, and the superficial learning that results from this multiplicity of contents. The upgrading of educational content also refers to the search for the integration of learning activities that make the learning more practical and useful in the students' lives. This search is being achieved not only through the piloting of methodologies for regional and local curricula, but also through experimenting with whole initiatives devoted exclusively to practical or life skills. One such initiative is the recently implemented project known as 'la main à la pâte' ('hands-on' learning) supported by the French cooperation programme in Morocco and aiming at enabling students to learn academic content through practical activities. Another example is the current 'Pertinence' programme undertaken by USAID-ALEF (2005), the purpose of which is to develop, with middle and primary schools, learning activities that create a strong link between school life and the demands of the real world. The challenge is for these initiatives to be fully transferred into the official curricula and to create a new pedagogical culture centred on learning 'relevance'.

2. *The introduction of an innovative pedagogical framework.* This new framework, based on competencies, is now in place and all the approved textbooks are designed in accordance to it. The main merits of this approach lie in the fact that – at least in principle – it focuses attention on the integration of knowledge, discrete skills, and attitudes and relates the learning to potential real-life needs. However, despite these merits, the introduction of this innovation is matched by problems. Important among these is the lack of clarity among teachers and even textbook authors and evaluators as to what the approach really means, how it differs from the objectives-based curriculum or the notional functional approach (in the case of language education), and how it should be applied in material design and in testing. This problem is further complicated by the absence of professional training on this new approach. When training is provided, it almost always turns into an exercise of 'selling' a particular textbook, rather than clarifying the approach for the common good.

3. *The total privatisation of textbook resources production and the implementation of the principle of plurality of references.* The implementation of these measures has been largely successful and seems to constitute a 'success story' for the system. Among other things, it opens the door for competition among creative material developers and thus liberates the official educational authorities from a heavy burden that they could not continue to bear. It also offers provincial authorities and eventually schools the possibility to make some choices, instead of relying on one single set textbook. Under this system, up to fifty-seven textbooks have been approved for the different subjects (COSEF, 2005), and it is expected that the cycle of privatised material production will reach the end of high school starting in September 2007. As would be expected, this innovation, as successful as it may be, is not without its imperfections. Among these are the vague and ambiguous 'Terms of Reference' given to potential textbook writers, the lack of a contractual relationship between the textbook evaluators and the Ministry in charge, and the relatively low professionalism of the textbook authors, designers and printers.

4. *Progress towards implementing regional and local curricula.* This provision constitutes another important innovation of the curriculum reform. It

provides a needed compromise and resolves the tension among the three forces competing for school time. Regarding the implementation of the provision, the educational system has developed methodologies for developing and applying regional and local curricula. The first, which was developed with the support of the USAID project known as the Morocco Education for Girls (MEG) project, makes use of the 'study of the milieu' and is more suitable for local curricula (Ministère de l'Education Nationale et de la Jeunesse – MENJ and United States Agency for International Development – Morocco Education for Girls', 2001). The second, on the other hand, was developed by the UNICEF programme in Morocco, on the basis of 'needs analysis' techniques, and is more suitable for the regional curricula (Ministère de l'Education Nationale et de la Jeunesse – MENJ and UNICEF, 2001). The two methodologies have been successfully trialled and delivered, through training, to various educational leaders. Naturally, the regional and local educational leaderships, including teachers and school directors, will need to face the difficult challenge of having to modify a substantial part of their instructional materials and activities. This requires not only skill but also a change of working culture.

5. *Improvements in the evaluation system.* The new evaluation system introduced by the reform has instituted continuous assessment in all educational cycles and has introduced major changes in the Baccalaureate. This involves a unified regional examination in eleventh grade and a final national examination in twelfth grade, and one session instead of two. These changes offer several advantages, especially in view of their impact on teaching and learning, including: giving importance to teachers' and students' work in class; multiple inputs into the students' final results; and testing students at different stages of the Baccalaureate. However, while all of these changes bring more 'fairness' into the system, still more improvements are needed in this area. Among other things, the system still requires greater attention to test validity and reliability by developing professional testing expertise. This must be done, not only at the national or regional levels, but also at the school level, so as to ensure quality testing in all evaluation components, including continuous assessment. These improvements will, it is hoped, be made easier with the work to be undertaken by the agency in charge of educational evaluation ('Instance Nationale d'Evaluation'), an agency created in 2006 under the auspices of the 'Higher Council for Education' or 'Conseil Supérieur de l'Enseignement'.

6. *Unchanged teaching methods.* This aspect of educational quality is perhaps the one that is most resistant to change, even in a major reform. Although the curriculum and the approach to textbook design has greatly improved, and although the reform calls for the implementation of active learning and teaching methods, teachers in the classrooms still conduct 'business as usual'. The teaching tradition continues to focus on academic content, rote learning,

teacher-fronted instruction, and teaching to the tests, with little attention to autonomous or cooperative learning. These modern interactive approaches, when they happen to be presented in training sessions, remain in the realm of theory. This stagnant and non-creative teaching tradition is further complicated by the scarcity of instructional resources, the weakness of quality control measures, such as too few visits by the supervisors and the limited role of parents' associations.

7. *Accumulated deficit translating into students' poor achievement.* Whatever the quality of the reform, the real test for its merits is the level of students' achievement in terms of results, which, judging from international assessment studies, are far from being satisfactory. For example, in the widely quoted Trends in International Mathematics and Science Study (TIMSS) (Institute of Education Sciences [IES], 2006), and taking only the sciences test scores of 2003, Moroccan eighth graders ranked forty-fifth out of fifty in the whole group of participating countries and seventh out of eight in the group of Arab countries. Improvement of the students' performance level clearly needs attention and should be taken as a collective responsibility, involving teachers, supervisors and administrators, as well as the students themselves.

ICT in Formal Schooling

In Morocco, as it is the case everywhere, ICT is currently being taken as a critical component of educational quality at all levels. In line with this perception, the charter (Article 10) calls upon the educational authorities to enable schools to close the 'digital gap', with the objectives of: (a) helping students' improve their learning and overcome their achievement difficulties, (b) facilitating access to information and documentation, especially for schools in remote areas; and (c) enabling teachers to pursue easily accessible in-service training. Among the actions recommended is integrating ICT in schools by creating, in each institution, one computer centre and one multimedia library in the course of the decade 2000-2010.

In application of these guidelines, the government of Morocco inaugurated in 2005 a three-year development scheme known as 'GENIE', aiming at equipping 8600 schools with multimedia centres and Internet connections. It also provides for ICT to all schools (Projet GENIE, 2006). For the immediate future, this scheme provides for equipping 3000 schools with computer centres by November 2006. It also provides for the training of 230,000 teachers, including 10,000 who will specialise in developing ICT learning packages. To be added to this are 700 technicians who will be trained to ensure the maintenance of the 100,000 machines that will be used during the period covered by the project.

To support the educational functioning of the equipment, an e-curricula programme is being developed, with the purpose of producing professional software dealing with the official instructional contents. The design of this content will be carried out by the private sector, but the guidelines, the follow-up and the validation will be overseen by an official specialiscd educational body. The channel of delivery is proposed to be an educational portal designed for this purpose. The first version of this portal, though originally planned to be on the Internet at the end of 2006, is to date not yet active. Although the project will be funded largely by public allocations, it is expected that it will be partially supported by international programmes operating in Morocco.

The scheme certainly presents some very special strengths. Among other things, it not only provides for the creation of computer centres in the schools, but also for the much needed support system: training of teachers and technicians; setting up a multimedia follow-up and development laboratory; and authoring of appropriate educational software. However, despite the considerable effort deployed in this strategy, and despite the experiences already gained from some pilot projects, there is a strong feeling among Moroccan pro-ICT educators that the official project, even when it is implemented, is not likely to meet the increasing and pressing needs. Among other things, the scheme is not likely to benefit the whole school population in that about 40% of the total student population (COSEF, 2005) are schooled in rural areas where access to electricity and to the Internet is a common difficulty. This is further complicated by the fact that one computer centre per school, even with the best use of the facility, is not likely to be enough, especially in view of the fact that the student population in each school is typically in the hundreds and sometimes in the thousands. Another potential difficulty has to do with the extent to which the teachers will actually 'come onboard' and fully integrate ICT in their teaching. Even if professional software is made available, it is not certain that this material will have the needed 'value-added' benefit or that teachers will make effective use of it in instruction and in testing. A third possible difficulty has to do with the sustainability of the entire investment. Teachers and students are accustomed to seeing new equipment arrive in their schools only to realise, after a while, that this equipment is out of service for good, because the spare parts are not available or the maintenance funding has run out or has not yet been allocated.

The Language Education Issue

The Guidelines

Given its critical importance to the quality of education, the issue of language instruction receives significant attention in the reform. The provision regarding this issue attempts to address the complex linguistic situation in Morocco. This complexity is demonstrated, primarily, by the multilingual make-up of Moroccan social and cultural life. In this make-up, different language systems co-exist and usually compete for prestige, communication functions, and of course for space in the curriculum. These language systems

217

include not only different varieties of Arabic (standard, semi-standard, and Moroccan Arabic), but also different varieties of Amazigh (the current label for the Berber varieties), not to mention the main foreign languages, especially French, Spanish and English. Matching this linguistic pluralism – or perhaps resulting from it – are the serious educational issues such as the observed weakness in students' communication skills, the mismatch between the pre-college and the tertiary levels regarding the medium of science education, and difficulties arising from having to learn to read in a linguistic system different from that of the 'mother tongue' (Moroccan Arabic or one of the varieties of Amazigh).

Aware of the complexity of this situation, and heeding the political and ethnic overtones associated with the different choices (e.g. Arabic vs. French or Arabic vs. Amazigh), the charter has opted for a line of reform characterised by a sense of realism, the need for careful change and for balance among the dominant forces, and most importantly by the dual concern with Morocco's Arabo-Islamic identity, coupled with the political determination to be open to – and indeed be a part of – the modern world. This sense of balance is reflected in the following provisions:

- A firm position on the status of Arabic as the (only) national language and the need to promote it through the modernisation of its teaching at all levels, the opening, in higher education, of scientific and technical branches to function in this language, the setting up of the 'Arabic Academy', and, of course, the use of Arabic as a medium of communication in different sectors, including science and technology.
- Recognising the important role of Amazigh in the educational system: the charter recommends that this language be dealt with under the regional authorities and be taught simply as a medium to facilitate the learning of subject content (taught in Arabic); in addition, the charter provides for the creation of research and teacher training centres so as to promote the language and culture of Amazigh.
- Facilitating the mastery of foreign languages, by (i) instituting an early start on the teaching of two of them, one as early as second grade, and the other as early as sixth grade, (ii) associating each foreign language with the teaching of cultural, scientific or technical modules in this same foreign language so as to reinforce the functional nature of the learning, (iii) providing a pre-college programme to bring the students' foreign language competence to the required level so as to help them make the transition from Arabic to the foreign language in their study of scientific and technical subjects, (iv) the recurrent in-service training of teachers, and (v) the integration of ICT in teaching and learning.
- Providing for the elaboration of a 10-year plan on the teaching of languages in the Moroccan school system. This plan is expected to cover propositions on the development of: instructional methods and materials, the elaboration of testing instruments, teacher training

strategies and content, the phases of the plan, and of course, the means of funding and supporting the implementation of all these activities.

The 'Balance Sheet' on Language Education

The reform measures on language education are in themselves of sound quality. If properly implemented, they should be expected to significantly improve not only the teaching of languages, but the total quality of education as a whole. Unfortunately, the quality of a reform does not only lie in its theoretical formulations. The problems that may be raised in this regard vary a great deal. Some have to do with the applicability of some provisions; others are more related to delays or to poor implementation. Regarding applicability, it is difficult, for example, to implement with success the provision of creating in higher education scientific and technical branches in Arabic, while the human resources continue to be trained in foreign languages, and also while the necessary references in Arabic continue to be scarce and of doubtful quality. But what is more serious is that the provisions about the language component of the reform have not yet been implemented, although the adoption of the Charter is already seven years old. The delays concern, among other things, the elaboration and approval of the ten-year language education plan, and the creation of the Arabic Academy. Equally serious is the fact that some of these measures are being implemented with little concern for careful planning or for quality instruction. For example, the second foreign language was introduced in the middle school without ensuring the preparation of the necessary number of teachers and the proper preparation of the needed textbooks. The improvised measures led, inevitably, to a largely disorganised launching of the new foreign language programme and is likely to adversely affect the expected outcomes.

A special note must be made here about Amazigh. This is perhaps the only matter where the implementation has far exceeded the terms of the charter. While the charter placed the teaching of Amazigh within the regional curricula and assigned to it the limited role of supporting the learning of Arabic, the actual implementation has stepped beyond the regional authority and has launched Amazigh instruction, albeit still on a limited scale, not as a means to facilitate the learning of the different subjects, but as a language and a culture in their own right. The credit here goes to the active role played by the IRCAM (the Royal Institute for Amazigh Culture of Morocco) and to the civil society forces that work for the promotion of Amazigh. Unfortunately, while it is recognised that the efforts undertaken to promote the teaching of Amazigh in public schools is a positive development for Morocco, both politically and culturally, no one can ignore the concerns over the factors that may limit the overall success of the entire project. Perhaps the most important of these factors is the adoption of Tifannagh as the Amazigh script instead of the Arabic or Latin script. This adoption means that the children who will learn Amazigh (presumably many if not all Moroccan children, as the promoters of this language wish) will have to struggle – as early as the first years of primary schooling – with three totally different alphabets: Arabic, Latin and Tifannagh, which certainly adds to the many factors responsible for the already heavy school wastage.

Conclusions and Perspectives

In this chapter, we examined some key aspects of formal schooling in Morocco, focusing on significant and pressing issues such as the universalisation of schooling, the curricula and methodology of teaching and evaluation, ICT in education, and language education. These issues are all dealt with extensively in the reform as presented in the charter; in fact, it is widely believed that this document is both sound and highly responsive to needed improvements. Taken to implementation, the reform has certainly brought some important positive changes, especially in the areas of first grade enrolment, curriculum development, textbook design, and evaluation. It has also generated some key legislative texts, including the laws on the generalisation of education and on pre-schooling. However, certain implementation difficulties are severely weakening the success level of the reform.

To improve the chance for the reform to achieve its goals, the course of immediate and future action should perhaps focus on the following initiatives:

- *Improving school resources.* The reform cannot achieve any of its major goals if schools present – or continue to present – a poor physical environment. Major investments are needed not only to improve the school physical plant, but also to make available the required learning resources, including laboratory and sports equipment, teaching aids, libraries and multimedia centres.
- *Strengthening student enrolment, retention and completion.* The system should maintain the focus on first-grade enrolment. Significant efforts are also needed to retain children at school and reduce the drop-out and absenteeism rates, especially among the rural student population and among girls in particular. These efforts should include support for such services as school meals, transport, school supplies, and boarding facilities for girls in middle schools. Needless to say here that a friendly school environment and quality instruction are important factors in this support system.
- *Continuing the improvement work on curricula and teaching methods.* In this area, the educational system needs to sharpen the competency-based approach through the development of a clearer vision on this approach and the delivery of professional training for the educational community, including textbook writers. This training should cover the application of the approach not only in teaching and designing instructional material, but also in evaluation. The system should also seek to make the

contents of the curricula more related to students' needs, by ensuring the connection between academic information with real-life activities, reinforcing the practical aspects of the academic subjects, building into the curricula such components as 'life skills', and fully implementing the project of regional and local curricula. Naturally, these curricular changes would need to be strengthened by the use of active teaching methods involving learner-centred principles, autonomous and cooperative learning, and the emphasis on higher-order thinking and 'time-on-task' in classroom instruction. The Moroccan educational scene is full of potentially productive experiences on useful learning and innovative pedagogies, some of which are achieved with inputs from international cooperation programmes, and it is being done by the ministry in charge of education with the partnership of USAID under the ALEF project (USAID-ALEF, 2005); others are developed by the initiatives of regular classroom teachers. Of course, these pedagogical innovations will not have much significance unless they are scaled up to a larger student population and unless they lead to real improvements in students' achievement results.

- *Speeding up the integration of ICT.* To support the innovations in the areas of curriculum and teaching methodology, the system needs to speed up the process of integrating ICT into teaching and learning practices. This integration needs full-scale training for teachers at both pre- and in-service levels and, of course, the ensuring of continuous maintenance of the equipment and the production of adequate educational software.

- *Special attention to language and communication skills.* Despite the efforts that are being made in language education, this component of the reform remains highly problematic. Improving students' communication skills cannot be achieved by increasing the number of languages to be taught, for there is already a widely shared feeling that the students are 'learners of several language systems, but masters of none'. Improving the teaching of Arabic cannot be done with declarations of intent, and foreign languages cannot be mastered simply by starting their teaching earlier. What is needed most is to provide good quality instruction, ensuring maximum 'time on task' in the classroom and using intensive communication-oriented activities, instead of focusing on rules or knowledge about language. What is also needed is a rich school environment with useful resources and meaningful extra-curricular activities in which learners develop fluency, independent learning, and confidence in their communication skills, both oral and written. To support this quality instruction, the system needs to make extensive use of ICT in language education and implement a standards-based evaluation for students' language performance at different levels.

Abdelkader Ezzaki

- *Improving the management of human resources*: It is clear that the reform is a highly ambitious enterprise and the problems to be solved are highly complex and demanding in terms of material and human resources. It is worth noting in this regard that the Moroccan educational system, under a general government scheme, released in 2005 several hundreds of educational personnel (teachers and administrators) who have not been replaced. This has happened at a time when the system is in need of more capacity, rather than less. The deficit in human resources needs to be addressed, and this should be done not only by the appropriate deployment of the remaining personnel, but also by strengthening their morale, providing proper incentives, and of course, putting into place a rigorous management and a strong accountability system. No improvement can be expected in the system if teachers and administrators are not inspired or required to deliver quality education to their students.

References

Commission Spéciale d'Education et de Formation (COSEF) (1999) *La Charte Nationale d'Education et de Formation*. Rabat. Also available on www.cosef.ac.ma.

Commission Spéciale d'Education et de Formation (COSEF) (2005) *Réforme du système éducatif et de formation 1999-2004*. Also available on www.cosef.ac.ma.

Institute of Education Sciences (IES). *Trends in International Mathematics and Science Study (TIMSS)* (International Comparisons in Education). nces.ed.gov/timss/.

Ministère de l'Education Nationale et de la Jeunesse (MENJ) (2004) *Cadre stratégique du système éducatif*. Rabat.

Ministère de l'Education Nationale et de la Jeunesse (MENJ) and US Agency for International Development (USAID) – Morocco Education for Girls (MEG) (2001) *Méthodologie pour les Curricula Régionaux et Locaux*. Rabat.

Ministère de l'Education Nationale et de la Jeunesse (MENJ) and UNICEF (2000) *Les Curricula Régionaux et Locaux*. Rabat.

Projet GENIE (2006) Actualité quotidienne sur les nouvelles technologies au Maroc et dans le monde. www.itmaroc.com/Les-details-du-projet-Genie, Sunday, March 12, 2006.

United Nations Development Program (UNDP) (2003) *Human Development Report–Morocco*. hdr.undp.org/reports/.

USAID-ALEF (2005) Note technique sur le Programme de Pertinence. www.alef.ma.

World Bank (2005) *Morocco Human Development Report*. web.worldbank.org.

Computerising Turkey's Schools

AYSE KOK

Introduction

Information and communication technologies (ICTs) have become key global tools in service delivery across various sectors of society. This phenomenon has given birth to the revolution of methodology in primary education in developing countries such as Turkey which is the primary focus of this chapter. However, this revolution is not yet widespread and needs to be strengthened to reach all schools in Turkey. What is required now is for government and all stakeholders to insist on the best standards and approaches so as to ensure effective ICT for education service delivery in all institutions of learning from early years to graduate studies.

ICT in Education and Society

The term ICT in this chapter designates multimedia, the Internet or the Web, as a medium to enhance instruction or as a replacement for other media (Pelgrum & Law, 2003). The idea that information technology (IT) can help developing countries is intriguing to many, because of the benefits that have apparently been realised in the West. As Avgerou (1990) wrote, the literature sometimes contains a naïve, taken-for-granted assumption that the success of the West is attributable to ICT, and therefore bringing the benefits of this development to poorer countries is simply a matter of delivering IT.

Moreover, education has a central influence on the idea of ICT and therefore it must be examined and re-examined in order to gain a better understanding of how ICT can have an impact on developing countries (Ezer, 2005). So, advantage should be taken of the power of technology to improve the conditions in the educational area. As Hawkin (2006) states, if this transformation could be realised,

> schools a hundred years from now will sit at the heart of a learning
> society and allow youth from any country in the world – rich or
> poor – to have the same opportunities to create a better world.

In order to address the questions of 'How can ICT be applied to support education change?' and 'How can its application in education in turn support

223

sustained economic development and social transformation?' Kozma (2005) suggests the following four types of approaches in general:

- ICT is used to improve the *delivery* of and *access* to education. This approach can improve education on the margins by increasing the efficiency by which instruction is distributed, but it need not involve fundamental change.
- ICT is the *focus* of learning. By learning ICT skills, students become better prepared for work that increasingly involves the use of ICT.
- ICT can be used to improve student *understanding*, increase the *quality* of education, and thereby increase the *impact* of education on the economy.
- Knowledge creation, technology, technological innovativeness, and knowledge sharing can contribute to the *transformation* of the education system and to sustained economic growth and social development.

Furthermore, Levine (1998) emphasises the importance of having a plan that is based on real school needs and that is realistic, achievable and effective. The plan should be produced, not for the sole purpose of putting technology in the classroom but to reflect the real needs of schools in order to make effective technology deployment and to produce enhanced learning environments. The involvement of all stakeholders in the preparation and execution of the plan has been identified as a catalyst in the integration process.

Similarly, Hepp et al (2004) caution that there is no universal truth when it comes to applying ICT in education, and that there is no advice that can be directly applied without considering each country's contextual priorities, long-term budgetary prospects and commitment.

Theoretical Lenses to ICT

The introduction and use of information technology in education is commonly associated with a process of 'educational innovation' (Fullan, 1996), either acting as a Trojan horse, as a catalyst (Hawkridge et al, 1990) or, more recently, as a lever, a tool that must be applied purposefully to a task to be of value. These different categories might show the evolution of the role that ICT plays in educational innovation and also show its prevalence associated to processes of educational innovation (Hinostroza et al, 2002). This has set an international scenario in which there is widespread presence of ICT in schools (Hinostroza et al, 2002).

Some authors are optimistic and argue that ICT can lower costs, provide users with more information, make markets more efficient, and improve public service delivery, while others are more sceptical. They point to the fact that often technology does not address a pressing need (Ezer, 2005). As Avgerou (1990) argues, ICT initiatives can often become a waste of valuable time and money. At the same time, some consider digital information and communication technologies as a powerful instrument with the ability to act as a catalyst to 'desirable' change in the structure of society (Trujillo, 2000). They think that characteristics of information technology (convergence and cost reduction) hold the potential for 'leapfrogging' development stages (Bell, [1985], Cane [1992] and Canning [1999], cited in Campbell, 2001).

Still others argue that the information revolution will change the structure of societies. They think that digital information technologies will 'level the playing field' by increasing access to sources of information to all sectors of society (Trujillo, 2000).

Education, ICT and Developing Countries

Regardless of theoretical approaches taken, one cannot deny the fact that developing countries in the Middle East face the same problems as other developing countries around the world: low levels of education and literacy, poor technology infrastructures, and a wide gap between the disposable income of the relatively few 'haves' and the more numerous 'have-nots'.

As the International Telecommunication Unit (ITU) described in their World Telecommunication Development Report (2003), education is a key component of a country's transformation towards actively and fully participating in the global information society. As Kozma (2005) illustrates, the development policy literature ascribes a very important role to education (Organisation for Economic Cooperation and Development [OECD], 2001, 2004). He notes that in the narrowest sense, education increases the productive skills of the labour force and these skills increase the productivity of the economy in general and increase the earning power of individuals in particular. In a broader sense, education has an impact on a person's sense of well-being, job satisfaction, and capacity to absorb new ideas and technologies, as well as an impact on increased community participation, improved health, reduced crime, and general well-being (Kozma, 2005).

Efforts such as the United Nations' 'Education for All' (EFA) initiative from 1990 (Jomtien, and Dakar, 2000), the 'Millennium Development Goals' and the 'Literacy Decade' commit developed and less developed countries to work together to provide universal primary education, increase adult literacy, eliminate gender disparities in education, provide youth with life skills, and generally improve the quality of education (Kozma, 2005).

Turkey at a Glance

Since the establishment of the Republic of Turkey in 1923, Turkish society has been going through an enormous transformation, involving social, cultural, intellectual, economic and structural dimensions. The government of the Republic of Turkey has been moving to integrate the country into Europe since its founding by Mustafa Ataturk in 1923 and in line with this long-term national aim, Turkey has been investing aggressively in ICT projects in recent years, building bridges between 'the West', especially Europe, and 'the East'. This long-standing agenda mirrors the country's geographical situation as literally a bridge between the two.

While diffusion and use of these technologies have been proceeding in Turkey, progress has been hampered by unfavourable economic conditions such as the November 2000 banking crisis, and rapidly shifting governments during the past ten years. Pak (2001) sums up the Turkish context admirably:

> Turkey has a penchant for surprising the world and this goes hand in hand with a reputation for not fitting any bill. While the cards on the table reveal a picture that conforms to lingering prejudices, the country always has something more up its sleeve that helps it keep its head well above the water. To name but a few: a dynamic and diversified economy which has survived years of runaway inflation and grown to disprove predictions of doom; a young and vibrant population with about a half under the age of 20, propelling more or less steady development; a well-trained and adaptive workforce that powers industrial growth; and an ever-growing ensemble of businessmen, willing and able to rise to the challenges of globalisation.

ICT in the Turkish Educational System

Turkey's contact with the information age, or, to be more precise, mass encounter with computers, has a history that spans no more than two decades (Pak, 2001) whereas the public's acquaintance with the Internet has been even more recent, going back just over a decade.

As the results of a study undertaken by Goktas & Yildirim (2003) show, the importance of integration of ICT into education is vital to Turkey. Turkey faces massive educational challenges with a great number of people to educate, a very large educational system, a poor economic situation, inadequate technologies and very large numbers of students and teachers. In spite of these challenging conditions, Turkey is required to take measures in order to catch up with the European Union (EU) standards in integrating ICT into its educational system as the country aspires to EU membership.

In comparison to many other countries of the Middle East, Turkey shows greater signs of realising an information revolution in education. Due to being a democratic country, Turkey is not constrained in government and civil society participation for successful employment of all dimensions of the potential of ICT for development.

As in many other developing countries, the Turkish Government has articulated a vision of an information society in which widespread access to technology can not only contribute to human capital, but also improve government services, promote Turkish culture, and support economic

226

growth. In other words, the ICT sector is seen as a vehicle for both economic growth and social development (Kozma, 2005). As one Turkish IT leader observed, 'the explosive impact of communications has not only eased people's lives, it has made the country more democratic and pluralistic' (Turkish IT Magazine, 1999, vol. 2).

With this belief in mind, several governmental bodies have ICT projects under way. For example, the Ministry of National Education (MoNE)) has begun deploying computer facilities with broadband connections to 75,000 schools within Turkey. All four rationales put forward by Hawkridge et al (1990) to justify mass computerisation in schools apply to Turkey. These are:

- *Social rationale*: This deals with all students' place in society and the demystification of the importance of computers at school level. So, all students of primary school age should be aware, and unafraid of, how computers work because computers are fundamental to operations in all countries. Consequently, all students should acquire computer awareness.
- *Vocational rationale*: This refers to the need to prepare learners for employment through providing computer education. According to this rationale, students should be able to operate computers, at least at a basic level, since this gives them vital skills for their employment and career prospects.
- *Pedagogical rationale*: This rationale calls for improved qualities of teaching and learning. Computers as sophisticated educational tools can extend and transcend traditional ways of presenting information to learners of all ages and enrich existing curricula.
- *Catalytic rationale*: This rationale states that schools can be changed for the better by the introduction of computers and that teaching, administrative and managerial efficiency may be improved. Computers help students to become less dependent on the teacher as expert. Moreover, they require students to do less memorising of facts and more information handling and problem solving. So, students will move away from rote learning and teacher-centred lessons by having more control of their own learning.

Integrating ICT into a centralised education system such as Turkey's depends on its successful design and application, which is an expensive and complex process (Akbaba-Altun, 2006). The scale of this policy is massive, comprising numerous objectives, as distinguished by Kocaoluk & Kocaoluk (2000):

- to obtain information about practical methods of using computers;
- to obtain information about the definition, developments and ways of using computers;
- to comprehend the numerical systems used in computers;
- to identify the basic parts of computers and their functions;

- to gain basic knowledge and skills on the use of computers and computer programming;
- to obtain precise knowledge from computers;
- to load the intended knowledge to the computers;
- to acquire knowledge of best practice in computer use;
- to practise basic programs on computers.

In this context, Turkey has also targeted the education system as an important component of its development strategy, and like many other countries – particularly less developed ones – it faces many problems and constraints when considering education reform in the context of economic and social development (Kozma, 2005).

As part of computer-assisted education, efforts have already been made to spread the use of computers. In the academic year 2000-01, the number of schools with computers reached 5536 (Ministry of National Education [MoNE], , 2005). Moreover, the average of pupils per computer in primary education in Turkey is 103.5 (Table I). Learning about ICT is not included in the compulsory primary curriculum, but offered as an elective course which depends on the school or students, but is approximately one or two hours a week (Kocaoluk & Kocaoluk, 2000).

Countries	Land area[1] (1000 km²)	Population[1] (2001)	GNP[1] (euros) (2000)	No. of comp. per 1000 people[1] (1999)	No. of students in primary and secondary education[2] (2000)	No. of teachers in primary and secondary education[2] (2000)	Pupils per computer at primary educ.[3]	Pupils per computer at sec. educ.[3]
Total or average of the EU	3,193,000	379,448,000	24,463	278	60,802,600	4,501,500	13.2	8.6
France	544,000	59,343,000	23,250	220	9,813,300	709,100	14.1	9.4
Germany	357,000	82,360,000	24,640	297	11,963,100	817,600	19.2	13.7
Italy	301,000	58,018,000	20,190	191	7,240,700	680,100	20.8	8.9
Spain	505,000	40,428,000	15,220	122	5,939,600	459,800	11.2	12.4
UK	242,000	60,075,000	25,970	304	12,930,400	710,000	11.8	6.4
Turkey	770,000	65,300,000	3,200	32	12,339,254	511,062	103.5	35.2

Table I. Comparison of the 2004 basic indicators
between selected countries of the European Union and Turkey.

Current Issues in the Turkish Educational System and ICT

Although ICT holds great potential to support ongoing educational as well as national development, several challenges have affected its large-scale deployment and utilisation for educational purposes, and these have very much reduced its capacity to do the nation good (Fouth, 2005).

Firstly, as a related study undertaken by Akbaba-Altun (2006) indicates, there are general capacity and systemic issues such as too few computers, slow Internet connections, insufficient software in the native language, and a lack of peripheral equipment in schools. Moreover, the IT classrooms in schools were placed in existing older classrooms that were not designed according to the needs of IT classrooms, so there is a need for future schools to be designed with adequate wiring, ergonomics and security in IT-dedicated classrooms. According to this study, another common issue is insufficient in-service training courses for teachers, especially in content areas. Training courses are provided by unqualified staff and are not appropriate for teachers' needs and levels. These in-service training courses also have a lack of hands-on activities.

Akbaba-Altun (2006) also claim that curriculum problems generally stem from the available software programs in schools. According to the findings of their study, these software programs were not considered to be suitable for the students' grade levels by the participants. Moreover, the suggested curriculum for fourth to eighth graders is almost the same, and upper grades do not build upon their knowledge (Akbaba-Altun, 2006). Another issue is the relatively high software prices which make it difficult for schools to purchase.

It is also claimed that school principals' lack of technical knowledge, their idiosyncratic interpretations of regulations, and their lack of support pave the way for the problems and issues outlined here. Although providing security is one of the roles of the principals related to IT classrooms, they mostly do not take necessary precautions in their schools for IT classrooms in particular, and so most computers are not protected against burglary (Akbaba-Altun, 2006).

Another important issue is that the supervisors do not consider themselves competent enough to be able to supervise IT classrooms. There needs to be a priori training and support before supervisors are sent to schools.

In this context, some of the factors which have affected the effective deployment and utilisation of ICT for educational purposes in Turkey are summarised by Fouth (2005) as follows:

- inadequate ICT infrastructure including computer hardware and software, and bandwidth/access;
- a lack of skilled manpower to manage available systems and inadequate training facilities for ICT education at the tertiary level;
- resistance to change from traditional pedagogical methods to more innovative, technology-based teaching and learning methods, by both students and academics;
- the overall educational system is under-funded, therefore, available funds are used to meet survival needs by the institutions;
- the over-dependence of educational institutions on government for everything has limited institutions' ability to find partners in the private sector or seek alternative funding sources for ICT educational initiatives;
- lack of effective coordination of all the various ICT for education initiatives.

The list is not exhaustive but represents the major problems faced in the development of ICT for education in Turkey. If these issues are adequately addressed, e-education could thrive in Turkey, and despite the negatives significant progress has been made.

Turkey's ICT Reform in Education

One should bear in mind that, not long ago – until 2005 – the pedagogy, curriculum, and textbooks within Turkey's educational system emphasised the memorisation of subject matter facts and principles. Similarly, student examinations were also based on memorisation. It is also worth mentioning that there are high-stakes tests that determine the educational (and consequently, the economic) future of the young people in Turkey. So, the use of ICT in schools was reinforcing the curricular and pedagogical emphasis on rote learning. Consequently, the Government introduced educational reforms to prepare students for a modern future in which Turkey is open to the cultures of other peoples and school learning becomes integrated into that of the outside world (Kozma, 2005).

With the adoption of a policy document for integrating ICT as an indispensable part of lifelong learning in 2004, MoNE made an effort to reach an enrolment ratio at basic education (Grade 1 through Grade 8) around 97%. However there are still ongoing efforts in order to bring this ratio up to 100% (Karip, 2005). Efforts are made to ensure that the children will attend and continue to attend basic education by providing financial incentives as direct payment to families. Several other measures to increase enrolment in basic education, including building more boarding schools, can be cited, such as the 'Support Campaign for National Education', the 'Campaign for Girls' Education' (Haydi Kızlar Okula), and '100% Support for Education Campaign'.

Moreover, a policy document outlining strategies to integrate the use of ICT in education and training systems for both teachers and students has also been adopted by MoNE. This policy document states that MoNE will provide continuously the most advanced ICT for schools. ICT initiatives that have been completed or are in progress indicate that the Government is committed to the use of ICT for management, education and training purposes (Karip, 2005). The significant improvement of the ICT infrastructure during the last several years is clearly evident in the following figures taken from the country report for the European Commission (2005):

- 8950 ICT classrooms have been established in year 2004;
- 6400 ICT classrooms have been planned for year 2005;
- distribution of 45,064 PCs for use of teachers has taken place in year 2005 and the hardware components are supported by related instructional and administrative software and web-based applications;
- broadband Internet access options like satellite, ISDN or ADSL have been provided for all of the 42,534 schools;

- connections for about 20,000 schools have been provided.

As indicated in the report, with regard to teacher training, the Board of Education has already established a website for teachers. Additionally, MoNE is establishing an 'education portal' to create a digital system to serve the educational needs of teachers, pupils and community to improve quality of education and to use ICT in education as part of educational policy (Karip, 2005).

Although significant improvement and progress has been shown during the last several years, resource constraints are very tight and it is unlikely that there will be more support available from the government budget (Karip, 2005). As Karip (2005) suggests, it is crucial to create tax incentives and to find other creative solutions to generate the necessary funding for education.

Turkey's ICT Initiatives in Education

Turkey's centralised education system began using computers more than twenty years ago when, in 1984, MoNE first introduced computers to secondary schools (Akbaba-Altun, 2006). In 1991, national educational policy included computer-aided instruction.

In 1998, the MoNE received a loan, equivalent to 600 million US dollars, from the World Bank to invest in a two-phase National Basic Education Program (BEP), which finished at the end of 2006. As a comprehensive educational investment project, the objectives of the BEP are to expand eight-year compulsory education, to improve the quality of education, and to make basic education schools become learning centres of their communities. In order to improve the quality of Turkey's education, one of the objectives of this development programme is to ensure that each student and teacher becomes at least literate in ICT. Phase I was completed in 2003 and Phase II is being prepared for implementation. The phases are described below.

Basic Education Programme Phase I (1998-2003)

One of the areas in which the modernisation/reform efforts of Turkey's education and training systems are concentrating is on building the ICT infrastructure (Karip, 2005). In relation to this, the following activities were completed within Phase I (Akbaba-Altun, 2006):

- MoNE created 3188 IT classrooms in 2802 elementary schools (K-8) and equipped them with computers, printers, scanners, televisions, videos, multimedia software and slides. All schools had the same number and type of IT tools, except for the number of computers;
- a total of 56,605 computers were distributed to 26,244 rural area elementary schools;

- 1630 laptop computers were supplied to 3000 primary education supervisors who were then trained in computer literacy, active learning, and teaching strategies;
- 25,000 elementary school teachers were trained in computer literacy in various in-service programmes provided by the MoNE. In addition, 15,928 elementary school teachers received advanced computer training by the contract firms who supplied hardware and software to those schools;
- 2308 computer coordinators were trained in using projectors and 18,517 schools were sent overhead projectors.

Since the full implementation of Phase I has been fairly recent, empirical research reports on the effectiveness of Phase I are limited but all suggest that the IT classrooms are not yet being used effectively (Akbaba-Altun, 2006).

Basic Education Programme Phase II

Upon implementation of Phase I, a loan agreement was signed in 2000 between Turkey and the World Bank for Phase II, according to which the objectives in Phase I were expanded. Within Phase II, there are pre-school education and special education programmes and consequently, the following initiatives were added to the BEP:

- develop an educational web portal site and provide ICT equipment to approximately 3000 more elementary education schools;
- provide educational materials to 4000 additional elementary schools;
- train more teachers, principals and supervisors;
- continue programme implementation support;
- continue programme progress and evaluation activities.

As Akbaba-Altun (2006) state, integrating computer technologies into education is a large investment that will continue, despite their research showing that IT classrooms are not being used effectively. Yet, because of the continual large financial investment in ICT s, the vital question of how can those IT classrooms be used more effectively urgently needs to be answered. Akbaba-Altun state that

> understanding the obstacles that have so far prevented effective IT classroom use will ... provide a framework for policy makers to retool the program, raise practitioners' awareness toward integrating information technology at their schools, and increase awareness that the ICT issues in culturally different contexts can contribute to Turkey's own understanding of technology transfer. (p. 22)

The strong belief that education could contribute to the development of Turkey's information society by improving the quality of its human capital, increasing knowledge creation and innovativeness, and fostering knowledge sharing (Kozma, 2005) is evident in MoNE's reform effort whereby technology has been identified as an important component. Needless to say, major systemic barriers have to be changed within the education system itself, such as the country's curriculum and assessment systems, which still emphasise the memorisation of facts, thus impeding innovative thinking and knowledge creation in schools. To participate in the information society, curriculum, pedagogy, assessment, and the use of technology need to be aligned with Turkey's vision of the future (Kozma, 2005).

Turkey's Journey as an EU Candidate

Turkey has been on a journey to becoming a participant in the EU for some years now. Not being quite sure whether it will get there, the country puts every effort into fulfilling the membership requirements, including the area of education. According to the country report for the European Commission (2005), Turkey's basic education (Grade 1 through Grade 8) curricula for core subjects have been developed, and curriculum development work for remaining subjects is continuing. To quote from this report:

> Basic education curricula for basic skill areas, including mathematics, science and technology, social studies, Turkish language and life skills have been piloted in 120 schools in 9 provinces. Moreover, new textbooks and instructional materials have been developed both by MoNE and private sector. Nationwide dissemination and implementation of new curricula for Grade 1 through Grade 5 has already started as of September 2005. (p. 7)

Karip (2005) states in the country report for the European Commission that reforming education and training systems is among the top priorities of the Turkish Government. The report continues:

> it has been mentioned in this report, reform efforts have been catalyzed by EU funded projects such as Support to Basic Education Program, Strengthening Vocational and Technical Education Project and Modernization of Vocational Education and Training Project. These projects provide support for developing and implementing national lifelong learning policies aligned with Lisbon objectives. (p. 93)

Current reform efforts are taking a holistic approach to improve quality and relevance of education and training. These efforts also include integrating the use of ICT with education and training and integrating secondary school curricula with higher education (Karip, 2005).

In a similar vein, the European Commission's report states that associated with curriculum development for lifelong learning, new textbook and instructional material developments have been in progress. In this context, new instructional materials are being designed for a student-centred and constructivist learning style. The report confirms that as part of the curriculum reform process, almost all of the supervisors have been trained and training for classroom teachers will continue. Multiple avenues for lifelong learning and continuous improvement of the quality of the teaching force have been opened up, such as distance learning opportunities with interactive ICT use, providing printed and multimedia materials as well as implementing locally organised, school-based training activities. Additionally, partnership between faculties of education and provincial-level management have been established for teacher training activities, primarily designed for dissemination and institutionalisation of new curricula.

Conclusions

ICTs are now understood in Turkey to be an indispensable means to increase the availability of educational services and the efficient administration of educational institutions:

> to be effective in this period of globalization is more difficult than
> meets the eye. With a set of good principles, a reasonable level of
> support, and an eye toward innovation, a great deal can be
> achieved to employ ICTs to educate the poorest of the poor –
> indeed more than has ever been thought possible before. (Wagner
> & Kozma, 2003, p. 67)

However, integrating computer technologies into education requires successful development of infrastructure, personnel, curriculum, administration, and supervision, which can also apply to general education development, and these issues are difficult to separate from general education problems and issues (Akbaba-Altun, 2006). The more problems and issues general education has, the more problems and issues citizens have to face in computer integration.

Having an education system that aims at leading toward a knowledge society, Turkey has put the integration of computer technologies into education high on the agenda. Believing in the promise that ICTs can enhance the basic education, literacy and livelihood of Turkey's next generation remains a profoundly challenging area of development work today. The question of whether ICTs will enable Turkey to leapfrog some development stages remains unanswered at the moment, but it is clear that there is determination and vision in the approach of successive governments. Prospective membership of the EU remains a driving force, and getting the record of Turkey somewhere near the ratios of pupils per computer in primary and secondary schools in EU states of comparable population size is a severe challenge. However, as widespread access to information and knowledge, and to how to achieve this, make for a more inclusive society, the objectives of widespread computer literacy and EU membership could be mutually supportive. What this would mean in respect of Turkey as a Middle Eastern country is another issue.

References

Akbaba-Altun, S. (2006) Complexity of Integrating Computer Technologies into Education in Turkey, *Educational Technology and Society*, 3, 40.

Avgerou, C. (1990) Computer-Based Information Systems and the Modernisation of Public Administration in Developing Countries, *Information Systems for Development*, 20, 45.

Campbell, D. (2001) Can the Digital Divide Be Contained? *International Labour Review*, 140(2).

Ezer, J.F. (2005) *Interplay of Institutional Forces behind Higher ICT Education in India*. London: Department of Information Systems, London School of Economics and Political Science.

Fouth, J.C. (Ed.) (2005) *Harnessing the Potential of ICT for Education – a multistakeholder approach*. New York: United Nations ICT Task Force.

Fullan, M.G. (Ed.) (1996) Implementation of Innovation, *International Encyclopedia of Educational Technology*. Oxford: Elsevier Science/Pelgrum.

Goktas, Y. & Yildirim, Z. (2003) A Comparative Analysis of the EU Countries and Turkey Regarding the Integration of ICT in Primary Education Curricula and Teacher Education Programs. European Conference on Educational Research, University of Hamburg.

Hawkin, R.J. (2002) *Ten Lessons for ICT and Education in the Developing World*. New York: Macmillan.

Hawkridge, D., Joworosky, J. & McMahon, H. (1990) *Computers into Third-World Schools: examples, experiences and issues*. London: Macmillan.

Hepp, K.P., Hinostroza, S.E., Laval, M.E. & Rehbein, L.F. (2004) Technology in Schools: education, ICT and the knowledge society. OECD. http://www.worldbank.org/education/pdf/ICT_report_oct04a.pdf (accessed 15 December 2005).

Hinostroza, J.E., Guzmán, A. & Isaacs, S. (2002) Innovative Uses of ICT in Chilean Schools, *Journal of Computer Assisted Learning*, 18, 459-469.

International Telecommunication Unit (ITU) (2003) World Telecommunication Development Report.

Karip, E. (2005) *Implementing the Education and Training 2010 Work Programme*. European Commission. http://ec.europa.eu/education/policies/2010/natreport/tu_en.pdf

Kocaoluk, F. & Kocaoluk, M.Ş. (2000) *İlköğretim Okulu Programı* 1-8. Istanbul: Kocaoluk Yayınevi.

Kozma, R.B. (2005) *ICT and Educational Reform in Developed and Developing Countries*. Istanbul: Kocaoluk Yayinevi.

Levine, J. (1998) *Planning Strategically for Technology Integration*. http://www.coe.uh.edu/insite/elec_pub/HTML1998/el_levi.htm (accessed 17 January 2006).

MEB (2005) *National Education at the Beginning of 2002.* http://www.meb.gov.tr

Organisation for Economic Cooperation and Development (OECD) (2001) *Information and Communication Technologies and Rural Development.* http://www.sourceoecd.org

Organisation for Economic Cooperation and Development (OECD) (2004) ICTs and Economic Growth in Developing Countries. http://www.oecd.org/dataoecd/15/54/34663175.pdf (accessed 15 December 2005).

Pak, N. (2001) The Impact of ICT Revolution in Turkey: tunneling through barriers, *Journal of International Affairs*, 3, 42.

Pelgrum, W.J. & Law, N. (2003) *ICT in Education around the World: trends, problems and prospects.* New York: UNESCO–International Institute for Educational Planning.

Trujillo, M. (2000) The Global Digital Divide: a practical and theoretical overview. http://studentweb.tulane.edu/~mtruill/diss/Chapter3-Overview.pdf (accessed 19 December 2005).

Notes on Contributors

Bilal Barakat is a doctoral research student at the Department of Education, University of Oxford. After having studied mathematics at Cambridge(BA) and Oxford (MSc), he developed his current research interest in educational planning, especially in developing countries. He has worked as a consultant on various aspects of international and UK educational development, including higher education quality assurance, education in post-conflict settings and teacher training and recruitment, for UNDP, UNESCO, and for national agencies in the United Kingdom.

Colin Brock is UNESCO Chair of Education as Humanitarian Response at the University of Oxford and a Fellow of St Hugh's College,Oxford. A graduate in geography and anthropology from the University of Durham, he initially taught in secondary schools and subsequently at the universities of Reading, Leeds and Hull before moving to Oxford in 1992. From 1972 to 1974 he was Education Adviser at the Caribbean Development Division of the then Overseas Development Agency, since when he has worked in the field of comparative and ÿnternational education. Colin has undertaken significant project work in the field in many locations in Africa, South and East Asia, the Americas and the tropical island zones. More recently he has become involved in the Middle East. He is the author or editor of about 30 books and over 100 chapters, articles and research reports.

Yossi Dahan received his PhD from the Philosophy Department, Columbia University, New York, USA. He teaches courses on law and society and labor law at Ramat Gan College of Law in Israel, where he heads the human rights division. He also teaches courses on ethics, political theory and education at the Open University. He is the chairman and one of the founders of 'Adva Center', a research and advocacy center devoted to the study of social and economic inequalities in Israel. Dr Dahan is currently working on a book on theories of social justice.

Abdelkader Ezzaki was, until recently, Professor of Education at Mohammed V University-Souissi. He has served as Visiting Professor and as an international education consultant in the USA, in Africa and in the Gulf region. Currently, he is an 'Education Specialist' with ALEF, a USAID project that works in Morocco on innovative initiatives in education and vocational training. He holds a PhD from Temple University (USA), and an MA from the University of Wales (UK).

Sally Findlow is a lecturer in Education at Keele University. She gained her first degree in Islamic Studies and her PhD from the University of Cambridge. Sally has lived, worked and conducted fieldwork across several countries in the Arab Gulf and also in Egypt. In research terms she is interested in the role of higher education in the production of culture seen as dynamic and mutable, and responsive to social and policy change.

Serra Kirdar is the Founder and Director of the Muthabara Foundation, which was established in partnership with the University of Oxford Middle East Centre and the Centre for Applied HR Research to help maximise the potential of Arab women to achieve managerial and professional roles in the private sector. Serra gained a BA in Middle Eastern Studies, an MSc in Comparative and International Education and a DPhil., all at the University of Oxford. Her doctoral thesis was entitled: 'Gender and Cross-Cultural Experience with Reference to Elite Arab Women'. Serra was a founding member of the New Leaders Group for the Institute for International Education (IIE), and also founded the Initiative for Innovative Teaching (INTEACH) under the IIE and Oxford University Middle East Centre. INTEACH aims to develop tailor-made locally geared professional training programmes for public sector teachers in the Arab world with the aim of enhancing pedagogical instruction in the region. She is also a Foundation Life Fellow of St Antony's College, Middle East Centre, University of Oxford.

Ayse Kok received her BSc degree in Management Information Systems from Bogazici University, Turkey in 2003. She subsequently worked as an IT consultant with Ernst & Young, a professional business advisory services firm, before joining the MSc in ELearning programme at the University of Oxford. After completing her MSc degree, she worked as a short term e-learning consultant at the United Nations Systems and Staff College in Turin, Italy. Ayse has also presented several papers at international conferences about e-learning such as iLearn in Paris (January, 2007) and EDEN workshop in Barcelona (October, 2006).

Lila Zia Levers was born in Tehran where she attended primary school, before moving to England for her secondary and university education, graduating in Politics at the University of Exeter. She subsequently held a series of posts in both education and administration, culminating in the post of Graduate Studies Administrator at the Modern Languages Faculty, University of Oxford. As a long-standing member of the British Association for Comparative and International Education, she has presented papers at its conferences on aspects of education in Iran. She presented a paper at the Royal Institute of International Affairs, Chatham House, London on 'The Iranian Revolution: ten years later'. These papers have been published. Her most recent publication is 'Ideology and Change in Iranian Education' in

Rosarii Griffin (Ed.) *Education in the Muslim World: different perspectives* (Oxford: Symposium Books, 2006).

André Elias Mazawi is Associate Professor, Department of Educational Studies, Faculty of Education, University of British Columbia (UBC), Canada. He is Co-Director of the Centre for Policy Studies in Higher Education and Training (CHET) at UBC and serves as Associate Editor and French Editor of the *Canadian Journal of Higher Education*. He is interested in higher education and educational policy, with particular reference to the Middle East. His recent publications include: '"Knowledge Society" or Work as "Spectacle"? Education for Work and the Prospects of Social Transformation in Arab Societies', in *Educating the Global Workforce: knowledge, knowledge work and knowledge workers*, edited by L. Farrell & T. Fenwick, pp. 251-267. (London: Routledge, 2007); and 'Globalization, Development, and Policies of Knowledge and Learning in the Arab States', in *New Society Models for a New Millennium – the learning society in Europe and beyond*, edited by M. Kuhn (New York: Peter Lang, 2007).

Golnar Mehran is Associate Professor of Education at Al-Zahra University in Tehran, Iran. She has also acted as education consultant to UNICEF (Iran, Jordan and Oman), UNESCO, and the World Bank. Her research interest and publications include: ideology and education in post-revolutionary Iran; political socialization of Iranian schoolchildren; presentation of the 'self' and 'other' in Iranian education; female education in Iran and the Middle East; and religious education in the Islamic Republic of Iran.

Iran Mohammadi-Heuboeck recieved her PhD in Sociology from the Ecole des Hautes Etudes en Sciences Sociales (EHESS), Paris, for a thesis on the role of school in the process of construction of identity among Kurdish schoolchildren in the Islamic Republic of Iran. Her current research focuses on various aspects of contemporary Iranian society: identities of ethnic minorities, sociology of education, women's studies and questions of religious identity in the Islamic Republic. She is working as academic supervisor at the London School of Oriental and African Studies .

Richard Ratcliffe is near completing his DPhil on the politics of non-formal education among the Negev Bedouin, Israel at St Antonys College, University of Oxford. As part of this study, he spent 3 years working with different educational institutions and initiatives, as a consultant, researcher and teacher. Prior to this, he worked for a number of different human rights organisations in Israel/Palestine and gained an MA in Arabic from Edinburgh University.

Barbara Freyer Stowasser is Professor of Arabic and Islamic Studies at Georgetown University in Washington, DC, USA. She holds an MA in Near

East Studies from UCLA and a PhD in Comparative Semitic and Islamic Studies from the University of Munster, Germany. Her publications include *Islamic Law and the Challenges of Modernity*, co-edited with Yvonne Haddad (AltaMira Press, 2004), a book-length study on *Women in the Qur'an: traditions and interpretations* (Oxford University Press, 1994), and an edited volume entitled *The Islamic Impulse* (Center for Contemporary Arab Studies, Georgetown University, 1987, reprinted 1989). Two of her shorter think-pieces appeared as *Center for Contemporary Arab Studies Occational Papers*: 'Religion and Political Development: comparative ideas on Ibn Khaldun and Machiavelli' (1983, reprinted 2000), and 'A Time to Reap: thoughts on calendars and millennialism' (2000). The latter is the text of Dr Stowasser's address as outgoing president of the Middle East Studies Association (1989-99).

Yossi Yonah received his PhD from the Philosophy Department, University of Pennsylvania, USA. He teaches political philosophy and philosophy of education in the Department of Education, Ben Gurion University of the Negev, Israel. He was Head of the Teacher Training Program there between 1995 and 2002. He is a senior research fellow with the Jerusalem Van Leer Institute. Professor Yonah has published extensively on topics pertaining to moral and political philosophy, philosophy of education and multiculturalism.